Beyond Nineteen E:

MW00619147

Beyond
Nineteen Eighty-Four

Doublespeak in a Post-Orwellian Age

Edited by
William Lutz
Rutgers University

National Council of Teachers of English
1111 Kenyon Road, Urbana, Illinois 61801

NCTE Editorial Board: Donald R. Gallo, Richard Lloyd-Jones, Raymond Rodrigues, Dorothy S. Strickland, Brooke Workman; Charles Suhor, ex officio; Michael Spooner, ex officio

Staff Editors: Mary Daniels, David A. Hamburg

Cover Design: Michael J. Getz

Interior Book Design: Tom Kovacs for TGK Design

NCTE Stock Number 02859–3020

© 1989 by the National Council of Teachers of English. All rights reserved. Printed in the United States of America.

It is the policy of NCTE in its journals and other publications to provide a forum for the open discussion of ideas concerning the content and the teaching of English and the language arts. Publicity accorded to any particular point of view does not imply endorsement by the Executive Committee, the Board of Directors, or the membership at large, except in announcements of policy, where such endorsement is clearly specified.

Library of Congress Cataloging-in-Publication Data

Beyond nineteen eighty-four: doublespeak in a post-Orwellian age /
    edited by William D. Lutz.
        p.   cm.
    Includes bibliographical references.
    ISBN 0–8141–0285–9
    1. English language—Errors of usage. 2. English language—
Jargon. 3. English language—Political aspects. 4. Communication—
Political aspects. 5. Communication—Moral and ethical aspects.
6. Orwell, George, 1903–1950—Knowledge—Language and languages.
I. Lutz, William. II. National Council of Teachers of English.
III. Title: Doublespeak in a post-Orwellian age.
PE1460.B48   1989
428—dc20   89–12707
                                                         CIP

Contents

Acknowledgments

I gratefully acknowledge the support of the Rutgers University Research Council for grants which helped in the preparation of this book. I would also like to thank Barbara Murphy and Jennifer Elmer for assisting in the preparation of the manuscript. Their efforts often went beyond the call of duty in tracking down information and figuring out my cryptic notes and instructions. Special thanks is also due Mary Daniels for her extraordinary work in editing this manuscript.

Resolutions
Passed by the National Council of Teachers of English at the Sixty-First Annual Meeting, 1971

On Dishonest and Inhumane Uses of Language

Background: As teachers of English we stress the need for clarity, directness, and honesty in the use of language. We also try to transmit and evolve a tradition of humane culture, of which literature forms a part.

Meanwhile, there is another system of education in language and literature—the media and the commercial interests that control them. In this system, too, language is not always used lucidly and honestly, but it is used with great power. The Council on Economic Priorities recently showed, for instance, that many large corporations are trying to capitalize on public concern about the environment by advertising campaigns that are at best misleading, at worst dangerously false. Similarly, a lyric poem (a literary form) is being used with musical accompaniment to suggest that the problem of air pollution had best be left to the corporations. And in other areas of advertising, language and literature have many uses not within our traditional definition of the humanities.

It would be proper for our organization to take an active interest in these matters. Be it therefore

RESOLVED, That the National Council of Teachers of English find means to study dishonest and inhumane uses of language and literature by advertisers, to bring offenses to public attention, and to propose classroom techniques for preparing children to cope with commercial propaganda.

On the Relation of Language and Public Policy

Background: Most English teachers accept Orwell's point, in "Politics and the English Language," that language is often used as an instrument of social control. At best it is not a "neutral" medium, but reflects and implements the interests of its users. For this reason, the way language is used by those with political power is a matter of concern to all of us.

During the past ten years we have seen public officials in our country use words like "pacification," "free-fire zones," "protective reaction," "incursion," "free elections," "aggression," "defense," and "systems" to mediate and sell a war to the American public. Although teachers of English do not make national policy, we should do what we can to free public language and thought from manipulation by the powerful. Be it therefore

RESOLVED, That the National Council of Teachers of English find means to study the relation of language to public policy, to keep track of, publicize, and combat semantic distortion by public officials, candidates for office, political commentators, and all those who transmit through the mass media.

Introduction

In 1971, members attending the 61st annual meeting of the National Council of Teachers of English (NCTE) passed two resolutions dealing with language; the first dealing with the dishonest and inhumane uses of language and the second with the relation of language to public policy. The members of NCTE passed these resolutions because of mounting concern over the manipulation of language by the government and the military in reporting and discussing the Vietnam war. The Watergate conspiracy had not yet occurred, but its discovery would later reveal even greater language manipulation by government officials, and indirectly confirm that the concern for the misuse of public language expressed in these two resolutions was certainly justified.

In 1972, NCTE established the Committee on Public Doublespeak and charged the committee with the rather awesome task of combating the advertisers, the politicians, and the major manipulators of public language in our society. In announcing the formation of the committee, Robert Hogan, NCTE's Executive Secretary at that time, said that

> It isn't that the interests of NCTE in the mechanics and the structure of language, as well as its history, are diminishing at all. Behind the appointment of the committee is a resurgent interest in the content of language. The question is not just whether subjects and verbs agree, but whether statements and facts agree.

Contrary to the stereotype, English teachers are not guardians of the purity of the language, waiting to pounce with red pencil and scathing criticism on any poor soul who makes a mistake in spelling, punctuation, grammar, usage, or pronunciation. As Hogan's statement emphasizes, there is more to using language, and to the teaching of English, than making subjects and verbs agree.

There is also more to being an effective consumer of language than just expressing dismay at dangling modifiers, faulty subject and verb agreement, or questionable usage. All who use language should be concerned whether statements and facts agree, whether language is, in Orwell's words, "largely the defence of the indefensible," whether language "consists largely of euphemism, question-begging and sheer cloudy vagueness" (4:136), and whether language "is designed to make lies sound truthful and murder respectable, and to give an appearance of solidity to pure wind" (4:139).

As part of its efforts to combat the misuse of public language, the Committee on Public Doublespeak gave its first annual Doublespeak Award in 1974, for language that is grossly deceptive, evasive, euphemistic, confusing, or self-contradictory and which has pernicious social or political consequences. In that same year, the committee began publishing a newsletter which later became the *Quarterly Review of Doublespeak* and now has subscribers in all fifty of the United States as well as twenty-one foreign countries. In 1975 the committee gave its first annual Orwell Award for the work that effectively treats the subject of public doublespeak and makes an outstanding contribution to the critical analysis of public language. The committee has published two books on doublespeak: *Language and Public Policy*, edited by Hugh Rank, was published by NCTE in 1974 and *Teaching About Doublespeak*, edited by Daniel Dieterich, was published by NCTE in 1976.

It has been over fifteen years since the publication of *Language and Public Policy*, a book designed to provide a perspective on the use of doublespeak in advertising, politics, the military, and the news media. And it has been over ten years since the publication of *Teaching About Doublespeak*, a book designed to provide teachers with practical information on how to teach students about doublespeak at every level, from elementary school to the college classroom. It seems appropriate that the Committee on Public Doublespeak, in its third book, surveys the extent and influence of doublespeak today.

Orwell was not a prophet, nor did he ever pretend to be one, yet much of what he wrote about language in both his novel *Nineteen Eighty-Four* and his essay "Politics and the English Language" has come to pass. But even Orwell would be surprised at the new and even more sophisticated and effective misuses of language which have been developed since he published his novel. He would also be surprised at the pervasiveness of language misuse; at how it has spread from the language of politics to the language of business, of education, and almost all aspects of life.

The essays in this book were written to explore the kinds and extent of doublespeak in our world. Some of these essays were written a few years ago. While the authors did update their essays, many decided that some of their original examples should remain because they illustrate so well the growth of doublespeak.

The essays collected here look at doublespeak in many of its manifestations. William Lutz begins by offering a description of four kinds of doublespeak and a method for analyzing language for its presence. Walker Gibson examines Orwell's view of language and finds that while Orwell's views may be a little old-fashioned in some ways, there is much we can still learn from him. Hugh Rank also takes a somewhat critical approach to Orwell's views on language and points out that while much of what Orwell said is worthy of consideration, there is much, too, that we should examine closely. Charles Weingartner discusses living in an "information rich" environment in which the counterfeit overwhelms the authentic, thus raising the question of how we know what we know. Edward White suggests that while the dangers of doublespeak can be readily determined, the more subtle dangers of singlespeak are equally great. The philosopher Dennis Rohatyn analyzes the concept of fallacy as it applies to doublespeak, while George Bramer examines the ethics of doublespeak, a topic long neglected but most important in its study. Donald Lazere analyzes disinformation—a new, subtle, and pervasive form of doublespeak, one which even Orwell could never have foreseen. Richard Ohmann offers reflections on the underlying semantics of foreign policy discourse, examining the origins of the vocabulary of diplomacy and foreign policy, and what this vocabulary really means. Harry Brent examines Orwell's experiences in the Spanish Civil War and the effects those experiences had on Orwell's views of language and writing. Dan Hahn explores the techniques used by politicians to say nothing, and the function of such language in the political process, while Frank D'Angelo analyzes one kind of doublespeak—jargon—which he calls "that social disease whose effects are no less upsetting to health and public order." Del Kehl examines the language of advertising and suggests a methodology that anyone can use to analyze it. Don Nilsen discusses a subtle linguistic process which can be used to produce multiple meanings in advertisements, meanings which are often communicated unconsciously. Scott Buechler analyzes the language used to discuss the philosophy of technology, arguing for the need for clear language if we are to understand the crucial decisions which need to be made in our technological age. Julia Penelope discusses the pervasiveness of doublespeak in higher education and the effects of the widespread use of such language on faculty, students, and administrators. Roy Fox explores sensationspeak, the language of the tabloid press, and suggests that such language, far from being harmless, can have serious effects on our society. Charles Suhor offers for consideration the doublespeak of the "pop grammarians," those who would purify the language and save us all from their version of substandard usages.

The eighteen essays in this collection are a starting point for the study of doublespeak and should be considered not definitive but representative. That is, they represent the work that is being carried on in the study of doublespeak and in the effort to combat it. Other resources for information about doublespeak can be found in the bibliography at the end of this book.

William Lutz
May 1989

Works Cited

Dieterich, Daniel. *Teaching About Doublespeak.* Urbana, Ill.: National Council of Teachers of English, 1976.

Rank, Hugh, ed. *Language and Public Policy.* Urbana, Ill.: National Council of Teachers of English, 1974.

Orwell, George. *Nineteen Eighty-Four.* New York: New American Library, 1961.

———. "Politics and the English Language." In *In Front of Your Nose (1945–1950),* 127–40. Vol. 4 of *The Collected Essays, Journalism and Letters of George Orwell.* Edited by Sonia Orwell and Ian Angus. New York: Harcourt, Brace & World, 1952. Reprint. New York: Harcourt Brace Jovanovich, 1968.

1 Notes toward a Definition of Doublespeak

William Lutz
Rutgers University

Language is a tool, one of many human tools. But language is arguably our most important tool, for with it we have developed society and built civilization. However, like any other tool, language can be abused, used not to build but to destroy, not to communicate but to confuse, not to clarify but to obscure, not to lead but mislead. Moreover, language is a unique tool used not simply to communicate but to apprehend and even give shape to reality. Edward Sapir, in his essay "The Status of Linguistics as a Science," writes:

> Language is a guide to social reality. . . . [I]t powerfully conditions all our thinking about social problems and processes. Human beings do not live in the objective world alone, nor alone in the world of social activity as ordinarily understood, but are very much at the mercy of the particular language which has become the medium of expression for their society. It is quite an illusion to imagine that one adjusts to reality essentially without the use of language and that language is merely an incidental means of solving specific problems of communication or reflection. . . . We see and hear and otherwise experience very largely as we do because the language habits of our community predispose certain choices of interpretation. (162)

Benjamin Lee Whorf later extended Sapir's thesis to what became known as the Sapir-Whorf hypothesis. In 1940 Whorf also argued in his essay, "Science and Linguistics," that each language conveys to its users a ready-made world view. "Every language . . . incorporates certain points of view and certain patterned resistances to widely divergent points of view" (212). Whorf adds:

©William Lutz. An earlier version of this essay was published in *The Legacy of Language: A Tribute to Charlton Laird*. Reno and Las Vegas: University of Nevada Press, 1987. An excerpt appeared in the *Quarterly Review of Doublespeak* 13, no. 2, 1987.

1

> Language is not merely a reproducing instrument for voicing ideas but rather is itself the shaper of ideas, the program and guide for the individual's mental activity, for his analysis of impressions, for his synthesis of his mental stock in trade. . . . [T]he world is presented in a kaleidoscope flux of impressions which has to be organized by our minds—and this means largely by the linguistic systems in our minds. (212–13)

Language thus reflects our perception of reality, which in turn influences and shapes our reactions to people, events, and ideas. Language is a kind of conceptual blueprint used to organize our thoughts. In this sense, language becomes the means by which we shape reality and the means by which we communicate our perceptions of reality to others. Language can easily distort perception and influence behavior and thus be a tool, or weapon, for achieving the greatest good or the greatest evil. Socrates and Aristotle understood well this power of language.

In his essay "Politics and the English Language," George Orwell writes that

> The great enemy of clear language is insincerity. When there is a gap between one's real and one's declared aims, one turns as it were instinctively to long words and exhausted idioms, like a cuttlefish squirting out ink. (4:137)

Orwell goes on to express his belief in "language as an instrument for expressing and not for concealing or preventing thought" (4:139).

> In our time . . . political speech and writing are largely the defense of the indefensible. . . . Thus political language has to consist largely of euphemisms, question-begging and sheer cloudy vagueness. . . .
> . . . Political language . . . is designed to make lies sound truthful and murder respectable, and to give an appearance of solidity to pure wind. (4:136, 139)

Orwell is reflecting here the Sapir-Whorf hypothesis on the relation of thought and language, but he is also raising the political implications of this hypothesis. If language can be used to control minds, then those who control language can control minds and ultimately control society. Language is power; those who control language control the world. Power may come out of the barrel of a gun, but without the control of language there can be no real control of society.

Orwell's belief in the power of language to achieve and maintain political control is most clearly expressed in his novel *Nineteen Eighty-Four*. The Party in Oceania understands the power of language, for it has based its control of society on the control of language. While the Thought Police terrorize and torture to preserve order, Newspeak prevents disorder, dissent, rebellion, and even independent thought. The thoughts, inspirations, and ideas that could lead to disorder are controlled, even eliminated, through the control of language. As Stephen Greenblatt (1974) observes,

> If language is abused, if words can have entirely contradictory meanings at the same time, if the language necessary to express political opposition is destroyed, if notions of objective truth and unchanging history are abandoned, then since thought is dependent on language, all unorthodox modes of thought can be made impossible, history can be altered to suit the needs of the moment, the individual can be reduced to an automaton incapable of thought or disloyalty. (114)

In such a world one must reject the evidence of one's eyes and ears, for the great sin, "the heresy of heresies was common sense" (*Nineteen Eighty-Four*, 69).

In *Nineteen Eighty-Four*, O'Brien, Winston Smith's torturer and guide to understanding the reality of life in Oceania, instructs Winston that

> reality is not external. Reality exists in the human mind, and nowhere else. Not in the individual mind, which can make mistakes, and in any case soon perishes; only in the mind of the Party, which is collective and immortal. Whatever the Party holds to be truth is truth. It is impossible to see reality except by looking through the eyes of the Party. (205)

And the only way to see reality properly is through the language of the Party. Language thus becomes the means of control in the world of *Nineteen Eighty-Four*.

The official language of the world of *Nineteen Eighty-Four* is Newspeak, a language that "was designed not to extend but to *diminish* the range of thought" (247). The purpose of Newspeak was not only to provide a medium of expression for the Party and its members, "but to make all other modes of thought impossible" (247). Newspeak is the medium used to express the mental process in

> the labyrinthine world of doublethink. To know and not to know, to be conscious of complete truthfulness while telling carefully constructed lies, to hold simultaneously two opinions which cancelled out, knowing them to be contradictory and believing in both of them; to use logic against logic, to repudiate morality while laying claim to it, to believe that democracy was impossible and that the Party was the guardian of democracy; to forget whatever it was necessary to forget, then to draw it back into memory again at the moment when it was needed, and then promptly to forget it again; and above all, to apply the same process to the process itself. . . . Even to understand the word "doublethink" involved the use of doublethink. (32–33)

The word *doublespeak* combines the meanings of *Newspeak* and *doublethink*. Doublespeak is language which pretends to communicate but really does not. It is language which makes the bad seem good, something negative appear positive, something unpleasant appear attractive, or at least tolerable. It is language which avoids or shifts responsibility; language which is at variance with its real and its purported meaning; language which conceals or prevents thought. Doublespeak is language which does not extend thought but limits it.

How To Analyze Language for Doublespeak

In his essay "The Teacher-Heal-Thyself Myth," Hugh Rank has written that identifying doublespeak requires an analysis of language "in context with the whole situation" (219). To identify the full context in which the language occurs, he asks these five questions:

1. Who is saying what to whom?
2. Under what conditions?
3. Under what circumstances?
4. With what intent?
5. With what results?

According to Edward P. J. Corbett (1976), this method of identifying doublespeak "encapsulates the whole art of rhetoric and provides a set of criteria to help us discriminate those uses of language that we should proscribe and those that we should encourage" (16–17). Applying this method of analysis to language will identify doublespeak in uses of language which might otherwise be legitimate or which might not even appear at first glance to be doublespeak.

There are at least four kinds of doublespeak: Euphemisms, jargon, gobbledygook or bureaucratese, and inflated language.

1. *Euphemisms are words or phrases designed to avoid harsh or distasteful reality.* When a euphemism is used out of sensitivity for the feelings of someone or out of concern for a social or cultural taboo it is not doublespeak. For example, we express grief that someone has *passed away* because we do not want to say to a grieving person, "I'm sorry your father is dead." The euphemism "passed away" functions here not just to protect the feelings of another person but also to communicate our concern over that person's feelings during a period of mourning.

However, when a euphemism is used to mislead or deceive it becomes doublespeak. For example, the U. S. State Department decided in 1984 that in its annual reports on the status of human rights in countries around the world it would no longer use the word "killing." Instead, it will use the phrase *unlawful or arbitrary deprivation of life.* Thus the State Department avoids discussing the embarrassing situation of government-sanctioned killings in countries that are supported by the United States. This use of language constitutes doublespeak because it is designed to mislead, to cover up the unpleasant. Its real intent is at variance with its apparent intent. It is language designed to alter our perception of reality.

2. *Jargon is the specialized language of a trade, profession, or similar group.* It is the specialized language of doctors, lawyers, engineers, educators, or car mechanics. Jargon can serve an important and useful function. Within a group, jargon allows members to communicate with each other clearly, efficiently, and quickly. Indeed, it is a mark of membership in the group to be able to use and understand the group's jargon. For example, lawyers and tax accountants will speak of an *involuntary conversion* of property when discussing the loss or destruction of property through theft, accident, or condemnation. When used by lawyers in a legal situation such jargon is a legitimate use of language since all members of the group can be expected to understand the term.

However, when a member of the group uses jargon to communicate with a person outside the group, and uses it knowing that the nonmember does not understand such language, then there is doublespeak. For example, in 1978 a commercial airliner crashed on takeoff, killing three passengers, injuring twenty-one others, and destroying the airplane, a Boeing 727. The insured value of the airplane was greater than its book value, so the airline made a profit of $1.7 million on the destroyed airplane. But the airline had two problems: it did not want to talk about one of its airplanes crashing, and it had to account for $1.7 million when it issued its annual report to its stockholders. The airline solved these problems by inserting a footnote in its annual report which explained that this $1.7 million was due to "the involuntary conversion of a 727." The term *involuntary conversion* is a technical term in law; it is legal jargon. Airline officials could claim to have explained the crash of the airplane and the subsequent profit. However, since most stockholders in the company, and indeed most of the general public, are not familiar with legal jargon, the use of such jargon constitutes doublespeak.

3. *Gobbledygook or bureaucratese is simply a matter of piling on words, of overwhelming the audience with words, the bigger the better.* For example, according to an editorial in the *Philadelphia Inquirer,* when Alan Greenspan was chairman of the President's Council of Economic Advisors he made this statement when testifying before a Senate committee:

> It is a tricky problem to find the particular calibration in timing that would be appropriate to stem the acceleration in risk premiums created by falling incomes without prematurely aborting the decline in the inflation-generated risk premiums. (12-A)

Did Alan Greenspan's audience really understand what he was saying? Did he believe his statement really explained anything? Perhaps there is some meaning beneath all those words, but it would take some time to search it out. This seems to be language which pretends to communicate but does not.

4. *Inflated language is language designed to make the ordinary seem extraordinary,* the common, uncommon, to make everyday things seem impressive, to give an air of importance to people, situations, or things which would not normally be considered important, to make the simple seem complex. With this kind of language car mechanics become *automotive internists,* elevator operators become *members of the vertical transportation corps,* used cars become not just *pre-owned* but *experienced cars,* grocery store checkout clerks become *career associate scanning professionals,* and smelling something becomes *organoleptic analysis.*

A World of Doublespeak

We live in a world filled with doublespeak. We are asked to check our packages at the desk *for our convenience* when it's not for our convenience at all but for someone else's convenience. We see advertisements for *previously distinguished* cars, not used cars, for *genuine imitation leather, virgin vinyl,* or *real counterfeit diamonds.* Television offers not reruns but *encore telecasts.* There are no slums or ghettos just the *inner city* or *sub-standard housing* where the *disadvantaged* or *economically non-affluent* live. Nonprofit organizations don't make a profit, they have *negative deficits* or they experience *revenue excesses.* In the world of doublespeak it's not dying but *terminal living.*

In the world of business we find that executives *operate* in *timeframes* within the *context* of which a *task force* will serve as the proper *conduit* for all necessary *input* to *program a scenario* that, within acceptable *param-*

eters, will *generate* the *maximum output* for a *printout* of *zero defect terminal objectives*. And when things don't turn out right, it's not a mistake just a *shortfall*.

Political language is the language of public policy and power. Through language our direction as a nation is defined for us by our elected leaders. The corruption of the language of power and public policy, therefore, can lead to the corruption of our political system and our sense of national purpose. If our leaders do not speak clearly to us, then we, the people, from whom all power ultimately derives, cannot have the requisite knowledge and understanding upon which to make important decisions. It takes some effort to determine that *advance downward adjustments* in the appropriations request is really a budget cut. Vietnam gave us *protective reaction strikes* (bombings), *resources control programs* (poisoning the vegetation and water supply), *preemptive counterattack*, (first strike), and *termination with extreme prejudice* (killing a suspected spy without trial). Watergate gave us *misspeak* and *inoperative statement* for lie, *inappropriate actions* for illegal acts, and *miscertification* for fraud and conspiracy. The Iran-Contra affair gave us *cleaning up the historical record* for falsifying official documents, *carefully crafted, nuanced answers* for lies, and testimony that is *fixed by omission* for false testimony. This is language which attacks the very purpose of language, communication between people. This is indeed language which, in Orwell's words, is "designed to make lies sound truthful and murder respectable, and to give an appearance of solidity to pure wind."

Identifying Doublespeak

Identifying doublespeak can at times be difficult. For example, on July 27, 1981, President Ronald Reagan said in a speech televised to the American public that

> I will not stand by and see those of you who are dependent on Social Security deprived of the benefits you've worked so hard to earn. You will continue to receive your checks in the full amount due you.

This speech had been billed as President Reagan's position on Social Security, a subject of much debate at the time. After the speech, public opinion polls revealed that the great majority of the public believed that President Reagan had affirmed his support for Social Security and that he would not support cuts in benefits. However, five days after the speech, on July 31, 1981, David Hess of the *Philadelphia Inquirer* quoted

White House communications director David Gergen as saying that President Reagan's words had been "carefully chosen." What President Reagan did mean, according to Gergen, was that he was reserving the right to decide who was "dependent" on those benefits, who had "earned" them, and who, therefore, was "due" them (6-A).

The subsequent remarks of David Gergen reveal the real intent of President Reagan as opposed to his apparent intent. Thus, Hugh Rank's criteria for analyzing language to determine whether it is doublespeak, when applied in light of David Gergen's remarks, reveal the doublespeak of President Reagan. Here is the gap between the speaker's real and declared aim.

Alexander Haig and Doublespeak

In 1981, Secretary of State Alexander Haig testified before congressional committees about the murder of three American nuns and a Catholic lay worker in El Salvador. Three of the women had been raped and all four were shot at close range, and there was clear evidence that the crime had been committed by soldiers of the Salvadoran government. As reported by Anthony Lewis of *The New York Times*, Secretary Haig said to the House Foreign Affairs Committee:

> I'd like to suggest to you that some of the investigations would lead one to believe that perhaps the vehicle the nuns were riding in may have tried to run a roadblock, or may accidentally have been perceived to have been doing so, and there'd been an exchange of fire and then perhaps those who inflicted the casualties sought to cover it up. And this could have been at a very low level of both competence and motivation in the context of the issue itself. But the facts on this are not clear enough for anyone to draw a definitive conclusion (E-21).

The next day, before the Senate Foreign Relations Committee, Secretary Haig claimed that press reports on his previous testimony were inaccurate.

When Senator Claiborne Pell asked whether Secretary Haig was suggesting the possibility that "the nuns may have run through a roadblock," Secretary Haig replied,

> You mean that they tried to violate . . . ? Not at all, no, not at all. My heavens! The dear nuns who raised me in my parochial schooling would forever isolate me from their affections and respect (E-21).

When Senator Pell asked Secretary Haig, "Did you mean that the nuns were firing at the people, or what did 'an exchange of fire' mean?" Secretary Haig replied,

> I haven't met any pistol-packing nuns in my day, Senator. What I
> meant was that if one fellow starts shooting, then the next thing
> you know they all panic. (E-21)

Thus did the Secretary of State of the United States explain official
government policy on the murder of four American citizens in a
foreign land.

Secretary Haig's testimony implies that the women were in some way
responsible for their own fate. By using such vague wording as "would
lead one to believe" and "may accidentally have been perceived to have
been" he avoids any direct assertion. The use of the phrase "inflicted
the casualties" not only avoids using the word "kill" but also implies that
at the worst the killings were accidental or justifiable. The result of this
testimony is that the Secretary of State has become an apologist for
murder. This is indeed the kind of language Orwell said is used in
defense of the indefensible; language designed to make lies sound
truthful and murder respectable; language designed to give an appearance of solidity to pure wind.

Doublespeak and Clear Thinking

These last examples of doublespeak should make it clear that doublespeak is not the product of careless language or sloppy thinking.
Indeed, most doublespeak is the product of clear thinking and is
language carefully designed and constructed to appear to communicate when in fact it doesn't. It is language designed not to lead but
mislead. It is language designed to distort reality and corrupt the mind.
It's not a tax increase but *revenue enhancement* or *tax base broadening,* so
how can you complain about higher taxes? It's not acid rain; it's *poorly
buffered precipitation,* so don't worry about all those dead trees. That
isn't the Mafia in Atlantic City, New Jersey; those are just *members of a
career-offender cartel,* so don't worry about the influence of organized
crime in the city. The Supreme Court Justice wasn't addicted to the
pain killing drug he was taking, the drug had simply *established an
interrelationship with the body, such that if the drug is removed precipitously,
there is a reaction,* so don't worry that his decisions might have been
influenced by his drug addiction. It's not a Titan II nuclear-armed,
intercontinental, ballistic missile with a warhead 630 times more
powerful than the atomic bomb dropped on Hiroshima; it's just a *very
large, potentially disruptive re-entry system,* so don't worry about the threat
of nuclear destruction. It's not a neutron bomb but an *enhanced radiation device,* so don't worry about escalating the arms race. It's not an

invasion but a *rescue mission,* or a *predawn vertical insertion,* so don't worry about any violations of United States or International Law.

Doublespeak which calls bus drivers *urban transportation specialists,* bill collectors *portfolio administrators,* and doorkeepers *access controllers* can be considered humorous and relatively harmless. But doublespeak which calls civilian casualties in a nuclear war *collateral damage,* lies *inoperative statements* or *plausible deniability,* and missiles designed to kill millions of people *Peacekeepers* is language which attempts to make the bad seem good, the negative appear positive, something unpleasant appear attractive; language which seems to communicate but does not. Such language breeds suspicion, cynicism, distrust, and, ultimately, hostility.

I offer these categories of doublespeak as a way of thinking about, identifying, and analyzing doublespeak and not as a definitive definition of the term.

Works Cited

Corbett, Edward P. J. "Public Doublespeak: If I Speak with Forked Tongue." *English Journal* 65, no. 4 (1976): 16–17.

Editorial. *Philadelphia Inquirer,* 25 December 1974: 12-A.

Greenblatt, Stephen J. "Orwell as Satirist." In *George Orwell: A Collection of Critical Essays,* 106–18. Edited by Raymond Williams. Englewood Cliffs, N.J.: Prentice-Hall, 1974.

Hess, David. "Reagan's Language on Benefits Confused, Angered Many." *Philadelphia Inquirer,* 31 July 1981: 6-A.

Lewis, Anthony. "Showing His Colors." *The New York Times,* 29 March 1981: E-21.

Orwell, George. "Politics and the English Language." In *In Front of Your Nose (1945–50),* 127–40. Vol. 4 of *The Collected Essays, Journalism and Letters of George Orwell.* Edited by Sonia Orwell and Ian Angus. 4 vols. New York: Harcourt, Brace & World, 1952. Reprint. Harcourt Brace Jovanovich, 1968.

———. *Nineteen Eighty-Four.* New York: New American Library, 1961.

Rank, Hugh. "The Teacher-Heal-Thyself Myth." *Language and Public Policy.* Edited by Hugh Rank. Urbana, Ill.: National Council of Teachers of English, 1974. 215–34.

Sapir, Edward. "The Status of Linguistics as a Science." *Selected Writings of Edward Sapir in Language, Culture and Personality,* 160–66. Edited by David G. Mandelbaum. Los Angeles: University of California Press, 1949.

Whorf, Benjamin Lee. "Science and Linguistics." In *Language, Thought and Reality: Selected Writings of Benjamin Lee Whorf,* 207–19. Edited by John B. Carroll. Cambridge: MIT Press, 1956.

2 Truisms Are True: Orwell's View of Language

Walker Gibson
University of Massachusetts at Amherst

Doubleness, if not double-talk, is of course a familiar gambit in modern life, and it's no doubt especially endemic among literary intellectuals. We treasure metaphor and irony for their balancing of different or opposing ideas in various relations of ambivalence and ambiguity. Seven types and then some. In science, we know that we must not ask of light if it is made of particles or waves, for the scientist will answer, "That is not a useful question. We physicists have stopped asking it; but if you insist, we may say that a beam of light is at one and the same time a set of particles and waves." At least that's the way James Conant put the situation thirty-five years ago in his book *Modern Science and Modern Man* (47). No doubt by now light has become some other pair of apparent incompatibles.

Or take the case recently proposed by my colleague Ernest Gallo, where two thinkers, observing the same phenomenon, offer absolutely opposing interpretations. The trend of modern mathematics, said Oswald Spengler, is toward abstraction, and so one is moving ever closer to the Infinite. The trend of modern mathematics, said Marshall McLuhan, is toward the concrete, and so one is moving ever closer to a tactile world and the global village. What does a contemporary mind do when confronted with two sages in violent disagreement over the same event? One response is amusement. Que voulez-vous? Or, we may serenely observe how each writer has taken his own inductive leap, aided by the notorious imprecision of language and the marvels of metaphor. There is a sense in which, we are fond of saying, both are right and both wrong. A response we rarely make is that of outrage. Nobody is really surprised at such oppositions, and nobody is morally shocked by them. Indeed, Gallo argues that such disagreements are necessary, in the very nature of nature.

Superficially at least, all this sounds something like Orwell's doublethink as he defines it in his novel *Nineteen Eighty-Four:* "To hold simultaneously two opinions which canceled out, knowing them to be contradictory and believing in both of them, to use logic against logic" (32). My sense is that Orwell *would* have found a head-on collision like Spengler-McLuhan discomfiting if not intolerable. He certainly would not have been amused.

The fact is, Orwell had a rather old-fashioned view of language and truth. As Samuel Hynes has observed, "Orwell's general attitude is conservative, taking the language of the past as ideal and urging a purer and more English language" (13). His great essay on "Politics and the English Language" has been much admired, and justly so. It is one of the most frequently anthologized documents of our time. It alerted us, very early on, not only to bureaucratic bilge and absurdity, but to the dehumanizing force of official styles. Orwell demonstrated, for example, how Latinized abstractions and dying metaphors were (and still are, of course) being employed to cover up hard facts so that human anguish is buried in pretentious verbiage. Yet it's worth noting that this brilliant essay was also the work of a firm linguistic conservative.

"Most people who bother with the matter at all," the essay begins in wonderful offhand style, "would admit that the English language is in a bad way" (4:127). The metaphor there seems to be that of a human patient, not doing too well. But language is not like a patient doing well or ill. Language is simply what people make it, and it serves their ends. Linguists tell us that the language of a particular period is never better or worse than that of any other period. Language simply *is:* it serves its users well or they wouldn't use it. They may be good or evil people, to be sure. And you can argue (though linguists generally don't) that one particular period is itself better or worse than some other. For many literary intellectuals, including Orwell, this argument usually comes down to saying that we live in a sad, drab age and that some other age would have been much nicer. People spoke better, wrote better, *were* better at some former time.

In *Nineteen Eighty-Four*, Orwell's nostalgia for traditional expression appears even in trivial incidents.

> "I arst you civil enough, didn't I?" said the old man, straightening his shoulders pugnaciously. "You telling me you ain't got a pint mug in the 'ole bleeding boozer?"
>
> "And what in hell's name *is* a pint?" said the barman. . . . "Liter and half liter—that's all we serve. There's the glasses on the shelf in front of you."
>
> "I like a pint," persisted the old man. "You could 'a drawn me off a pint easy enough. We didn't 'ave these bleeding liters when I was a young man."

> "When you were a young man we were all living in the treetops,"
> said the barman, with a glance at the other customers. (75)

One can feel some sympathy for the bartender. The old man's stubbornness in the face of linguistic change reflects Orwell's own attitude toward words and things as they used to be.

Immediately after this barroom scene, Winston Smith pays his second visit to the antique store or junk shop, whose proprietor

> was wearing an aged jacket of black velvet [which] gave him a vague
> air of intellectuality, as though he had been some kind of literary
> man, or perhaps a musician. His voice was soft, as though faded,
> and his accent less debased than that of the majority of the proles.
> (80)

Here, with the proprietor's help, Winston manages to complete the ancient rhyme that has fascinated him: "Oranges and lemons, say the bells of St. Clement's / You owe me three farthings, say the bells of St. Martin's!"

> It was curious, but when you said it to yourself you had the illusion
> of actually hearing the bells of a lost London. (84)

But the Oldspeak that Winston yearns for, like the coral paperweight he cherishes, relates to a London lost long before 1948, when the book was completed. Admirers of the novel today who are seriously interested in language have to take into account this fundamental linguistic conservatism on the part of its author, a conservatism that sometimes comes close to sentimentality.

Orwell's view of language makes it possible for a downright reactionary critic to applaud his work. My example is one Donald McCormick, in a British book called *Approaching 1984*. McCormick ingeniously includes an appendix listing Orwell's Newspeak terms alongside some other terms that are currently fashionable in our society and that, in McCormick's judgment, are "parallels to those thought up by Orwell" (175). Actually what they do is dramatize McCormick's own stand-pat prejudices; his list includes *sensitivity training, chill factor, tactile deprivation, teach-in, computerese, caring*. Nobody has to like these terms, but they are hardly in a class with Thought Police or doublethink. A phrase like "chill factor," for example, is a useful addition to the vocabulary of weather broadcasting. How quickly one's alarm at *some* changes in the language can become resistance or hostility to *any* change.

This is not to say that Orwell was always naïve about the tenuous relation of words and human experience. He knew that all language is a kind of lying. There is an essay of his, written about 1940 and posthumously published in *Collected Essays, Journalism and Letters of George Orwell,* called "New Words" that makes the point explicitly.

> Our language is practically useless for describing anything that goes on inside the brain. . . .
>   . . . [T]he lumpishness of words results in constant falsification. Is there anyone who has ever written so much as a love letter in which he felt that he said exactly what he intended? . . . Is not anyone with any degree of mental honesty conscious of telling lies all day long? (2:3, 6)

Art may thrive in this situation, with its "roundabout" ways of suggesting the inexpressible. Orwell's solution, however, is characteristically direct and unsophisticated. We need some new words, he suggests, that *will* express inner feelings, and he seems to think such inventions practical. (Can he be frivolous? But Orwell is never frivolous.) In any case he did not publish this essay during his lifetime, and for good reason. "I have written all this down hastily, and when I read through it I see there are weak patches in my argument" (2:12). He was right about that.

Newspeak offered the very opposite of "new words," for its essence was restriction of the lexicon. "Newspeak was designed not to extend but to *diminish* the range of thought, and this purpose was indirectly assisted by cutting the choice of words down to a minimum" (*Nineteen Eighty-Four,* 247). Throughout the appended "Principles of Newspeak" where this sentence appears, we can hear Orwell's conservative attitudes toward diction. For example, in Newspeak all strong verbs have become regularized: *thinked, runned.* That this development was already, in 1948, going on in the language (however slowly) would presumably not have pleased him.

It seems evident that his experience in the Spanish Civil War influenced Orwell's views of language, particularly his feelings about the reporting of news and the writing of history. In his essay "Looking Back on the Spanish Civil War," he wrote that

> Early in life I had noticed that no event is ever correctly reported in a newspaper, but in Spain, for the first time, I saw newspaper reports which did not bear any relation to the facts, not even the relationship which is implied in an ordinary lie. . . .
>   . . . This kind of thing is frightening to me, because it often gives me the feeling that the very concept of objective truth is fading out of the world. [Again Orwell is not utterly simplistic in his views of objective truth about the past.] I know it is the fashion to say that most of recorded history is lies anyway. I am willing to believe that history is for the most part inaccurate and biased, but

> what is peculiar to our own age is the abandonment of the idea that
> history *could* be truthfully written. (2:256, 258)

Winston Smith, we remember, is professionally engaged in the rewriting of history. His work is a parody of our own "revisionist" interpretations of the past. Every so often, in Oceania, the historical record has to be completely reversed in order to accommodate new political alliances. When Oceania abruptly stops fighting Eastasia and starts fighting Eurasia, all documents have to be rewritten to show that such has always been the case. At one point during the course of his work, Winston accidentally becomes aware that the confessions of some executed traitors had to be lies: a newspaper photograph clearly shows the three men at a Party meeting in Oceania on the day when they had confessed to being in Eurasia plotting against their country. "There was only one possible conclusion: the confessions were lies" (*Nineteen Eighty-Four*, 67). (Realistically speaking, it's a little hard to see why Winston is so upset by this, for his own profession has been lying from the start.)

In his consternation, Winston proceeds to face questions raised for Orwell by the Spanish War:

> For, after all, how do we know that two and two make four? Or
> that the force of gravity works? Or that the past is unchangeable? If
> both the past and the external world exist only in the mind, and if
> the mind itself is controllable—what then? (69)

This passage is immediately followed by the sternest of denials. "But no!" Those are not questions that Winston, or Orwell, can afford to entertain.

> But no! Truisms are true, hold on to that! The solid world exists, its
> laws do not change. Stones are hard, water is wet. . . . (69)

Any effort to make moral distinctions among uses of language, any effort to discriminate truth from lies, involves a step something like the one above. It is a step back into innocence, perhaps, and it operates by asserting the reality and force of human values. Very often it requires, too, an expression of outrage. Those of us concerned about doublespeak have to have taken just such a step.

Linguistic science has taught us much: a language is a constantly changing creature of society, and talk of "good" and "bad" language can lead to moralistic fuzziness. To their credit, linguists have also in recent years turned their attention to more human implications, as the disciplines of socio- and psycholinguistics attest. Nevertheless, some uses of language are plain evil, as Orwell brilliantly perceived, and as you and I believe.

The lesson of Watergate is said to be that you can only lie for so long, even in the White House. We are still a considerable distance from Newspeak, at least in the West, and it's possible to feel some complacency in the face of Orwell's drastic predictions. But he meant them as warnings, not predictions, and as warnings they are as real as they ever were. We need to appreciate, as Orwell did not, the shifting meanings of words and the inevitability of change. But without his base in traditional human values, and his capacity for outrage, our sophistication can turn to dust in our mouths.

Works Cited

Conant, James. *Modern Science and Modern Man*. New York: Columbia University Press, 1953.

Gallo, Ernest. "The Game of Analogy." *Western Humanities Review* 37, no. 1 (1983):62–66.

Hynes, Samuel, ed. *Twentieth Century Interpretations of 1984*. Englewood Cliffs, N.J.: Prentice-Hall, 1971.

McCormick, Donald. *Approaching 1984*. London: David & Charles, 1980.

Orwell, George. *Nineteen Eighty-Four*. New York: New American Library, Signet Edition, 1949.

———. "Politics and the English Language." In *In Front of Your Nose (1945–1950)*, 127–40. Vol. 4 of *The Collected Essays, Journalism and Letters of George Orwell*. Edited by Sonia Orwell and Ian Angus. 4 vols. London: Secker & Warburg, 1968.

———. "New Words." In *My Country Right or Left (1940–1943)*, 2–12. Vol. 2 of *The Collected Essays, Journalism and Letters of George Orwell*. Edited by Sonia Orwell and Ian Angus. 4 vols. London: Secker & Warburg, 1968.

———. "Looking Back on the Spanish Civil War." In *My Country Right or Left (1940–1943)*, 249–67. Vol. 2 of the *Collected Essays, Journalism and Letters of George Orwell*. Edited by Sonia Orwell and Ian Angus. London: Secker & Warburg, 1968.

3 Mr. Orwell, Mr. Schlesinger, and the Language

Hugh Rank
Governors State University

In 1946, George Orwell published "Politics and the English Language," an essay reprinted so often in school texts that it's usually introduced as the Classic-Statement-about-the-Abuse-of-Language-by-Politicians. Orwell has been canonized as a certified Good Guy, Freedom Fighter, Lover of the People, Popular Instructor of the Masses (via *Animal Farm* and *Nineteen Eighty-Four*) about the evils of totalitarian Socialism and Communism. In brief: Saint George. In 1974, Arthur Schlesinger, Jr., published an essay, "Politics and the American Language," which began with this sentence: "It takes a certain fortitude to pretend to amend Orwell on this subject" (553).

Schlesinger, too, is a good guy (solid credentials: at the right hand of JFK, etc.) and a good writer (urbane, informed, insightful, scholarly, prolific, etc.) who does say some interesting things in his essay about the language in the Vietnam and Watergate era. But because he's offering an "amendment" to update Orwell, perhaps he has missed some of the implications in the premises and assumptions of the original essay. It probably wouldn't bother the world too much, except that I do have the feeling that the Orwell and Schlesinger essays are going to be reprinted in future textbooks as a "matched set" to be read by thousands of future students of language. If so, before we start the official coronation ceremonies, let me point out a few of the shortcomings of the emperors' new clothes.

Not only because Orwell's essay is often "assigned reading" in classrooms and held up as some kind of model, but also because Orwell himself is raging against bad writing, lack of verbal precision, vagueness, and incompetency, it should be noted early that Orwell's essay suffers from serious stylistic flaws. Orwell opens by begging the question, by assuming to be true that which needs to be proven: "Most

Previously published in *College Composition and Communication* 28, no. 2 (1977).

people who bother with the matter at all would admit that the English language is in a bad way." A few lines later: "Now, it is clear that the decline of language must ultimately have political and economic causes" (4:127). (Beware of writers who seek assent to their ideas by casually, perhaps unconsciously, using phrasing that begs the question: *obviously, certainly, clearly, it's obvious, it is apparent, it's clear,* and so on.)

Orwell's openers are followed by a paragraph of weak analogies, massive overgeneralizations, a pleading for our sympathetic understanding ("I will come back to this presently, and I hope that by that time the meaning of what I have said here will have become clearer"), and an awkward paste-and-scissors listing of examples of bad writing ("Meanwhile, here are five specimens . . ." [4:128]).

Orwell's essay does have some good sentences in it, which are often quoted or used as epigrams. The most famous line is probably this one:

> In our time, political speech and writing are largely the defense of the indefensible. (4:136)

This is immediately followed by good examples, written in 1946 about the Soviets, which sound now as if they were taken from Pentagon communiqués during the Vietnam war. Elsewhere, Orwell creates some powerful sentences, which (if you can tolerate the paranoia or misanthropy) can be admired for their syntactical construction:

> All issues are political issues, and politics itself is a mass of lies, evasions, folly, hatred, and schizophrenia. (4:137)

Even when Orwell's tight writing fails, a good editor can use ellipsis to squeeze out a good quote from Orwell's conclusion:

> Political language . . . is designed to make lies sound truthful and murder respectable. (4:139)

Thus, at times within the essay, Orwell does write well; and in general, he is a well-intentioned critic of those who would exploit or oppress.

In addition to those parts of Orwell's essay that can be criticized for incompetent writing, readers who rigorously analyze the prose here will find some interesting patterns of thought surfacing obliquely through Orwell's dominant metaphors of disease and war. The imagery of battle permeates the essay, as does the metaphorical stress on sickness—with the implications also of "curing" and "healing." Near the end of the essay, Doctor Orwell is ready to give us his prescription: "One needs rules that one can rely on when instinct fails" (4:139). RX: Orwell's list of six rules. Take as often as needed, I presume. Three of his rules are strict *Nevers.* Two are hedgy *Never . . . ifs.* And the final rule, at the bottom line of the prescription, hedges against all the rest: *"Break any of these rules sooner than say anything outright barbarous"* (4:139, my emphasis).

In one way, this list seems simply a rather somber and awkward echo of D. H. Lawrence's very funny list of "rules" in his essay on Ben Franklin, but such hedging in a very serious essay brings attention to another noticeable pattern of Orwell's thinking. If I didn't like Orwell, I could call him mealymouthed, wishy-washy; more politely, I'm apt to say that he frequently hedges his bets, plays both sides, qualifies so much (*probably, unless, if, seems*) that it's almost doubletalk:

> Yet *without a doubt* it is the second kind of sentence that is *gaining ground* in modern English. *I do not want to exaggerate. This kind of writing is not yet universal, and outcrops of simplicity will occur here and there in the worst-written page. Still if. . . ."* (4:134, my emphasis)

What are Orwell's chief complaints about people abusing the language? What is his "catalogue of swindles and perversions," as he calls it? His examples, he states, have two common qualities that he dislikes: "staleness of imagery" and "lack of perception" (4:133, 129).

Concerning staleness of imagery: Orwell hates *dying metaphors* (clichés) and *mixed metaphors.* He likes the "newly invented" metaphor which evokes fresh images, and he tolerates and accepts the kind of metaphor that he calls "technically dead"—one that "has in effect reverted to being an ordinary word and can be generally used without loss of vividness" (4:130). But Orwell rages against the "in between" metaphors, those clichés "merely used because they save people the trouble of inventing phrases for themselves" (4:130). Orwell, however, doesn't set the limits, the boundaries, between the acceptable "dead" and the odious "dying"; nor does he tell us who is the Official Coroner or the Inquest Jury that certifies a phrase as "technically dead."

Orwell's second major complaint about modern writers is their "lack of precision" (4:129). Orwell ticks off a number of specifics that he objects to as contributing to "vagueness and sheer incompetence": mixed metaphors, padding, the passive voice, *-ize* and *de-* formations, *not . . . un-* formations, polysyllabic words, intensified adjectives, foreign words and phrases, and high-level abstractions (4:129–32). He lumps these techniques as errors and doesn't allow for their deliberate use by competent writers as a tactic to achieve an end.

Misdemeanors and Felonies

My objections to the attitudes of Orwell and Schlesinger fall into two general categories: the first grouping is *misdemeanors* of lesser importance because they are problems internal to these particular essays (The Good Old Days; Fast-Shuffling of a Stacked Deck). The second category, *felonies*, involves some important general attitudes about the use of language and about the analysis of language and politics (Virtue Triumphs! Hand-Wringing; Shoulder-Shrugging).

The Good Old Days

"Modern English, especially written English, is full of bad habits," Orwell begins, frequently stressing the evils of the *present:* "This mixture of vagueness and sheer incompetence is the most marked characteristic of Modern English prose. . . . The whole tendency of modern prose is away from concreteness" (4:129, 133). Schlesinger agrees that our modern language is corrupt and argues that it is becoming even more corrupt since the publication of Orwell's essay (553). Both men claim that the situation is growing worse in the present generation, a complaint (especially by elders) not new in human history. Things-Are-Going-to-Hell-Fast propositions are usually paired (as here) with the corollary of a Golden Age in the past, a Camelot, the Good Old Days when things were better.

Fast-Shuffling of a Stacked Deck

Orwell says, without any supporting data or examples, that there's an "increase in slovenliness and vagueness" in modern prose; in brief, he states or implies that the language is declining or decadent and needs to be defended (4:132). Schlesinger follows suit, but at least he devotes two sentences to shuffle quickly from the 1850s to the 1970s, attributing the increase in "linguistic pollution" to "the rise of mass communications, the growth of large organizations and novel technologies, the invention of advertising and public relations, the professionalization of education" (556).

Offhand, I can't produce statistics, word counts, facts and figures, or computer printouts of a quantitative analysis of language manipulation in previous eras. But memory, at least, reminds me that I've read a lot of windy, verbose, bombastic rhetoric from ages past; I know that such padding didn't start in our century. My recollections of Victorian prose (circa 1850) conjure up sentences dragging on forever, long-winded, inflated, and pompous. I also recall Shakespeare (circa 1600) playing around in *Hamlet,* satirizing the verbal maneuvers and the courtly cant of Polonius, Rosenkrantz and Guildenstern. Chaucer's Pardoner (circa 1400), I recall, knew a thing or two about word play, manipulating his sermons so as to free his audiences from their material goods to benefit their spiritual enrichment. I've read enough scholastic philosophy to know that the medievals were not above hair-splitting, nit-picking, padding, and circumlocution. Contemplating the Roman orators and rhetoricians, then going back even further, to the rhetors and sophists of the Greeks, I don't believe I can recall any era in which there wasn't a whole lot of hanky-panky going on with words.

The notion that people (and their languages) are getting worse is a myth and an illusion. I think I could accurately predict that there is going to be more "misuse" of language in America twenty-five years hence, simply because there will be another one hundred million more talking heads here by then. My prediction may be accurate, but it's not very profound. I remain unimpressed by Orwell's and Schlesinger's vague carping about how things are getting worse.

Orwell stacks the deck humorously by pitting the simple, beautiful style of *Ecclesiastes* against a modernized version in pretentious so-ciological jargon (4:133). Good clean fun, but still deck-stacking. I'll grant that *Ecclesiastes* is well written, and Saint Paul too; but I could select some of the "begat" passages from the Good Book which aren't very inspired writing.

Schlesinger is more sober and serious in his deck-stacking. For example, he used the *Federalist Papers* as an example of how intelligent writers—and readers—were in the good old days of the Founders: "One can only marvel at the sophistication of an audience that con-sumed and relished pieces so closely reasoned, so thoughtful and analytical" (554). Indeed, the *Federalist Papers* were well written, but they were not typical; not representative of the literally thousands of political tracts in that decade. Junk political pamphlets and junk ser-mons were as common in that era as junk mail is in ours. Nor can the collective mind of their audience be read from an analysis of the *Federalist Papers;* it was almost the same audience, after all, that a decade earlier had made Thomas Paine's emotional diatribe *Common Sense* the bestselling, most influential political work in the era.

Virtue Triumphs!

Schlesinger quotes Ralph Waldo Emerson as an "authority" to make the point that good people say good things, corrupt people use corrupt language: "The corruption of man is followed by the corruption of language" (556). Emerson, too, is a good guy, lofty and inspiring at times, but pretty flaky as a philosopher, misty and muddy at times, and his simplistic equation need not be accepted as gospel truth. In fact, it's this Virtue Triumphs attitude—that Good People say Good Things, that Corrupt People use Corrupt Language, that there are Bad Guys Out There—it's this attitude that is so dangerous. This polarized view of human nature, that there are Good people (Our Side) and Bad people (Out There), often leads to catastrophe. Persecutions, crusades, and wars have been carried out in the past as "good" people, with the best of intentions, sought to punish or to eradicate the "bad."

A more realistic attitude toward human nature is that every individual has the potential and capacity for good and evil and that all people are complicated mixtures of these qualities. Virtue doesn't always triumph (at least in this world); some of the most corrupt people can use the language most effectively, and some of the nicest people can be the most awkward, unskilled users of the language. Aristotelians, Thomists, and other realistic philosophers have always insisted on these points, which stress the complexity of the human situation.

It's probable that neither Orwell nor Schlesinger would consciously endorse any polarized, Good-Bad dichotomy; both men were sufficiently exposed to the ubiquity of human error and evil. But it appears that both men have made certain unconscious assumptions about how humans communicate, about "language manipulation"—a key term used here in a special way.

Hand Wringing

Emerson's buddy, Henry David Thoreau, once observed, "There are a thousand hacking at the branches of evil to one who is striking at the root." In my judgment, the root cause of much of our confusion about language today is the implicit assumption, seldom recognized or articulated, that language manipulation is intrinsically bad; that only bad guys manipulate language.

People who unconsciously accept this premise are condemned to hand-wringing, to feelings of guilt, to frustration (due to their call for impossible conditions) and possibly even misanthropy, because it can be observed that all people, in all eras, in all lands, have done—and continue to do—this "bad" thing of language manipulation.

Many people today intuitively sense their own language manipulation. Because they do not want to be hypocrites, any sense of moral outrage they may have against the language of the political or commercial propagandists, whether the Kremlin or the Pentagon or Madison Avenue, is countered from within; from their own sense of personal guilt that they, too, manipulate language. So the call for reform is usually very personal: "Let's reform ourselves first, then, once pure, we can go after others."

Indeed, most of the reformers and the critics of political language and commercial advertising, the texts and the teachers, I've encountered have assumed this premise that language manipulation is bad. (In my essay, "The Teacher-Heal-Thyself Myth," [NCTE, 1974] this is more fully developed.) In contrast, let me state the premise that *language manipulation is a neutral, natural human activity and that any "goodness" or "badness" depends on the context of the whole situation;* on who is saying what to whom, under what conditions and circumstances, with what intent, and with what results. Because such judgments are demanding, complex, and often tentative, they are much less emotionally satisfying that the "certitude" afforded by relying upon an a priori judgment that language manipulation is bad in and of itself.

Such hand-wringing and personal guilt feelings can be recognized in Orwell's essay. After inveighing against language "abuses," he feels guilty: "Look back through this essay, and for certain you will find that I have again and again committed the very faults I am protesting against" (4:137). You're right, George. You do "commit faults." For example, even in your closing paragraph (after you've already repented!), your writing is pretty trite, using dead metaphors ("One need not swallow such absurdities . . .") and padding ("one ought to recognize . . . that the present political chaos . . . one can probably bring about some improvement by starting at the verbal end." [4:139]).

Schlesinger, too, gets into the hand-wringing business. He begins his essay by linking it to the Orwell essay:

> In 1946 we comfortably supposed that Orwell was talking about other people—Nazis and Stalinists, bureaucrats and sociologists. . . . Now recent history has obliged us to extend his dispirited analysis to ourselves. (553)

Much of Schlesinger's essay makes favorable comments about the great political writings of our Founders; but, after praising the noble rationality and lucidity of their writings, Schlesinger admits, "It must not be supposed, however, that even this great generation was immune to temptation." To win votes, "they changed their tone and relaxed their standards" (555). Schlesinger quotes some of Jefferson's overblown flattery of farmers and calls it a "lapse" from realism:

> For, as society grew more diversified, new interests claimed their places in the sun; and each in time had to be courted and flattered as the Jeffersonians had courted and flattered the agriculturists. The desire for success at the polls thus sentimentalized and cheapened the language of politics. (555)

Flattery is not new, was not born in this country nor with the advent of democracy. Flattery, often in terms of inflated language, has always been a human way of courting power. Power, however, in past eras, existed in the Court or the Crown—Queens and Kings, Czars and Czarinas, Empresses and Emperors—and ample "literature" exists, written by earlier poets and playwrights praising the virtues of their royal patrons. Democracy shifted power away from the monarch, giving some power to the people and to the many diverse groups which now became the new target audiences for flattery. "Success at the polls" simply *replaced* "success at the courts." To suggest that democracy is a cause that "cheapened the language" ignores the courtly cant of the literary lackeys of previous eras.

Several paragraphs later, Schlesinger modifies or changes his position. After discussing the language manipulation and the vulgarity of Nixon as revealed in the White House tapes, Schlesinger wonders about Tocqueville's idea that "such deterioration is inherent in democracy" (559). Now, Schlesinger, speaking of what he calls "linguistic decay," points out its widespread existence today:

> But a moment's reflection suggests that the process is by no means confined to the United States nor to democracies. Language degenerates a good deal more rapidly and thoroughly in communist and fascist states. . . . Nowhere is meaning more ruthlessly manipulated, nowhere is language more stereotyped, mechanical, implacably banal and systematically false. Nowhere is it more purged of personal nuance and human inflection than in Russia and China. In democracies the assault on language is piecemeal, sporadic and unorganized. (559–60)

Here Schlesinger surveys the contemporary world and finds (correctly) that "everyone does it." In his next paragraph, he looks back in American history and notes how "the Constitution is in many respects a document of calculated omission and masterful ambiguity" (560). Earlier, Schlesinger had praised the "quest for precision" by the Founding Fathers (559), and now he's praising their deliberate ambiguity. Underneath this confusion is a shifting major premise; but predominantly the assumption is that language manipulation is bad, per se.

Shoulder-Shrugging

The major weakness of both Orwell's and Schlesinger's essays (as well as of a score of others by lesser-known writers responding to the language of the Vietnam war, the Pentagon, and the Watergate affair) is that these scolding essays end with a vague, shoulder-shrugging attitude. Such essays are sincere but ineffectual. They may accurately describe the language manipulation or itemize the jargon, but they offer a weak diagnosis of cause and a weaker prognosis of "cure."

Orwell and Schlesinger recite a litany of horrors about how language is being used by politicians and the powerful in such a way that there are terrible human consequences: war and violence, pain and suffering. But at the end of Orwell's essay, at the end of the listing of horrors, Orwell feels guilty about his own "sins," mildly shrugs his shoulders and urges us as individuals to reform and to disapprove (to mock? to purse our lips? to arch our eyebrows? to smirk?) of others who abuse language.

Classical rhetoricians recommended that in the closing passages of such a speech or essay basically designed to persuade an audience, the writer should call for *specific action*—not a shoulder-shrugging, nor a vague, wishy-washy, hand-wringing "let's do *something*" ending. After showing the horrible examples and moving the audience, the writer should climax the discourse with specific things to do or at least clarify for the audience that there are specific things which can be done.

I'm not suggesting that the writer oversimplify or promise a panacea, nor am I faulting Orwell or Schlesinger for not "solving" the problem of political language-manipulation; but I am criticizing those who would so revere Orwell's essay as to consider it the "classic" statement and who would recommend it to others as being a "brilliant example" of what we ought to do. What? What should we do? Orwell doesn't say, except for the vaguest generalities about reforming ourselves. Would you accept this from a writer or speaker who had just shown you example after example of horrible auto accidents? Would you be content with a mild admonition to "drive carefully"? A pleasant truism, but hardly a significant statement.

If Orwell and Schlesinger had started with the premise that language manipulation is a natural and normal human activity, then they could have concentrated their attention on the context (who is saying what to whom, with what intent and what result); on the growing inequality between the professional persuaders and the average persuadee; on making value judgments about the relative degrees of significance, merit and importance of various persuaders and subject matters; and on establishing priorities for our attention.

If Orwell and Schlesinger had assumed that all people will always try to persuade others; that money and power tend to concentrate; that there will always be an inequality in persuasion situations (on one side the powerful persuader, whether Monarch or Church, government or corporation; on the other side, the individual); then this cluster of assumptions could have been a reasonable starting point to suggest how people could move toward a greater degree of equality. In a democratic society, for example, such movement toward equality for the individual might be accomplished through both legislation and education.

Thus far, no one has written the Classic-Essay-about-What-to-Do-about-Language-Manipulation-by-Advertisers-and-Politicians. Nor is it likely that any one person, one essay, or one book will come up with a "solution." No one has fully itemized or specified those needed kinds of legislation (such as disclosure laws, open-meeting laws, "shield" laws covering journalists, standardized systems, Truth-in-Lending, Truth-in-Advertising, Freedom of Information laws, and so on) that will help balance the situation between organized persuaders and individual citizens. Nor has anyone organized coherently a comprehensive educational program (beginning with preschoolers' TV) that will train masses of people in the sophisticated literacy necessary to recognize the persuasion patterns in the many forms of human language and to understand the techniques of the various media.

It's this very absence of any satisfactory plan that ought to be stressed to students. Probably both Orwell and Schlesinger would agree that their essays were meant to provoke, not to solve; to awaken, not to lull; to begin, and not to end a quest for a better understanding of language and politics. Orwell's essay is not the "last word" on the subject; it is one of the first.

Works Cited

Fairfield, Roy P., ed. *The Federalist Papers: A Collection of Essays Written in Support of the Constitution of the United States from the Original Texts of Alexander Hamilton, James Madison, John Jay.* 3rd Ed. Baltimore, Md.: Johns Hopkins University Press, 1981.

Lawrence, D. H. "Benjamin Franklin." *Studies in Classic American Literature.* 13–31. New York: Thomas Seltzer, 1923.

Orwell, George. "Politics and the English Language." *In Front of Your Nose (1945–1950),* 127–145. Vol. 4 of *The Collected Essays, Journalism and Letters of George Orwell.* Edited by Sonia Orwell and Ian Angus. New York: Harcourt, Brace and World, 1968.

———. *Nineteen Eighty-Four.* New York: Harcourt Brace Jovanovich, 1949. Reprint, New American Library, 1983.

———. *Animal Farm.* London: Secker & Warburg, 1945.

Paine, Thomas. *Common Sense and Other Political Writings.* Edited by Nelson F. Adkins. New York: Liberal Arts Press, 1953.

Rank, Hugh. "The-Teacher-Heal-Thyself Myth." In *Language and Public Policy,* 215–34. Urbana, Ill.: National Council of Teachers of English, 1974.

Schlesinger, Arthur, Jr. "Politics and the American Language." *The American Scholar* 43 (1974):553–62.

4 What Do We Know?

Charles Weingartner
University of South Florida

Recently, on some television talk show (was it "live"? Live on tape? A tape of animatronic devices? Or even, perhaps, an electronically produced simulation of "actual" persons? How to tell?), the author of a newly published book on "propaganda" made a statement that the interviewer just let go by, but that made me do a double take. What he said was, "We don't know what we don't know."

For a moment, this sounded to me to be pretty much like most of the "profound" utterances that characterize talk shows: they cut right through to the surface. But as I ruminated about it, I recalled Alfred North Whitehead's observation that it takes an unusual kind of mind to analyze the obvious. The statement seemed to me to state what was so obvious it didn't warrant stating. Of *course* we don't know what we don't know. But then I started thinking about it in relation to what we do know, or, rather, think we know.

What Do We Think We Know?

As Norbert Wiener noted in his book *The Human Use of Human Beings* (Cambridge: Riverside, 1950), one of the great paradoxes of the "communications revolution" is that as we have access to more and more media of communication, we simultaneously have access to less and less information. It might be helpful at this point to note Wiener's precise definition of what he meant when he used the term "information." "Information . . . is a name for the content of what is exchanged with the outer world as we adjust to it, and [as we] make our adjustment felt upon it" (124). Wiener also argues that the more probable the message, the less information it gives.

It is necessary to note here that Wiener's definition is essentially a "mechanical" one in that it is based upon the Transportation Theory of

Communication. This theory has as its basic paradigm the "transmitter, channel, receiver" schema, and holds that the meaning of a message is exclusively in the message itself; the media merely move the message from source to receiver. As research in perception (i.e., the process of information getting from outside of us through our various senses to inside of us) unequivocally demonstrates, however, messages do not move like letters through a postal system. They do not "contain" meaning. Messages consist of "cues"; i.e., words or numbers or other signals or symbols that suggest to us which meanings we might assign to them out of the corpus of meanings that our experience has enabled us to accumulate and that our consciousness permits us to recall. This is a very different kind of process from the one represented by the transportation theory of communication. What it means is that we do not "get" meanings from messages, we *assign* meanings to messages, and can do so only as our experiences and purposes in a given context permit.

The Many Faces of "Information"

Wiener, however, permits us to make some distinctions that can be useful in trying to figure out what we know. His definition of information provides a base line for us to make further—necessary—distinctions among messages[1] and I suggest, in a most limited way, the need for making distinctions among the different kinds of "information" that the messages ostensibly encode in the various media. Remember, the information is not in the messages; it is in us. We assign meanings (i.e., generate information) from the cues embodied in the messages as our experiences and our purposes permit. We cannot assign a meaning that our experience has not previously recorded or that our purpose in a given context does not permit us to assign, irrespective of whether or not it is recorded in our experience. So it can help, in our attempt to assess what we know, to make distinctions between misinformation, disinformation, anti-information, and semi-information. A brief description of each of these terms is as follows:

Misinformation is what might be called deliberate lying. This kind of "information" is often associated with the military. We were introduced to it during the Vietnam war and met it again during the invasion of Grenada.

Disinformation is a particularly elusive form in that it can be a result of deliberate lying or mere stupidity. It is usually comprised of utterances that do not easily permit the assignment of any meaning with any degree of assurance. The limits of meaning that can be assigned are determined solely by the needs of the hearer or reader. The one characteristic that it does have is the conscious purpose of diverting interested parties from the pursuit of information.[2] We learn today that banks do not make bad loans, they have "nonperforming assets," or we do not have economic recessions, we have "periods of negative economic growth."

Anti-information is a more complex form of disinformation in that it is composed and disseminated specifically for the purpose of stopping a line of inquiry. Anti-information provides a "concluding" statement; i.e., a statement that seems to make it unnecessary to pursue the inquiry at hand any further. Politicians, for example, accept "responsibility" for their actions—but none of the consequences. Anti-information can also divert a line of inquiry from the original target to another, either real or imaginary. Guns don't kill people; people kill people. Anti-information is generally less ambiguous than disinformation and so is less susceptible to unlimited inferences. It is provided in order to conclude a given pursuit of, or inquiry into, information relating to a specific matter.

Semi-information is, in a way, the most insidious form of noninformation since it consists of partial bits of information, any or all of which are accurate and verifiable—up to a point—but none of which are adequate for the purpose of understanding either the matter involved or its possible consequences. The official statement of the Soviet Council of Ministers said that the Chernobyl accident resulted in "a certain leak of radioactive substances."

As can be seen, semi-information, like anti-information, can fulfill the same function as disinformation. There are degrees of difference rather than differences in kind involved. Lest there be a tendency to dismiss "mere degrees of difference," it is worth remembering that Norbert Wiener pointed out, with reference to questions relating to adequate and accurate information, that "the difference between a medicinal dose of strychnine and a fatal one is only one of degree" (33).

The Semi-Informative Nature of News Media

Virtually any—and, for that matter, every—news report, whether in print (as in a newspaper) or in oral form (as on radio or television) is, at best, semi-information since it is virtually impossible to make adequate and accurate information available about anything. The less complex and less significant (in a larger sense) the matter being reported, the closer the report can be to both adequacy and accuracy. But the more complex and more significant the matter being reported, the farther away from both adequacy and accuracy the report will be. This is a result of both data-gathering problems and the volume of data to be presented. Most persons, except those professionally involved in a given matter to be reported, reach "information overload" at some point early in any report, in any medium.

Given the marginal role of print in the lives of most persons today, other media (radio and television in particular) are the primary sources of "information" about almost everything. The television news format atomizes to an excruciating degree even such semi-information as is witlessly presented between commercials. To say that the television news show format barely scratches the surface of any story—an "in depth" presentation might take three or four minutes for example—fails to grasp the significance of *what is omitted from every story*.

Beyond this, as Wiener also pointed out, the atomized semi-information is presented within a persistent frame of fixed bias that the commercial (i.e., financial) bases of conventional media (newspapers, magazines, radio, and television) *require*. The audience cannot be upset or antagonized or it will defect from the product-purchasing role that makes all messages (predominantly packaged in non-information forms) available. Each mass medium is a flea market whose primary reason for being is to deliver prospective purchasers to peddlers. Apart from all other considerations, this economic fact about all mass media—the primary sources of "information" for all of us—precludes any possibility of adequate and accurate information being made available even about the most innocuous of subjects.

There is no doubt that as a medium of communication, print makes available much more adequate, if not more accurate, information than any other medium. There are, of course, tremendous variations in the adequacy of the information made available. Not only are there vast disparities between newspapers with regard to both adequacy and accuracy of information (despite the fact that most newspapers depend entirely on two, or at most three wire services for all of their "information" about anything other than local matters), but there are also vast disparities between the various, so-called "news" magazines such as *Time* and *Newsweek*. As any perusal of their advertisements illustrates, the most widely circulated news magazines see their readership as consisting mostly of business executives. This audience is not characteristically liberal in its point of view. The result is that neither are the news magazines. There are other sources of information in magazine format such as *In These Times* and *Mother Jones*. These focus on specific audiences and some even include "liberal" information in the form of detailed coverage resulting from substantive investigative reporting of matters either completely ignored or grossly slighted by the larger, popular magazines.

The point, then, is that to be even nominally well-informed, it is *necessary* to read something on the order of a dozen magazines representing a wide spectrum of editorial biases in parallel with a variety of newspapers, in order for a reasonable perspective to be maintained. Most newspapers in the United States, however, are dismally inadequate as sources of information about national and international events, to say nothing of events or matters that the local power élite prefers not have publicized. And those who depend primarily, much less solely, on a local newspaper for their impressions of the world around them are virtually operating in a psychotic state, so far from reality does such a parochial perception leave them.

The Inadequacy of Our Best Sources of Information

While print is far superior to any other medium as a source of information, it, too, is far from adequate. Especially is this true of newspapers. A. J. Liebling spent his life cataloging the inadequacies and inaccuracies of newspapers. His book, *The Press* (New York, Ballantine, 1961), is replete with details as to why he came to fill this role. His critical reviews of the press, incidentally, pre-date television by some time.

No one has filled Liebling's critical role in relation to television and radio. It is one of the least often made points that there is virtually no media criticism outside of print. Radio does not include any substantive or continuing critical analysis of radio, nor does television include any substantive or continuing critical analysis of itself. And neither says or does much even to acknowledge the existence of print. Since print is about the only medium in which one can find any information that can be useful in developing a perspective on itself and other media, the lack of media criticism is a grievous omission that leaves all of us at a serious disadvantage when we try (if we ever do) to assess the adequacy and/or the accuracy of any information made available to us through the media.

The exotic role of print in our society; that is, the limited degree to which print media are used by the "average citizen" as a significant source of important and useful information, simply intensifies the problem of getting such information to the public. Yet without that information, the public cannot make sensible (assuming that rationality ever affects judgment) decisions and choices, not only in personal terms, but also in relation to larger social and political questions. While print is largely ignored (and always has been) by the majority of Americans, there are even more depressing points to be made about print, such as (1) *TV Guide* is the most widely read print in the United States (*Advertising Age,* 18 April 1988: S-13), and (2) the most widely read portion of newspapers in the United States (even by schoolteachers) is Ann Landers. Ponder the implications of those two items.

Military Sources of Misinformation

It surely is not news to anyone that lying—both public and private—is the most common form of activity engaged in by those in politics and in the military. Whether politicians lie more to generals than generals do to politicians, however, is open to question. Generals "depend" upon politicians for their money, but they also use the virtually unchallengeable claim that they are interested only in "national defense" to overcome any political reluctance to provide more money.

National defense is a corollary of "national security." Probably the most effective strategy every employed by the American military was the shift in its nomenclature from "War" Department to "Defense" Department. Everyone, including generals (at least publicly), is "against" war. In our society this produces, simultaneously, the effect of being "for" peace. According to the military, we need to spend more and more money every year for weapons systems not to be prepared to conduct a war but to *"protect the peace."* This form of lunacy seems always to have been popular, but after almost forty years of media-assisted training in paranoia, the American public now "requires" any presidential candidate (and subsequent President) to vow a commitment to national defense. This produced spending of over $1.5 trillion on the military during the eight years of the Reagan administration.

In contemporary American society, the language of defense is more potent emotionally than the language of religion—any religion. And most of it, as history and current investigative reporting shows, is inaccurate. Whole books have been written about this phenomenon, including at least a dozen relating to Vietnam alone. The military lied to *everyone,* including itself, for thirteen years, at least, in and about Vietnam.

Jonathan Schell's book *The Fate of the Earth* (New York: Knopf, 1982) provides a vivid description of military policy, especially as it relates to nuclear weapons, that is not available in wire-service-fed newspapers or on commercial radio and television programs. The media receive, instead, the standard military description, routinely amplified by the President, the Secretary of State, and "national security" advisers. The bizarre notion that it is "safe" to have a "limited nuclear war," for example, is now official policy.

One of the oldest aphorisms about the military goes: "Generals are always fighting the last war." The military rhetoric about nuclear weapons goes on as if it merely described extensions of conventional explosives, and in the process reveals how limited (and paranoid) the military perception is. That we can have an arsenal of nuclear weapons sufficient to destroy the whole planet several times over, is a tribute to the military misinformation program, which is conducted relentlessly with sympathetic assistance from all media.

In any case, the point here is that any information contrapuntal to the standard military and political and economic establishment line is not easily come by. It exists almost exclusively in print, and then in forms that the vast majority of the population seldom—if ever—even sees, much less reads and contemplates as a basis for personal action. Just one example of the significance of this point: Twice as many people read the *Golf Digest* as read the *New Yorker;* three times as many buy *Hustler;* ten times as many buy *Playboy;* and to no one's surprise, thirty-five times as many buy *TV Guide* (*Ulrich's International Periodicals Directory*, 1988–89). Print as a medium for making information available to the vast majority is almost as quaint as stone tablets.

The Inadequacy of Television
as an Information Source

Television and its massive maceration of information is far and away the most popular source of "information" for Americans. Even the twenty-four-hour-a-day news channels (mostly on cable) turn out to present a random catalog of disparate—and mostly trivial—stories. Their "in-depth" efforts consist mostly of ninety-second or two-minute "pieces" from a teletype machine that cut right through to the surface, or interviews with "experts," or celebrities of one kind or another, who respond to mainly dumb questions with opinions that turn out—as subsequent events clearly reveal—to be erroneous. It is worth noting at this point that one of the least mentioned—and most crucial—points about television "news" and "information" is its very relentlessness, and not just on twenty-four hour programs. The relentless deluge of "news" and "information" via television erases the public memory. Accordingly, there is no public memory—at least of any significant political or military or economic event—irrespective of the mode of "reporting." There never has been much public interest in substantive matters—of any kind—anyway, but with the advent of television the possibility of a public memory functioning in any practical way was simply obliterated. The interest in television that sustains any memory at all is confined to soap operas and soap-opera-like dramas that not only do little to keep the public informed, but also serve to distract them from matters that they need to know about for both their own personal welfare and the welfare of society. It is now commonplace, for example, for viewers to complain if their soap opera programming is displaced by the coverage of some other event—any other event—no matter how potentially important it might be.

In a survey of high school students on the relative amounts of time and attention they give to newspapers and television, one said, "We frequently talk about television programs and ask each other whether or not we saw something on television, but we never talk about newspapers and say we saw a really neat or important story about anything."

The Message Is Not the Meaning

While most attention is paid to the media (i.e., the press, television, magazines, and even, sometimes, radio) by those concerned about the relative level of information (in any or all of its forms) made available to the public, little attention seems to be paid to the public which, it is assumed, will behave rationally on the basis of adequate and accurate information. This assumption derives from an unquestioned acceptance that the media merely move the message from source to receiver. As was pointed out above, however, the only place that meaning can reside is in the head of some human being. It is no secret that different people do make different meanings of the same message, event, or observation. Eyewitness testimony, contrary to popular belief, is unreliable. The disparity of meaning-making abilities is also illustrated by the Letters to the Editor column in any periodical with a wide (even though relatively homogeneous) readership. If any meaning at all is associated with anything on a conscious level, it occurs only inside of the head of the person whose consciousness is impinged upon. So, there is no sensible way to consider "the meaning" of any message, in any form, apart from the audience that somehow perceived it.

An Audience Deceived

Where does this leave us with the American audience? How good at making accurate, reasonable, and rational meanings is this audience? What is the audience like for newspapers, periodicals, radio, film, and television?

First, it should be noted that the American audience is probably not substantively different in its meaning-making ability from any other audience. This amounts to its being much more likely to miss the point or to come up with a colossal non sequitur than it is to get anything—even on the simplest, most literal level—straight. This, in turn, is one of the main reasons why politicians, especially, utter routinely (and most solemnly) the by now obligatory and ludicrous reminder that "the American public is much too intelligent to be deceived by blah, blah. . . ." It is too bad that it simply is not true.

The American public is deceived by almost everybody who deliberately addresses it—for any reason: politicians, military, advertisers, automobile manufacturers, utility companies and peddlers of almost everything that is advertised in print or on television. This is so unsurprising that it is surprising if any claim made by anybody about anything turns out, later, to be true. Nonetheless, given the amount of schooling that is available free, along with all of the books, magazines, newspapers, radio, and television—all of which nominally make "information" available, the American public is just plain dumb. Now dumb is not the same as ignorant—it is worse, much worse. Josh Billings caught the essence of the difference in his observation (made more than one hundred years ago) that "The trouble ain't that people are ignorant; it's that they 'know' so much that ain't so."

The best way to determine what people know and believe (that is, *value*) is to look at how they spend their time and money, as well as the other choices and decisions they make which reveal their beliefs and values.

According to the *New York Times* (3 July 1988, 2:24), the television set is on for an average of six and one-half hours a day in the average American home. (This does not include video games.) For six and one-half hours a day it fills the house with soap operas, bowling matches, golf tournaments, baseball games, football games, tennis matches, celebrity "athletic" contests, game shows, and assorted other mind-numbing activities including prime time evening dramas like "Dallas" (which drew the largest television audience in history with the program that revealed the answer to the question that even brought England to a virtual halt—"Who shot J.R.?"), "Dynasty" and "Falcon Crest." If you added up all of the people watching, and all of the hours watched, and multiplied one by the other to determine the total hours devoted to this kind of mental masturbation, you would come up with something like 260 million hours *per day*. That is an impressive number of hours to be spent each day at *not* becoming aware of anything useful—to put it in the best light possible.

The stories are endless about how dumb the ordinary American is. At Miami International Airport, a special telephone, colored blue, was installed for business executives who make only collect or credit card calls. It has *no* coin slot. The directions appear where the coin slot would be on a conventional coin phone. They state "Lift the receiver. Dial '0' and then the area code and number." Period. Endless numbers of people try to force coins into any crack they can find, or they try to use the phone to call taxis or hotels or motels or almost anything other than making a collect or credit card call. These are the people who deplore the state of American schooling (which is worth deploring) and especially the inability of kids to read. They are so dumb that they don't even move to the regular telephone next to the blue one.

These are the people who support "National Defense," and favor "limited nuclear war," and especially the use of the neutron bomb (because it only kills people, it does not destroy property); who support the Moral Majority, and join cults, and slap on bumper stickers that say "Buy American." They learned that from American television commercials about automobiles. As a matter of fact, Chrysler's Champ, Colt, and Arrow models are built in Japan by Mitsubishi, and Ford advertises its Escort model as a "world car." The parts for this car come from nine different foreign countries. "Buy American."

It would take too much space to enumerate even just a few other examples of American Dumb, so let me just cite two examples:

1. A U.S. Office of Education (USOE) study finds that 55 million adult Americans (less than half the population 18 to 65) are competent in reading, writing, computation, and problem-solving skills.

2. In the above-mentioned USOE study, findings included:
   - 15 million could not address an envelope for mailing;
   - 68.5 million could not read and understand a simple paragraph;

- 35 million could not read an airline schedule;
- 30.7 million could not determine the best unit price among three sizes of cereal boxes.

The study was conducted by a University of Texas team over a period of four years. The study noted that there were no significant differences between males and females or between social and economic groups.

So that's the great, intelligent, knowledgeable, sophisticated American public in the fourth decade of the nuclear space age.

If our adult population enjoys a level of knowledge, belief, and behavior appropriate to a kind of continuing Gong Show, what of our youth? What do they know? Believe? Value? How do they act out what they know, believe, and value?

Remember that they comprise, by a vast majority, the audience for rock concerts, the consumers of junk food, the most dangerous drivers, the most dangerous criminal element, the most predictable audience for fantasy and horror films, carriers of portable stereo radios, the most devout followers of the dumbest fads, the most misinformed portion of the population, that part of the population that reads the least and with the worst comprehension of what it does read, and so on.

What's the worst thing to say about teenagers and what is inside their heads? The worst you can say about them is that the content of their heads is almost identical to that of the content of the heads of adults. What adult Americans have inside their heads (as revealed by their theology, their philosophy, their political views, their beliefs about people different from themselves, and their understanding of how their own bodies function) is indistinguishable from the contents of the heads of medieval peasants. Having the use of microwave ovens, deep-freezers, self-starters, automatic transmissions, television tape recorders, and hand-held calculators does not only not make people any smarter, it makes them even dumber. Medieval peasants had many more practical skills, for example, than the present day consumer in our technologically sophisticated society. It is part of the Faustian bargain with technology.

Availability of Information
Does Not Presume Knowledge

It is too easy to get at knowledge (or "information") in our technological society. Indeed, it is almost impossible to avoid it. Yet, one of the curiosities of "progress" is that as more knowledge has become available, less of it is in use by the ordinary person. Even given the fact that the vast majority of information so easily available is trivial and superficial, it is impressive that so many people manage to avoid knowing even the trivial. That there is some correlation between schooling (at least the quantity of time spent in school) and the affinity for dumb ideas, movements, and cults is incontrovertible. Smart people can handle (however poorly) complexity—that's what makes them smart. Dumb people require and insist upon simplicity, preferably provided by a few simple aphorisms and rules to be followed.

New knowledge has no effect on ingrained attitudes. That is one of the reasons for the curious lack of effect of schooling on values and behavior. Most abstract knowledge (which is anything unrelated to our personal experience) is inert anyway. We can "know" it, but it doesn't make any difference as far as our decisions, choices, beliefs, and behavior are concerned, because there is little point to knowing something if we do not behave as if we do.

Most of the "knowledge" made available via schooling, television, film, or print is abstract and emotionally null and void. Plato observed more than 2,500 years ago that "In order for education to accomplish its purpose, reason must have an adequate emotional base." The point is that we cannot know anything unless it is emotionally significant to us. And the probability of abstract information being emotionally significant is zero.

So, what are we to make of this? Well, even if television were capable of presenting adequate and accurate information (which it is not) we would continue to know only what we already knew before we saw whatever it was on television. In a literal sense, people can only see and hear what they already "know," i.e., what is emotionally important to them. Anything that diverges from what they already know constitutes an emotional threat because it requires them to abandon the security of what they already "know" for the insecurity of learning something new. People prefer to hang on to what makes them feel secure. Abstract knowledge (like mathematics, or geography, or parts of speech) isn't affected by this and so doesn't make much difference one way or the other. Whether or not we ever get to know any of that stuff is mostly a function of whether or not we need to use any of it in a relatively routine way. If we don't use it we forget it. (Maybe that's the best part.) How come we don't forget how to ride a bicycle?

The problems, the serious problems with news and information that is sprayed at us via the media, derive from the incredibility (read: lack of credibility) that this flimsy stuff deserves. The main sources of such "information" for Americans of all ages, in order of frequency and quantity of use, are television, radio, film, and some form of print. So, for all practical purposes, most Americans live in a world that television builds: what they "know" of the world around them filters through the wire services (primarily AP and UPI), the biases of the reporters (both local and network) whose station or network executives have already imposed their biases (strongly conservative despite the claims of politicians and other critics) on the thin stuff that the wire service employees have gathered.

News and the Half Truth

Years ago (1952), Elmer Davis (one of America's most distinguished journalists but now unknown to all but a small number of people, including journalists) wrote in an article titled "News and the Whole Truth,"

> Truth has three dimensions; but the practices of the American news business—practices adopted in a praiseworthy ambition to be objective—too often give us only one-dimensional news; factually accurate so far as it goes, but very far indeed from the whole truth. (*Atlantic Monthly* 90, no. 2:34)

Davis was referring to the then-common practice of "reporting" the allegations of the late Senator Joseph McCarthy of Wisconsin. None of McCarthy's allegations turned out to be true, but the reports neglected to mention their inaccuracy or unreliability. As a result, untold numbers of people were damaged by his allegations—allegations which received wide, national publicity without any mention of their being groundless. This, please note, was the grossest kind of misinformation because it was reported not with malice, but with "objectivity."

Such "objective" reporting, in any medium of misinformation, disinformation, anti-information, or just plain outright lies, is as dangerous and as malignant (perhaps even more so) as the flat-out, known-to-all distortions presented by an open advocate of an identifiable position or perspective, such as the Grand Dragon of the Ku Klux Klan. The pernicious problem of widespread, seemingly objective amplifications of one kind of misinformation or another via the media is probably without any practical solution.

The central problem is this: In order to detect a lie one must already know what is true; in order to identify the counterfeit, one must already know the authentic; in order to identify the bogus, one must already know the bona fide. While someone, somewhere, sometime, might have access to information that would permit the identification of something specious in the media, this is a relatively rare event, confined in any case to persons with access to privileged information. Your ordinary citizen is seldom, if ever, in such a position. What this means is that the ordinary citizen is condemned to having to somehow cope with an endless stream of misinformation, disinformation, semi-information, and anti-information from all media.

There is, in addition, the annoying but predictable paradox of there being a higher level of adequacy and accuracy to reports as their subject diminishes in significance: The more trivial a "story," the more likely it is to be adequate and accurate. The very complexity of significant stories militates against any medium (with the exception of journals devoted to novel-length treatment of the details of the stories they cover) presenting them adequately and accurately—even if they wanted to. Any commercially based medium which depends upon revenue from advertising to make a profit is, itself, a "big business" and so reflects the bias of big business.

Adequate and accurate information, then, is hard to come by. Misinformation, however, is not only available to all of us all of the time, it is inescapable. We are drowning in it. It comes, relentlessly, from all directions all of the time: from the executive branch of the government, from the President himself, however "unwittingly";[3] from the Pentagon; from the CIA; from the FBI; from the "official spokespersons" of just about every federal agency; from local politicians; from judges; from lawyers; from used-car salespeople; from utilities company executives; from cemetery plot vendors; from pharmaceutical manufacturers; from nuclear power advocates; from the British military; from the Israeli military; from the PLO; from the Syrian military; from the government of El Salvador; from the manufacturers of cosmetics and deodorants and shampoos and diet pills; from real estate brokers; from condominium "time sharing" agents; in other words, just about any statement made publicly by anybody about anything for any reason publicly via the media is probably inaccurate and inadequate or it would not be made publicly "via the media." Diogenes would just sit down and cry.

Ronald Reagan was routinely referred to as "The Great Communicator." It is a commentary on our times that this appellation was proudly and patriotically bestowed on a man whose public statements were so widely "misinterpreted" by those who heard or read them. Addressing a VFW convention, Ronald Reagan referred to the Vietnam disaster as "a noble cause"! Even given the context in which it was made, that statement raises serious questions about Reagan's perception of one of the nation's worst, from every possible point of view, mistakes. A mistake which was characterized by more than a decade of lying by the military to everyone—the American people, the President, and each other—regarding what was really going on.

Ronald Reagan posed one of the most dismaying examples of the irrationality of the whole business of communicating information. Over and over again he "misspoke" himself, and some of the public even became aware of it. But, no matter how visible his inaccurate utterances and the incongruous results of his policies, his personal popularity (at least as reported in national polls) remained consistently high.

The Fragments of What We Know

So, the question remains in the face of all of this, "What do we know?" Most of us have access (either by choice or circumstance) only to fragments of some form of misinformation via the media, primarily television. Even this flimsy supply of bits and pieces is rendered even more inadequate by virtue of the fact that the supply is endless. It was a big enough problem prior to cable television when there were only three network and a few "independent" channels plus, perhaps, a public channel. Cable now makes available thirty-five, fifty, or one hundred and more channels, turning the trivia stream into a flood. Perhaps one of the most pernicious effects of all of this stuff via all of these channels is that everything gets "leveled." It all blends into an undifferentiated mass of unrecallable images and a few one-syllable words. There is simply too much to cope with for any of us to be able to distinguish the most blatant misinformation, disinformation, semi-information, or anti-information, even if we are inclined to try. There is no way for members of the public to know anything that bears much relationship to any reality, including their own personal variety.

Compounding the problem is the fact that there is simply no method of "analysis," nor any paradigm, nor any "system," nor any chart, nor any anything other than direct knowledge of "the truth" that permits anything other than suspended judgment. Who is telling the truth? How would one go about determining that? Who is doublespeaking? Or not? Or propagandizing? Or not? In the absence of direct, unimpeachable, verifiable, adequate, accurate information, there is simply no way to make a feasible judgment.

I am aware of only one instance where someone provided documentation via primary evidence (i.e., videotapes) demonstrating unequivocal, blatant, reiterated misinformation. This unique use of network television news occurred during the first week of March 1982 on the NBC "Nightly News." It involved a piece showing Vice-President George Bush repeatedly stating in a speech that it was a dastardly lie that he had ever accused Ronald Reagan of "voodoo economics." He denied several times ever having used that term, and challenged anyone to find any record of his ever having done so. Someone in the news department at NBC found a videotape of a speech made by Bush while he was campaigning for the Republican presidential nomination during which he called Reagan's economic platform voodoo economics, and not just once, but several times. The next day a "White House spokesperson" said that Bush was just kidding around when he denied having said what he had in fact said.

Since we cannot rely on the television networks to provide us regularly with such daring documentation of this kind of deliberate misinformation, the question remains "What are we to do?" Buy our own videotape recorders and tape *everything* and then develop a videotape library with all of the time, expense, and effort involved in cataloging, storage, and retrieval? Who could afford to do this, even if so inclined?

You see the problem. We are nominally in the midst of an information-rich environment in which the counterfeit overwhelms the authentic. Most of us have access *only* to the counterfeit. So, what do we know? Just as the man quoted at the outset said, "We don't know what we don't know." But that isn't all. We don't know what we do know either! And there isn't much that we can do about it—really.

We are all, whether we like it or not, ready to make our most crucial life decisions and choices on the basis of the misinformation, disinformation, semi-information, and anti-information that we find most comfortable emotionally.

And we don't know the basis for our emotional preferences either.

Notes

1. One of the abilities an "expert" enjoys that comprises the essence of expertise is the ability to make distinctions that the nonexpert cannot. These distinctions are made possible by their being given specific names. A botanist, for example, can make distinctions between a wide variety of lilacs that look the same to a non-botanist. Each "discipline," each category of human knowledge, has its own unique lexicon that it employs in developing its specific taxonomies for making distinctions among the items that comprise the focus of its inquiry.

2. "No comment" is not a form of disinformation since it does not produce the illusion that some information has been made available, except by inference on the part of the hearer or reader of the "No comment" response. None of us has any control over the inferences that anyone who hears or reads

anything we say or write might make. That is one of the compounding elements omitted from the transportation theory of communication.

3. The presidential press secretary spends much time explaining that everyone "misinterpreted" what the President has just said, causing the White House staff consequently to make extra efforts to keep the President from making extemporaneous remarks—most of which have turned out to be inaccurate, almost irrespective of the subject.

5 The Dangers of Singlespeak

Edward M. White
California State University

> Oh God us keep
> From Single Vision and Newton's Sleep.
>
> —William Blake

The evils of doublespeak are plain, and no sensible person concerned about the moral uses of prose can defend language designed to deceive. The pages of the *Quarterly Review of Doublespeak* are certainly filled with enough egregious examples of deliberate dishonesty in usage, of language "with pernicious social and political consequences" (to quote from the statement accompanying the Doublespeak Award), to earn the amused contempt of all morally sensitive readers.

But let us turn our attention to a less obvious evil, one that normally stands virtuously beside us in our opposition to the dishonest use of language. If we spend time on such matters as doublespeak in college composition classes, we are often surprised to find that our students are perfectly ready to condemn as doublespeak any metaphor at all, any prose of substantial complexity, any long words or long ideas. For many of our students, the distinction between the evils of doublespeak and the virtues of art (a distinction we tend to assume is real and important) simply does not exist. These well-meaning and supportive students have some theoretical justification for confusing art with deceit. When Picasso argues that "Art is a lie that tells the truth," he suggests that duplicity of a certain kind is a necessary part of an artist's work. But the simplemindedness and literal-mindedness that I am calling Singlespeak maintains itself in virtuous opposition to art or to any but the simplest meanings. When Blake calls the single vision "Newton's Sleep" (and, elsewhere, simply, "blindness"), he identifies the profound simplemindedness that is unable to notice or respond to complex visions; a reductionism far from the unequivocal virtue that simplistic notions of doublespeak might suggest as its opposite.

The singlespeak that is at least as pernicious as doublespeak is that particularly complacent form of simplicity that sees language as ideally a clear glass; because all meanings must be simple, or single, any language that suggests complexity or ambiguity is like a dirty window, to be cleaned or broken. Writing and speaking are seen as transmissions of already-shaped (encoded) ideas which are then to be decoded by readers or hearers with as little interference as possible. Writing itself is imagined to be a simple product, not a process of inquiry or discovery; abstractions and metaphors interfere with unambiguous communication and should be replaced by simple, concrete nouns; all concepts can be and ought to be reduced to a briefing paragraph for a busy executive; Henry James is unreadable. The prose model is Hemingway, whose hero in *A Farewell to Arms* finds abstractions "obscene" and can find comfort only in the names of places and dates.

George Orwell, the patron saint of opposition to doublespeak, seems to use the same window metaphor for prose when he says, in "Why I Write," "Good prose is like a window pane." But the context makes clear that he is not arguing for simplicity, but rather for a clear fusion of "political purpose and artistic purpose into one whole" (7). The "window pane" of his metaphor should be as clear as possible, but it offers at best a streaked view into an artistic unknown: "All writers are vain, selfish and lazy, and at the very bottom of their motives there lies a mystery" (7). Indeed, it is hard to say which he opposes more strongly: the obfuscation of doublespeak or the simplemindedness of slogans and false simplicity that reveal singlespeak. The Newspeak dictionary in *Nineteen Eighty-Four,* after all, is designed to give authority to the lies created when a complex language disappears. It is true, however, that Orwell's most overt statement on the subject, the ubiquitous "Politics and the English Language," argues so strongly against political doubletalk that it overstates the need for simple, concrete expression. We need occasional reminders, such as Richard Ohmann's sarcastically entitled article, "Use Definite, Specific, Concrete Language" (1979), that abstract words are also important tools for thought and vision.

The underlying "blindness" that Blake warns us against is the insistence that reality is simple and knowable, and that language should reflect that simplicity. For Blake, the name that came to mind was Newton; for others it is more likely to be the archetypal strong, silent type, one of few words and unerring judgment. James Fenimore Cooper's Natty Bumppo and his successors, the stolid sheriffs and solitary soldiers of fortune of our Westerns and war movies, neither reflect nor read. Such myths enforce the view that simple and unlettered good sense is to be preferred to sophisticated wisdom which, like sophisticated wine, smells of corruption. It is precisely this appeal to the stolid virtues of the Frontier that makes singlespeak even more dangerous than doublespeak.

Doublespeak at its most appalling needs only to be cited to be exposed; singlespeak masquerades as opposition to doublespeak, as simple good sense, as clarity. To many of our students cursed with singlespeak, our admiration for such verbal reflections of complexity as irony, metaphor, and literature itself, appears to be admiration of doublespeak. Why can't Swift just *say* what he means? Who has the time to figure out what Austen really has in mind? If Marvell wants to take his coy mistress to bed, why doesn't he just tell her so, or, better still, just do it and not talk about it?

Thus, both double- and singlespeak are manifestations of the same kind of solipsistic naiveté: the use of language to adapt reality to our own ends, without awareness that both reality and language are very complex. But there are important differences, such as those I have begun to suggest here. I suspect that subsuming singlespeak under the umbrella of doublespeak blurs these differences, making it a bit too easy for those who would dismiss valid complexity as doublespeak, and letting singlespeakers cloak themselves in too-easy virtue.

In our zeal to ferret out and expose the dishonesty of doublespeak, we need to be particularly careful not to endorse or reward the blindness of singlespeak. As we shake our heads over the *pre-dawn vertical insertion* that invaded Grenada, let us remember the *America—Love It or Leave It* that prepared the way. The direct diction of *I Found It* on the bumpers of heaven-bound chariots is part of the seamless web of theological obfuscation that shapes the bountiful collection baskets and public hypocrisies of TV preachers. The supposed law of supply and demand is singlespeak, behind which lurks a thousand dishonest explanations for outrageous conduct: A "bribe" is a rebate, is it not? High authority does not excuse singlespeak, indeed it adds to the offense: *Avoid foreign entanglements; A poem should not mean but be.* Wherever common sense asserts false and simple answers to complex questions, singlespeak declares its blindness to be most excellent vision.

The student allegiance to singlespeak, of course, reflects the admiration for simplemindedness that afflicts much of our society. We find it everywhere, though usually in the guise of "straight talk" or something called "realism." Since it hides more readily than doublespeak in its mask of rude virtue, we must be unusually vigilant to identify singlespeak and expose it for what it is.

Take, for instance, the following editorial from *The Wall Street Journal* of December 11, 1986. Entitled "Seeing Red," it seeks to set straight those who feel that the issues of American military intervention in Nicaragua are complicated:

> An intriguing Media General–Associated Press poll reports that 60% of the people interviewed oppose military aid to the Nicaraguan contras, but 42% don't even know which side the U.S. is on. Meanwhile, 58% think communist governments in Latin America threaten U.S. security. We think we see the problem here: It's hard to tell anymore who the communists are and who the good guys are. Years ago, such struggles were divided into communists and anti-communists. This view was ridiculed as ignorant of various "indigenous liberation movements." Flattered, the communists started giving themselves colorful names: the Sandinistas, the Tupemaros, Shining Path, M-19. The Sandinistas shrewdly called their anti-communist opponents "contras," a word without content for most Americans. If clarity of meaning is important, perhaps we should return to the ancient but clear classifications. Communists are communists. The people who are against them are anti-communists. Anyone who still can't figure out which side he's on is entitled to be listed under the column labeled "Don't Know." (32)

If this were the house organ of some right-wing military splinter group, we could smile and let it go. But this is, after all, *The Wall Street Journal,* the voice of responsibility for American capitalism. So we must notice the skill and force calling for singlespeak. If we follow the editorial, we must not, despite all knowledge of differences among those who call themselves communists, think that those people are different from one another; the Soviets, the Chinese, the Hungarians, the Cubans, the Italian or French Eurocommunists, the opponents of dictators wherever they may be—all, all of them are to be seen as the same. If they seem to have different names, they have "shrewdly" chosen them solely to confuse Americans, a gullible tribe who have trouble with clear classifications. Everything is simple, if people would only realize that there are only two possible positions in the world. The singlespeaker is ever ready to provide the scorecard with the lineup on it, so we can tell our team from theirs. Doublespeak may cover over what happens in military action, but it is singlespeak that starts the war in the first place.

We ought not to be surprised to find that professional educators have a particular affinity for singlespeak. Their job is to make complicated matters accessible to the untrained and it seems all too easy for them to fall into the grossest kinds of oversimplifications. Nonetheless, when such a habit of mind shows itself "resolving" educational problems barely perceived, we experience the shock of the singlespeaker.

I recall an official from the California State Department of Education saying at a meeting, "Now that we have solved the problem of reading, it is time to turn our attention to writing." I smile privately at the outraged parent holding forth at a school board meeting, berating the schoolteachers who had allowed children to raise questions on forbidden subjects: "We're paying you to educate our kids, so stop messing with their *minds!*"

Perhaps the neatest example of educational singlespeak as I write this is the concept of "value-added education." That slogan has momentarily replaced "merit pay for teachers" as the simple answer to the complex problem of improving education. By the time you read this, no doubt a new slogan will be in the news; nonetheless, we might as well look at this one, since it so nicely embodies the aspects of singlespeak which educational slogans have in common.

Value-added education, as espoused by educational politicians such as Governor Ashcroft of Missouri, is based on the commercial concept of molding raw materials into processed goods. Thus, when raw rubber is turned into automobile tires at a manufacturing plant, the tires are worth more than the rubber. A "value-added tax" (common in many European countries) is then assessed on the difference in cost.

While the value-added tax may be European, the concept of value-added education is truly American. It not only uses the analogy of molding raw material as a way of thinking about education, but it also assumes that a readily ascertainable and measurable difference from raw material to molded product in fact defines education. It thus sees education as something that is done to students (not something students do or become) and restricts the value of education to that which can be measured by pre- and posttesting. Since anyone can see that rubber tires are different from raw rubber, our seniors should be similarly and obviously different from our freshmen. The difference, when quantified, becomes the value of the education they have received, and that derived statistic becomes the basis for funding educational institutions.

Newton's Sleep, indeed! It is the essence of singlespeak to reduce complex phenomena or activities to the readily quantifiable. Even sophisticated thinkers find that task daunting. A generation ago, Albert Kitzhaber (1963) tried to assess the difference between the writing of freshmen and seniors at Dartmouth College. Unfortunately, he did not have the refined techniques of essay testing that are now available, so he chose a series of error counts as his assessment device.

To his dismay, he found that the seniors wrote "worse" than the freshmen; that is, that the seniors made more errors in their writing. Later research has demonstrated that most writers make more errors in first draft work as their writing tasks become more complex and ambitious. (For example, if you write only simple sentences and use only a basic vocabulary, you are not as likely to make sentence or spelling errors as you will with more advanced verbal materials.) The Dartmouth seniors were, in fact, writing far more advanced work than they did as freshmen, but the measurement of that advance was wholly beyond the tools available. The measurement that was available "proved" what everyone knew to be untrue. If Dartmouth had been foolish enough to use those results to revise its curriculum, we would now see its general education program reduced to exercises in spelling and sentence structure. Unhappily, less enlightened institutions deceived by educational singlespeak are cheerfully following that path. Those institutions now committed to "value-added" education are, in fact, using their relatively simpleminded evaluation devices to shape and reduce their curricula.

In theory, of course, we could come up with evaluation devices sufficiently complex to measure the real value of education—but don't count on it. Such devices are costly, complicated, and hard to quantify. The singlespeak metaphor of "value-added" demands quick weights and measures, practical budgetary action, and unambiguous decision-making: Either you have learned double entry bookkeeping or you have not; don't bother with poetry if you can't come up with similar numbers. Singlespeak requires simplicity and has no interest in Einstein's qualifier: "Everything," he said, "should be as simple as possible—but no simpler."

Singlespeak, thus, is the vocabulary of those who need no Newspeak for self-deception; Oldspeak does the job perfectly well. Doublethink is unnecessary and rather too much trouble because halfthink manages the world very nicely, thank you. Singlespeak is sometimes comic (the character Zero in the *Beetle Bailey* comic strip forever at attention before the sign "Watch this space for important announcements"), but usually it is serious and quiet. Singlespeak is most deceptive when it pretends to simple honesty; most dangerous as it asserts its simple virtue. We may at last have a committee to defend us from doublespeak, but where is the task force to protect us from the more subtle, pernicious, and pervasive power of singlespeak?

Works Cited

Blake, William. Letter to Thomas Butts, 22 Nov. 1802, lines 84–88. In *The Letters of William Blake*. 3rd Ed., 46. Edited by Geoffrey Keynes. Oxford: Clarendon Press, 1980.

Editorial. "Seeing Red." *The Wall Street Journal,* 11 Dec. 1986: 32.

Hemingway, Ernest. *A Farewell to Arms.* New York: Scribner's, 1957.

Kitzhaber, Albert R. *Themes, Theories, and Therapy: The Teaching of Writing in College.* New York: McGraw-Hill, 1963.

Ohmann, R. "Use Definite, Specific, Concrete Language." *College English* 41 (1979): 390–97.

Orwell, George. "Why I Write." In *An Age Like This (1920–1940),* 1–7. Vol. 1 of *The Collected Essays, Journalism and Letters of George Orwell.* 4 vols. Edited by Sonia Orwell and Ian Angus. London: Secker & Warburg, 1968.

———. "Politics and the English Language." In *In Front of Your Nose (1945–1950),* 127–40. Vol. 4 of *The Collected Essays, Journalism and Letters of George Orwell.* 4 vols. Edited by Sonia Orwell and Ian Angus. London: Secker & Warburg, 1968.

6 The Fallacies of Doublespeak

Dennis Rohatyn
University of San Diego

For the past fifteen years, fallacy pedagogy for the teacher of philosophy has undergone a quiet revolution. It used to be easy to teach the subject of fallacies; lately (for very good reasons) it has gotten more difficult. I will explain why.

What Is a Fallacy?

Some textbooks define a fallacy as an incorrect pattern of reasoning (Seech 1987). But what makes it incorrect? What causes or produces logical error? In short, why is a fallacy a fallacy? In lieu of an answer, the textbook tradition simply divides fallacies into two chief classes: formal and informal.

Formal fallacies involve violation of a rule. Denying the antecedent and affirming the consequent are the best known examples.

Informal fallacies are all of the rest. Informal fallacies comprise several subcategories:

- irrelevance (ad hominem attacks, "straw arguer," appeals to pity or force, appeals to the people or to authority, arguments from ignorance)
- semantic fallacies (equivocation, composition, division)
- inductive fallacies (hasty generalization, post hoc, false cause)
- fallacies of presumption (begging the question, suppressed evidence)

An earlier version of this essay appeared in *Critical Thinking News* 6, no.4, March-April 1988. I want to offer special thanks to Mary Daniels for her work in the preparation of this chapter—D.R.

But what, if anything, do these different types of fallacy have in common? A mere list or grouping of mistakes gives no clue as to what makes them taboo.

In recent years, logicians have devoted considerable energy to analyzing what fallacies are, as opposed to taking them for granted as though their meanings were self-evident. Concisely defined, fallacies are errors or flaws in reasoning; mistakes that make arguments invalid, unsound, or inaccurate. More expansively, "we reason fallaciously whenever we (1) reason from questionable premises, (2) fail to use relevant information, or (3) reason invalidly" (Kahane 21). Using this approach, there are at least three ways in which fallacies can and do occur:

1. When we make inferences or draw conclusions that simply don't follow from a given set of premises
2. When we accept one or more false assumptions or adopt a false conclusion, not as a tentative hypothesis or thought experiment, but finally—and in earnest
3. When we abuse or pervert the life of reason; for example, when we hide relevant facts from an audience or dishonestly assume just what needs to be proved.

This third category reflects the etymology of the word "fallacy," whose Latin root means "to deceive."

This typology of fallacies is not exhaustive, but it helps. Why is there so much fuss about fallacies? It has taken so long for philosophers to abandon traditional classifications and seek better ones for two reasons. The first is technical; the second, political.

Redefining Fallacies

The technical reason for redefining fallacies is that many arguments seem fallacious but aren't. For example, suppose a defense attorney assails the credibility of an eyewitness to an auto accident: "Mr. X says that he saw car *A* viciously slam into car *B*. But Mr. X is a habitual drunkard. Therefore, I ask the jurors to disregard X's testimony." Is this simply an ad hominem attack on X's character? Or does it serve a legitimate purpose by allowing an attorney to refute the credibility of the witness?

Or consider Christ's admonition to those who were about to pelt the adulteress: "Let him who is without sin among you be the first to cast a stone at her." We might respond, "Do two wrongs make a right?" Yet if Christ did commit a tu quoque fallacy, he had an excellent excuse for doing so because by shifting the burden of moral proof to her assailants, he emphasized that self-criticism is the basis of all moral and ethical reasoning (Rohatyn 1987).

Thus, if there are times when a fallacy isn't a fallacy, we must revise our traditional definitions in an ad hoc manner to admit (or to prohibit) exceptions to each purported rule as they arise. One method is messy; the other, clumsy. The moral is that except for formal fallacies, we cannot erect an algorithm or provide what logicians call a "decision-procedure" to establish the (in)correctness of a given argument in advance. We can only determine this contextually, case by case, by relying on rules of thumb rather than hard-and-fast rules which allegedly require no interpretation.

Some logicians (Lambert and Ulrich 1980) find this fact so distressing that they ban fallacies from their curriculum. But that's like pretending (as the United States did for twenty-five years) that mainland China doesn't exist because their ideology differs from ours.

The Sociology of Fallacies

The second reason for a growth of interest in fallacies both in research and in the classroom is the changed climate of American higher education since Vietnam and Watergate.

Like many of their academic counterparts, philosophers since the 1970s have (re)discovered the "real world," by applying their conceptual skills to such problems as nuclear war, world hunger, ecology and economic justice, not to mention medicine, law and other professions in which life and death issues are routinely at stake. The "legitimation crisis" of North American society has spurred my discipline to stop being smug about itself. As a consequence, logic (once taught as a high-powered mathematics course primarily intended to prepare prospective graduate students for the rigors of Russell, Whitehead and Frege) is no longer detached from more "practical" applications, such as serving as an intellectual antidote to the gratuitous suffering often inflicted by advertisers, politicians, and bureaucrats, not to mention philosophers thirsting for scapegoats.

No one goes fallacy hunting anymore, though we do find fallacies in abundance. Logicians have become far more careful about whom they accuse of error, and on what grounds. Twenty years ago, teachers and authors who prepared drills and exercises did not hesitate to compile lists of four-line quotations to illustrate various blunders, as though fallacies were discrete specimens to be housed under glass. Today we quote an entire passage or a chapter if need be, to give the students enough background to understand the subject, and then we ask them to perform a sensitive argument reconstruction and diagnosis (Johnson and Blair 1983; Fogelin 1986). When an argument is broken we try to repair it, and we encourage our students to do likewise. This is known as the Principle of Charity, or giving one's opponent the benefit of the doubt. And that's as much a part of our moral code as the avoidance of fallacies.

Finding the Golden Mean

Comparing doublespeak to fallacies involves more than matching members on two or more lists, as though (forgive the cliché) we were ordering food from a Chinese menu. Yet, when I first began to write this essay, despite my years of experience I fully expected to say something like "euphemism and inflated language are semantic fallacies, jargon is an indirect appeal to authority, and gobbledygook commits the fallacy of vagueness. QED." Now I realize how naïve I was about facile treatments of argument pathology.

Accordingly, those who are still committed to traditional fallacy pedagogy should be committed before they commit more fallacies than the textbooks enumerate! (Please pardon the equivocation, plus the hint of slippery slope.) It would, however, be equally rash to dispense with tradition altogether. As my colleague Dorothy Berger remarks, "Even the best cook uses or consults a cookbook every now and then." We do so, not out of weakness or faulty memory, but in order to test our strategy before it's too late. When confronting novelty or danger, the best training in the world is hopelessly inadequate; yet without it we are lost. To spark an insight or generate the intuition needed to resolve a dilemma, prior guidelines mean both everything and nothing. Whether we set out to master fallacies, to examine doublespeak, or to do anything (Dreyfus and Dreyfus 1986), it is advisable, indeed necessary, to start with a "cookbook"—provided that eventually we learn how to operate without one, not just in an emergency but all of the time. That's what "self-reliance" means. That is also the essential meaning of self-transcendence: of learning rules that eventually enable us to avoid following them blindly. It follows that contempt for rules is as misguided as rule-worship, and just as disastrous. Rules were meant to be broken, sometimes for our sake, sometimes for the sake of the rules themselves. It's fine to invent new rules, as long as we don't become slaves to them.

The Meaning of Inconsistency

Although we must beware of imposing an artificial unity on doublespeak, it does not follow that doublespeak has no essence. Since
doublespeak is "language which is at variance with its real or its [pur-
ported] meaning" (Lutz 1987), in all four of its varieties the common
denominator is (self-)deception in the form of lies, mystification, and,
above all, inconsistency.

Ever since Aristotle, logicians have tried to prove that contradictions
are untenable. Unfortunately, such proofs are circular because they
presuppose the principle of non-contradiction, or something equivalent to it.

Logicians contend that from a contradiction, anything follows. That
is true: if we assume both p and $\sim p$, it is easy to prove both q and $\sim q$, r
and $\sim r$ and so on, to infinity. This is objectionable because, we usually
argue, some propositions are true while others are false; because not
every inference we make or propound is as likely or probable as the
next; because abolishing or suspending the law of non-contradiction
(LNC), as Hegel attempted to do, would lead to a night in which all
cows are black, all distinctions equally (in)valid. This leaves us with the
fictional universe of *Nineteen Eighty-Four*. As both Goldstein and
O'Brien (who may or may not be the same person) describe it, it is a
world governed entirely by two axioms:

   I. Whatever the Party says, is right.
   II. Every statement is both true and false simultaneously.

A little thoughtcrime suffices to show that I and II entail

   III. Whatever the Party says, is wrong.

And also

   IV. Axiom II is (both true and) false.

No wonder Orwell's protagonist, Winston Smith, goes mad just trying
to comprehend Party logic, let alone abide by it. Granted, as he devel-
ops political consciousness Winston tries repeatedly to defy the law.
But in Oceania there are no laws. Hence his—or by bizarre implication
anyone's—rebellion is pointless, futile, and doomed from the outset.
Only the reader can escape from this nightmare, not just by closing the
book, but by ensuring that it remains a mere fantasy.

Let me share two reflections concerning this scenario. First, it para-
lyzes the Party even more than its victims. Second, knowing this makes
no difference to the institutions or the people who are bent on complete (self-)destruction.

Aristotle thought that anyone who denied the LNC was either a sophist or a fool, but in any case a hypocrite: "for one is not indifferent to all things alike when one wants a drink of water" (*Metaphysics* 1008b20–21). Thus he devised a *pragmatic test* for would-be adherents of the law of contradiction (LC). If they really mean what they say, let them try to live by or up to its dictates, not just to debate it abstractly or espouse it as a (substitute) logical norm. Once they do try, they are guaranteed to fail; to expose their utter inability to practice what they preach, because at some point they must choose between alternatives. Aristotle expresses himself quite vehemently:

> But clearly no man who says these things . . . really is so stupid. For if he wants to go to Megara, why does he go there instead of staying where he is? Why doesn't he . . . wander into any well or fall into any abyss that happens to be there, instead of carefully avoiding it, if he really thinks falling in equally good and not good?" (*Metaphysics* 1008b12–17)

From this viewpoint, we needn't fear our inability to prove the law of non-contradiction. The burden of proof is on those who deny it (or who both deny and affirm it). Their clever theoretical alternative dissolves as soon as we stop arguing against it and simply challenge them to put it into practice. We need not refute them; they refute themselves.

This is very reassuring, but is it true?

Why Doublespeakers Must (Mis)use the Language of Logic

A universe filled with doublespeak (and emptied of everything else) is impossible and cannot even be coherently described. If doublespeak were all there was, we could not even say "doublespeak" unless the Party commanded it! That is why *Nineteen Eighty-Four* mimics Newspeak but is composed primarily in the language of Oldspeak. Yet there are times when we almost succeed in reaching negative infinity, in historical moments that annihilate discourse; not just in Nazi Germany or during the Stalinist era, but far closer to home and to the present moment.

Doublespeak is insane yet undeniably real, and therefore all the more threatening to those whose sanity, as Orwell would say, is not yet a statistic. Doublespeak is also self-defeating, but its proponents and practitioners don't seem to notice, much less care about, linguistic or moral suicide. So it is up to us to prevent doublespeak from having or being the last word.

This suggests that the study of contradictions and of those systems which exclude (or on occasion, include) them is central to the logical enterprise. Here, as elsewhere, it is important to avoid dogmatism. Quantum mechanics (Heisenberg's uncertainty principle, Bell's inequality) spurred and justified the efforts of Lukasiewicz, Reichenbach, and other pioneers of "many-valued logic" (Rescher 1969) who challenged the "sacred" Law of Excluded Middle (a variation of the LNC) because it didn't fit certain experimental situations in subatomic physics. Thus, like fallacies, *contradictions aren't always bad* or aren't always contradictions. Again, we must never revise old rules just to suit a whim, or to take contradictions lightly. In logic as in life, tradition has prima facie validity, no more, no less.

The same is true of human ambivalence (love-hate relationships, for example), where ordinary logic is often a poor guide to understanding complex feelings and moods. Even so, we are rational animals, not least in struggling to understand and sometimes approve of the ways in which we are irrational (Elster 1983). Even when reason fails to resolve or overcome a deep-seated human paradox, we abandon reason at our peril. Perhaps that is the deepest paradox of all. Of course, it is easily explained, thanks to the paradox that human beings are born paradox-generators! (Hofstadter 1979, 1985)

Inconsistency Equals Doublespeak

Inconsistency is hardly the only form of doublespeak, yet arguably it underlies all such phenomena. Hence it is both easy to spot and troublesome to remove, not least when (like Aristotle, and despite his bluster) we obey conscience by giving our opponents a full hearing, no matter how perverse, unfair, or inconsiderate they may be. As in politics so, too, in logic: we must tolerate the intolerant and safeguard even (or especially) the rights of those who would not think twice about discarding the norms that make their own dissent possible. This seems foolish if not suicidal. Yet this, and only this, is noble. It keeps us slightly "above the brutes," i.e., slightly above ourselves at those times when we are brutes. It also provides the desired link between the concepts we have just critiqued.

Like any fallacy, but perhaps more pointedly, doublespeak violates canons of (self-)respect in word and deed. Doublespeak commits many fallacies, yet in the end it commits just one: it makes it more difficult for everyone—speakers and audiences, arguers and bystanders—to be fully human. Difficult, yes, but as our conversation proves, not yet impossible.

Bibliography

Aristotle. *Metaphysics*. Translated by Richard Hope. New York: Columbia University Press, 1952. Reprinted Ann Arbor: University of Michigan Press, 1960.

Barker, Stephen F. *The Elements of Logic*. 4th ed. New York: McGraw-Hill, 1985.

Bencivenga, Ermanno. "On Good and Bad Arguments." *Journal of Philosophical Logic* 8 (1979): 247–59.

Dreyfus, Hubert L., and Stuart E. Dreyfus (with Tom Athanasiou). *Mind Over Machine: The Power of Human Intuition and Expertise in the Era of the Computer*. New York: Free Press, 1986.

Elster, Jon. *Sour Grapes: Studies in the Subversion of Rationality*. Cambridge: Cambridge University Press, 1983.

Fogelin, Robert J. *Understanding Arguments: An Introduction to Informal Logic*. 3rd ed. San Diego: Harcourt Brace Jovanovich, 1986.

Govier, Trudy. *A Practical Study of Argument*. 2d ed. Belmont, Calif.: Wadsworth, 1988.

Hamblin, Charles L. *Fallacies*. London: Methuen, 1970.

Hofstadter, Douglas R. *Goedel Escher Bach: An Eternal Golden Braid*. New York: Basic Books, 1979.

———. *Metamagical Themes: Questing for the Essence of Mind and Pattern*. New York: Basic Books, 1985.

Johnson, Ralph L., and J. Anthony Blair. *Logical Self-Defense*. 2d ed. Toronto: McGraw-Hill Ryerson, 1983.

Kahane, Howard. *Logic and Contemporary Rhetoric*. 5th ed. Belmont, Calif.: Wadsworth, 1988.

Lambert, Karel, and William Ulrich. *The Nature of Argument*. New York: Macmillan, 1980.

Lifton, Robert J. *The Nazi Doctors: Medical Killing and the Psychology of Genocide*. New York: Basic Books, 1986.

Lutz, William. "Notes Toward a Description of Doublespeak (Revised)." *Quarterly Review of Doublespeak* 13, no. 2 (1977): 10–13. (An expanded version of this essay appears in this book.)

Orwell, George. *Nineteen Eighty-Four: Text, Sources, Criticism*. 2d ed. Edited by Irving Howe. New York: Harcourt Brace Jovanovich, 1982.

————. *Nineteen Eighty-Four.* New York: New American Library, 1961.

————. "Politics and the English Language." In *In Front of Your Nose (1945–1950)*, 127–40. Vol. 4 of *The Collected Essays, Journalism and Letters of George Orwell.* Edited by Sonia Orwell and Ian Angus. 4 vols. New York: Harcourt, Brace & World, 1968.

Rawls, John. *A Theory of Justice.* Cambridge: Harvard University Press, 1971.

Rescher, Nicholas. *Many-Valued Logic.* New York: St. Martin's, 1969.

Rohatyn, Dennis. "When Is a Fallacy a Fallacy?" *Proceedings of the 1st International Conference on Argumentation.* Vol. 3, 45–55. Edited by Rob Grotendoorst and Frans van Eemeren. Amsterdam: Foris Publications, 1987.

Seech, Zachary. *Logic in Everyday Life: Practical Reasoning Skills.* Belmont, Calif.: Wadsworth, 1987.

Thomas, Stephen N. *The Uses of Argument.* Rev. ed. Cambridge: Cambridge University Press, 1964.

Walton, Douglas. *Dialogues, Language-Games and Fallacies.* Lanham, Md.: University Press of America, 1984.

7 Doublespeak and Ethics

George R. Bramer
Lansing Community College

Concern about ethics, or rather about ethical behavior, has reached an unusually high level in the United States during the late 1980s. In these years we have had dramatic accounts of illegal insider trading in the stock market, ethics investigations aimed at unprecedented numbers of federal government officials in the executive branch, the Iran-Contra scandal, televangelist scandals, and public censure of the behavior of two leading presidential candidates and a nominee for the United States Supreme Court. The May 25, 1987, issue of *Time* magazine was indicative of intense media attention to these concerns. Announcing a cluster of cover stories, including one titled "What's Wrong," the outside caption read, "What Ever Happened to Ethics." Much of the media attention was focused on unethical language, on lying and deception. The February 23, 1987, issue of *U.S. News & World Report* captioned its cover story "A Nation of Liars?" with this statement: "Public Concern Over Honesty and Standards of Behavior Has Reached the Highest Level Since Watergate."

In this climate, the NCTE Committee on Public Doublespeak has had plenty to work with. Its *Quarterly Review of Doublespeak* has consistently exhibited pages of doublespeak from the business world, from government and the military, from medicine and education, and from many other sectors of society. Prominent recipients have been identified annually for the committee's Doublespeak Award, which is reported regularly by national media. These circumstances—the continuing flow of doublespeak and the intense national concern about ethics—raise some fundamental questions: What's wrong with using doublespeak? How serious a problem is it? Is it an ethical or a moral issue?

An earlier version of this essay was presented at the annual meeting of the National Council of Teachers of English in Los Angeles, 1987.

Perhaps because English teachers generally seem reluctant to be moralistic, the words "unethical" and "immoral" have not been prominent in the literature of the committee. However, in its first book, *Language and Public Policy*, Hugh Rank as editor included the NCTE resolutions on which the committee was founded, resolutions focusing on "dishonest" and "inhumane" uses of language and on "semantic distortion" (vii). In describing the committee's functions in its 1988 *Directory*, NCTE used the expressions "irresponsible" and "misusing the language" to describe the committee's concerns. And William Lutz, chair of the committee, stated when announcing the 1987 winners of the Doublespeak Award that the award was restricted "to misuses of language with pernicious social or political consequences" (Lutz 1988, 1). The official language about doublespeak has been strong, even if the question of ethics has been somewhat elusive. With the official language in mind, as well as events and concerns of the 1980s, it seems reasonable to bring the question into sharp focus.

Some valuable beginnings were made in the early work of the committee, most notably in their book *Language and Public Policy*, published in 1974. At that time Watergate was fresh in our minds and much of that volume was devoted to analyses and indictments of Watergate language. However, Robert C. Jeffrey's contribution, "Ethics in Public Discourse," carried a stirring appeal for increased attention to ethics in speech criticism, research, and theory (177–79), while Hugh Rank's essay, "The Teacher-Heal-Thyself Myth," argued for making moral judgments about language situationally—in the context of "who is saying what to whom, under what conditions and circumstances, with what intent, and with what results" (219). In 1988 the *Quarterly Review of Doublespeak* carried D. G. Kehl's article entitled "Doublespeak: Its Meaning and Its Menace." Writing against the background of language such as that of the Iran-Contra scandal, Kehl considered the destructive consequences which doublespeak can have. He concluded that "doublespeak is so pernicious because it is a form of psychological violence" (9).

Those valuable contributions might be extended by asking the basic question: Is doublespeak unethical? Related questions naturally follow: If or when doublespeak is regarded as unethical, what is being adversely criticized—ends, means, or both? And by what criteria is the adverse judgment made? Before I approach these questions, I would like to define the terms "doublespeak" and "ethics."

The Concept of Doublespeak

William Lutz has identified several kinds of doublespeak (euphemism, jargon, gobbledygook or bureaucratese, and inflated language), and he offers this tentative definition:

> Doublespeak is language which pretends to communicate but really does not. It is language which makes the bad seem good, something negative appear positive, and something unpleasant appear attractive, or at least tolerable. It is language which avoids or shifts responsibility, language which is at variance with its real meaning. It is language which conceals or prevents thought. Doublespeak is language which does not extend thought but limits it. (1987, 10–11)

Building on Lutz's article, D. G. Kehl has suggested this definition:

> Doublespeak, constituting the linguistic manifestation of doublethink and involving incongruity between word and referent, is language used to confuse or deceive, serving less to express than to impress, less to communicate than to manipulate, and which, by means of elevation, obfuscation, inundation, circumambulation, dissipation, equivocation, and prevarication, violates both language, the purpose of which is to communicate, and people, whose human dignity demands truth, honesty, and a degree of autonomy. (1988, 9)

Kehl's suggested definition is particularly interesting in that it attempts to identify the inherent semantic quality of doublespeak ("incongruity between word and referent"), the intent of the doublespeaker ("to confuse or deceive," etc.), various functions of doublespeak ("elevation," etc.), and its consequences (violation of language and people). Doublespeak can be quite complex, but I think we can draw on the central elements in the suggestions of Lutz and Kehl to formulate a rather simple, yet serviceable, definition.

One element, a distinction between doublespeak and lying, is only implicit in the essays of Lutz and Kehl. That distinction was stated explicitly by Metta Winter in the *Christian Science Monitor:*

> Doublespeak is not lying, nor is it merely sloppy language; it is the intentional use of euphemisms, synonyms, jargon, and vagueness which pretends to communicate but really does not, or which implies the opposite of what it would appear to be communicating. (18)

I think it is useful to define a lie as a clear, unequivocal, intentional statement of a falsehood, and to distinguish lying from other verbal deception. Keeping the distinction in mind, and hoping not to oversimplify, I believe the central elements in those suggestions can be condensed tentatively into this definition: *Doublespeak is deliberately deceptive language other than lying.* That is the definition which I will assume in this discussion.

The Concept of Ethics

The second key concept in this essay is ethics. By "ethics" I simply mean principles of morality. Ethics is the philosophy of human acts, and it supplies rules of human conduct, or principles of right and wrong. Those rules and principles are more fundamental and more broadly applicable than either professional codes of ethics or legal codes; hence, they can be used to evaluate such codes, while the reverse generally is not true. People sit down periodically to revise professional or legal codes, but a moral code is not so readily alterable.

If moral codes are relatively stable, however, they are not uniform. There is no single, universal morality to which we can appeal in discussing ethics and doublespeak. In his book *Ethics and Persuasion,* Richard Johannesen asks, "Should the ethics of persuasion be absolutistic, relativistic, or a blend of both?" (xii) We are faced with the same question in attempting to evaluate doublespeak by ethical principles.

Absolutist ethical philosophies identify certain human acts as intrinsically evil, regardless of the circumstances in which they occur. Regarding language ethics, Sissela Bok, in *Lying: Moral Choice in Public and Private Life,* describes the absolutist position as "prohibiting all lies, even those told for the best of purposes or to avoid the most horrible of fates" (40).

Relativist philosophies hold that the morality of human acts is not intrinsic but relative to something outside the act, perhaps to the values of a given society or to the specific elements of a given situation. Richard L. Johannesen, in *Ethics in Human Communication,* describes some relativist positions, particularly those of some situationists, who "focus primarily on the elements of the specific communication situation at hand to make ethical judgments" (57).

But the lines between absolutist and relativist positions are not always so sharp and consistent as the two terms suggest. Many absolutists, for example, have modified their prescriptiveness by defining various degrees of culpability or by offering other, less convincing moral distinctions (Bok 41, 48). And situationists might appeal to some absolute principle such as the general welfare or the sacredness of human life in evaluating specific circumstances (Johannesen 61).

Is Deceptive Language Unethical?

Ethics and doublespeak are not simple concepts, but I have attempted to define them sufficiently for the present discussion. Now I turn to the principle question—Is doublespeak unethical?—and to related questions. Although I have defined doublespeak as "deceptive language other than lying," I submit that ethical judgments about lying are also applicable to doublespeak. Because both are deceptive language, I believe both are properly judged by the same principles. Thus, the essential question here is whether or not deceptive language is unethical. The best answer, I believe, will attempt to draw on the insights both of absolutist ethics and of relativist ethics. My tentative answer is that doublespeak, like all deceptive language, is unethical, or immoral—usually. In an attempt to validate that view, I will offer some considerations which I think might qualify as principles for making ethical or moral judgments about doublespeak. The suggested principles are meant merely as explorations, but hopefully they can contribute to some forward movement on this important topic.

Nine Principles For Evaluating Doublespeak

1. *Using language is not neutral but is an inherently good human act, except in destructive circumstances.* Some other inherently good human acts, it seems, are eating, using any of the five senses, sexual intercourse, and thinking. Shouting or picking something up and moving it around seem neutral. Attributing positive value to acts which sustain and enrich human life seems reasonable, and sexual intercourse is usually accorded special reverence because of its association with the beginning of human life and with the strengthening of human bonds. Yet sex, like eating and using the five senses, is experienced by lower animals as well as by humans. The attribution of special value to language appears even more reasonable because language, the instrument and vehicle of thought, elevates humans above lower animal forms. Language is at the center of our full humanness, which it (perhaps more than anything else) sustains and enriches.

2. *Truthfulness is a moral virtue.* Aristotle said that virtue is a mean between extremes, and that truthfulness is the mean between the extremes of exaggeration and understatement (343). (The extremes of overstatement and understatement are reflected in Hugh Rank's *Intensify/Downplay* schema for analyzing communication, persuasion and propaganda.) Sissela Bok, while allowing that "there are at least some

circumstances which warrant a lie" (48), accepts Aristotle's view that falsehood "is in itself mean and culpable" (24). She asserts a "principle of veracity," the presumption that truthfulness has positive worth and is to be preferred over lying "in the absence of special considerations" (32). One reason Bok attaches importance to truthfulness is that she believes deception undermines trust (19–20). Bok writes that "trust in some degree of veracity functions as a foundation of relations among human beings; when this trust shatters or wears away, institutions collapse" (33). Thinking about the deception of doublespeak, we can add to this Kehl's idea that it "violates the dignity of the audience/ reader, for truth, honesty, and individual autonomy are basic human rights" (9).

3. *The ethics of truthfulness and deception apply to doublespeak just as they do to lying, even though doublespeak might be defined as something other than lying.* Bok explains that ethicists in some absolutist traditions have attempted to justify forms of deception by defining them as something other than lies (37–38). A notable example is the "mental reservation," by which one supposedly validates misleading ambiguity and incomplete statements by mentally supplying clarification or missing elements. Bok does not object to defining such strategies as something other than lies "so long as one retains the prerogative of morally evaluating the intentionally misleading statements" (15). That view applies to doublespeak, and such strategies as the mental reservation should be considered forms of doublespeak. Perhaps President Reagan employed mental reservation in a 1981 statement quoted by Lutz in "Notes": "I will not stand by and see those of you who are dependent on Social Security deprived of the benefits you've worked so hard to earn." Lutz writes that a White House spokesperson later said the President "was reserving the right to decide who was 'dependent' on those benefits, who had 'earned' them, and who, therefore, was 'due' them" (11).

4. *Doublespeak must always be justified, whereas its opposite, truthfulness, usually need not be.* This does not mean that doublespeak is never justified, or even that truthfulness is always justified. It does mean that there should be, in Bok's words, an "initial imbalance in our weighting of truthfulness" and its opposite—an imbalance in favor of truthfulness (32). She contends that

> in any situation where a lie is a possible choice, one must first seek truthful alternatives. . . . [O]nly where a lie is a last resort can one even begin to consider whether or not it is morally justified. (33)

In her view, if there are no apparent alternatives, lying (and I would substitute "doublespeak") must be further justified by weighing benefit against harm, and by asking how "a public of reasonable persons" might evaluate the deception (59, 112).

5. *A sound ethical evaluation of doublespeak should be a blend of absolutism and relativism.* That blend is desirable because each approach has its strengths and its weaknesses. A pure absolutist view of deceptive language—the view that it is never morally permissible, regardless of the circumstances—has been taken by some philosophers and theologians. A strength of that position is that it implicitly asserts the fundamental positive value of truthfulness. A weakness, however, is that it seems to imply that nothing can ever be more important than telling the truth. Probably few would agree with that position. Quite likely few of us would object to deceiving a would-be murderer in order to save the intended victim. And that observation suggests the strength of the relativist approach, which allows us to weigh contending values and, when a societal value or a personal principle weighs more heavily than truthfulness, to justify deception. The weakness in the relativist approach, however, is precisely in its lack of definitiveness. The deceptive mind can find endless justifications favoring its own desires over truthfulness. A blend of absolutism and relativism, sensitively and conscientiously applied, would forestall the destructiveness of both simplistic truthfulness and of self-serving deception.

6. *Doublespeak, like lying, can be wrong in varying degrees, depending on the circumstances and the consequences.* A useful concept might be borrowed from the tradition in moral theology that makes a distinction between mortal and venial sins. Distinctions among degrees of seriousness in wrongdoing appeal to common sense, and they are embodied in civil and criminal law. Such a distinction may be implied in the "Guidelines for The Doublespeak Award," which indicate that it is given for misuses of language believed to be "more worthy of censure than the kind of garden-variety jargon, gobbledygook, or solecisms emphasized by many current critics of language" (4). I would suggest that minor deceptions, such as "unleather handbags," while not deserving the Award, should not be automatically dismissed as harmless. Because of the fundamental importance of truthfulness, it seems more salutary to identify at least some minor deceptions as little wrongs, or venial sins, rather than no wrongs at all. Through repetition, as in the case of theft, they can become habitual and grow into much more serious wrongs, including, as Bok says, harm to oneself—loss of integrity (25–27). Regarding doublespeak, Kehl again is helpful; he writes that "doublespeak violates the users and their thought processes, for as Orwell expressed the Whorfian principle, 'If thought corrupts language, language can also corrupt thought'" (9).

7. *The speaker's or the writer's intent, although significant, may not be definitive in determining whether or not inaccurate or misleading language is unethical.* Aristotle considered intent a key determinant in distinguishing right from wrong (350), and deliberateness is part of the definition of doublespeak which I have suggested. We can say that deceptive language is not ethically wrong if the deception is not intended, but there is another dimension to be considered. If one does intend to deceive, but for a worthy purpose, the intended desirable outcome does not always justify the deception. In other words, the end does not always justify the means. Ordinarily, it would not be justifiable to burn down a neighbor's house in order to beautify the environment. Likewise, the goal of harmony within an organization or the goal of patriotism hardly seems to justify the use of doublespeak. Another important consideration is the uncertainty of motives, or intent. Leaders may convince themselves, and/or others, that they are deceiving the public out of concern for national security when in fact their motive is to promote a party cause. It can be difficult to determine one's own motives, and even more difficult to determine those of someone else.

8. *The semantic quality of one's language is, itself, of central importance in determining whether or not it is ethical.* Language which is truthful and accurate, corresponding closely with the facts, seems consistent with its nature and generally good. On the other hand, language which is inaccurate and actually (or potentially) deceptive seems inconsistent with its nature and generally suspect. Referring to doublespeak, Kehl writes that it "violates language, which is intended to communicate rather than to manipulate" (9). Certainly accuracy is only one important consideration in making a moral judgment about language. The total context of a statement must be considered, including intent, audience, and effects. But if intent is sometimes elusive, the mind of an audience seems even more uncertain. Consequently, it can be very difficult to predict the effects of inaccurate language before the fact or to assess the effects afterwards.

Although all the variables in a language situation are important in making a judgment about ethics, the variable over which the speaker or writer has most control, it seems, is the language itself. Language is what Aristotle would call the object of the human act. Lawrence Flynn, interpreting Aristotle, has explained:

> The object, considered as the act in the abstract and stripped of intent and circumstances, becomes the primary moral aspect of the act itself because it is the core of every act. (119)

9. *Ethical evaluations of doublespeak should place as much emphasis as possible on means toward an end, while also giving due attention to the end, or purpose.* Words, with a few possible exceptions in imaginative literature and word play, seem only to be means to various human ends beyond language, and thus may seem relatively insignificant in themselves. But the importance of the means, of the words themselves, should not be underestimated. Each use of language, if undertaken with knowledge and free choice, is a fully human act and therefore should be given full moral attention in itself. Coarse references to sexual functions or to specific ethnic groups, without context, would probably be objectionable to most of us. They might be redeemed by some contexts or purposes, but most of us would insist on that kind of justification. It seems that inaccurate and misleading statements should be no less seriously received and evaluated.

Doublespeak is Usually Unethical

These suggested principles, then, furnish a tentative answer to the central question posed earlier in this exploratory discussion: Doublespeak is usually unethical. In evaluating doublespeak we should focus on its undesirable qualities as means—even when it seems used for a good end—because doublespeak, unlike truthfulness, is presumed to be harmful unless fully justified. Some criteria by which doublespeak would be judged adversely are these:

1. It is deceptive
2. There are alternative means in the situation at hand
3. A public of reasonable persons would not judge the ends as justifying the deception in this particular case.

Language is indeed a means toward many ends, but it appears that its capacity for serving constructive ends is diminished as its natural communicative function is subverted, either for harmful purposes or for good ones. Deception, including doublespeak, seems too dangerous to be employed lightly or often. Truthfulness seems so life-enriching, in itself, that it can seldom fail us or often be overdone. Certainly it seems that more of it would significantly improve the quality of our national life, as events of the 1980s have dramatically demonstrated.

Works Cited

Aristotle. *Ethica Nichomachea.* Translated by W. D. Ross. In *Introduction to Aristotle.* Edited by Richard McKeon. New York: Modern Library, 1947.

Bok, Sissela. *Lying: Moral Choice in Public and Private Life.* New York: Vintage, 1976.

Flynn, Lawrence J. "The Aristotelian Basis for the Ethics of Speaking." In *Ethics and Persuasion,* 113–29. Edited by Richard Johannesen. New York: Random House, 1967.

"Guidelines for Doublespeak Award." *Quarterly Review of Doublespeak* 13, no. 4 (1987): 4.

Jeffrey, Robert C. "Ethics in Discourse." In *Language and Public Policy,* 176–83. Edited by Hugh Rank. Urbana, Ill.: National Council of Teachers of English, 1974.

Johannesen, Richard L., ed. *Ethics and Persuasion: Selected Readings.* New York: Random House, 1967.

———. *Ethics in Human Communication.* Columbus: Charles E. Merrill, 1975.

Kehl, D. G. "Doublespeak: Its Meaning and Its Menace." *Quarterly Review of Doublespeak* 14, no. 2 (1988): 8–9.

Lutz, William. "1987 Orwell Award and 1987 Doublespeak Award." *Quarterly Review of Doublespeak* 14, no. 2 (1988): 1–2.

———. "Notes Toward a Description of Doublespeak (Revised)." *Quarterly Review of Doublespeak* 13, no. 2 (1987): 10–12. (An expanded version of this essay appears in this book.)

"A Nation of Liars?" *U.S. News & World Report,* 23 February 1987: 54–61.

1988 Directory. Urbana, Ill.: National Council of Teachers of English, 1988.

Orwell, George. *Nineteen Eighty-Four.* New York: New American Library, 1984.

Rank, Hugh. *Intensify/Downplay Approach.* Park Forest, Ill.: Counter-Propaganda Press, 1976.

———, ed. *Language and Public Policy.* Urbana, Ill.: National Council of Teachers of English, 1974.

———. "The Teacher-Heal-Thyself Myth." In *Language and Public Policy,* 215–234. Edited by Hugh Rank. Urbana, Ill.: National Council of Teachers of English, 1974.

"What's Wrong?" and related articles. *Time,* 25 May 1987: 14–29.

Winter, Metta L. "Doublespeak—Care in Language Use, a Defense against Deception." *The Christian Science Monitor,* 22 November 1982: 18.

8 Post-Orwellian Refinements of Doublethink: Will the Real Big Brother Please Stand Up?

Donald Lazere
California Polytechnic State University

> Everything spiritual and valuable has a gross and revolting parody, very similar to it, with the same name. Only unremitting judgment can distinguish between them.
>
> —Jonathan Swift (paraphrased by William Empson)

In mid-1971, as various investigations have subsequently revealed, the White House Plumbers Unit had already been formed and was planning the burglary of Daniel Ellsberg's psychiatrist's office and other illegal adventures. The Justice Department, the FBI's Cointelpro operation, the CIA's Operation CHAOS, the Defense Department, and the Internal Revenue Service had all been contributing in various ways to a program of illegal surveillance, secret dossiers, provocation, forgery, assault, slander, and other forms of harassment against tens of thousands of American citizens ranging from militant activists, to nonviolent civil rights workers, to liberals mildly critical of government policy. The CIA was also engaged in various covert actions abroad, such as disseminating false information about (and otherwise subverting) the democratically elected Allende government in Chile, laying the way for the coup by a junta there in 1973, and the subsequent installation of a brutal dictatorship under General Augusto Pinochet.

At this time Attorney General John Mitchell made a speech accusing the liberal press of lying, first, in its reports that the Nixon administration was attempting to suppress the civil liberties of its political opponents, and second, in its suggestions that Mitchell's "no-knock" law (which was later repealed as unconstitutional) was one such restriction on civil liberties. UPI gave the following account of Mitchell's speech:

> "Actually, the no-knock provision gives more citizen protection, not less," he said, "because the decision to enter and search is taken from police and given to a judge, who must approve a 'no-knock'

entry." [As though police previously had the authority to enter and search without a warrant.]

"These are only two public issues that arose out of a shocking contempt for truth and a cheap surrender to instinct," Mitchell said. "Nor do I blame the public, so much as the sharp erosion of professionalism among many who have the public's ear."

"Whether parents or students, the people are no better informed than the quality of their information sources. Can we now allow ourselves, in our national decisions, to abandon fact in favor of emotion?"

Mitchell said some news media reporting reminds him of George Orwell's novel *1984* and its language of "Newspeak," in which words assume opposite meanings—wrong becomes right, and fiction becomes truth. "I believe that we Americans are not now, and never will be, ready to speak that language," Mitchell said.

Not even Orwell could foresee that the most exquisite refinement of doublethink would be for Big Brother to invoke *Nineteen Eighty-Four*, thus reversing his role with that of Winston Smith by portraying himself as the victim rather than the perpetrator of doublethink and Newspeak. Today those in power have learned not simply to commit misdeeds and lie about them, but to accuse those who would expose them of being Orwellian confounders of the truth. The Nixon administration, which wrought this rhetorical ploy to perfection, should be memorialized in a permanent title for it: Agnewspeak.

Agnewspeak—Lessons in Intentional Doublethink

In a speech given in January 1972, five months before the Plumbers were flushed in Watergate, Vice-President Agnew cited a column by Norman Podhoretz in the previous month's *Commentary:*

> The editor of *Commentary* magazine recently examined the charge that we are living in a repressive society and concluded, as others have, that the charge is totally absurd. In analyzing this rhetorical attack on America, he wrote, "Never has there been so much talk of repression, but never has there been so great a degree of civil freedom, probably in the history of the world, as exists in the United States today." (Nobile 1974, 6)

In earlier speeches, Agnew had attributed these allegedly fraudulent criticisms of the Nixon administration to the celebrated "effete corps of impudent snobs who characterize themselves as intellectuals" (Porter 1976, 43). He further charged that

> The elite consists of the raised-eyebrow cynics, the anti-intellectual intellectuals, the pampered egotists who sneer at honesty, thrift, hard work, prudence, common decency, and self-denial. (Nobile 1974, 5)

In 1973 Agnew was indicted for taking bribes and evading income taxes as Governor of Maryland and as Vice-President. He pleaded no contest and resigned the vice-presidency, after which Nixon appointed as his replacement Gerald Ford, who in turn pardoned Nixon after the latter resigned under impeachment.

One could continue ad infinitum to retell Orwellian tales from the Watergate archives—and it *is* necessary to retell them periodically, considering the recent tendency to let the history of Watergate disappear down the memory hole under the pretext that it's stale old stuff— and besides, as my students (whose ignorance of this chapter of history is staggering) are always saying, "Nixon may have pulled one dumb stunt, but he didn't deserve to be crucified for it." However, two more recent revelations from the Agnewtonian Age will suffice for present purposes. One is the information revealed by the *Columbia Journalism Review* that the FBI in the early seventies attempted to discredit the left-wing Liberation News Service (LNS) by circulating anonymous letters to leftist newspapers and organizations which falsely accused LNS of being an FBI front (Mackenzie 1981). The other is a confidential memo, reprinted in *Assault on the Media: The Nixon Years,* by William E. Porter, from Nixon aide Jeb Magruder to White House Chief-of-Staff H.R. Haldeman and Communications Director Herbert Klein, dated July 17, 1970, and titled "Tentative Plan: Press Objectivity." The following were some of Magruder's proposals to counter what was perceived to be anti-Nixon bias in the news media:

> Plant a column with a syndicated columnist which raises the question of objectivity and ethics in the news media. Kevin Phillips could be a good choice. (271)
>
> Arrange for an article on the subject in a major consumer magazine authored by Stewart Alsop, Buckley, or Kilpatrick. Also, request Hobe Lewis to run a major article. (271) [Lewis was editor-in-chief of *Reader's Digest.*]
>
> Arrange for an "expose" [sic] to be written by an author such as Earl Mazo or Victor Lasky. Publish in hardcover and paperback. (272) [In 1977, Lasky published a book defending Nixon, titled *It Didn't Start With Watergate.*]
>
> Generate a massive outpouring of letters-to-the-editor. (273) [Jonathan Schell's *The Time of Illusion* presents evidence that Nixon and Haldeman's method for generating such letters, not only to

the press but to members of Congress and the White House itself, was to forge them and send them out over the signatures of ordinary citizens around the country.]

Unintentional Doublethink—
Lessons in (Self-)Deceit

In the previous examples, doublethink resulted from deliberate manipulations of the truth. Often, however, it is unintentional, involving the process of rationalization that Orwell described in *Nineteen Eighty-Four* as leading into "the labyrinthine world of doublethink" (Orwell 1949, 25). The Communists, for example, are Orwellian twisters of truth and threats to democracy, who believe that the end justifies the means; the only way to thwart them is to fight fire with fire, so *our* end justifies the same means as theirs, including lying. "To repudiate morality while laying claim to it, to believe that democracy was impossible and that the Party was the guardian of democracy. . . ." (25)

Furthermore, what is and what is not doublethink is often a subjective judgment upon which rational people disagree. In current American discourse, the most dizzying confusions between Big Brother and Winston Smith are found not among the professional politicians and paid disinformers, but among some of our most respected journalists and scholars. Even more than the contemporaries of Orwell whom he berated for this trait, the present intellectual left and right mimic one another's language uncannily; and now part of that mimicry is regularly citing Orwell against each other.

Orwell vs. Orwell—Enter the Hall of Mirrors

Orwell's own key words and ideas have become victims of the corruption of language and thought he deplored. As was almost inevitable in this age when any rhetorical ethos quickly gets clichéd, coopted, and travestied, the great Orwell texts are becoming such a debased currency, by being cited on all sides of every issue, that they may soon no longer be usable toward any legitimate purpose. The appeal to Orwell as an authority has simply been added to the "mass of lies, evasions, folly, hatred, and schizophrenia" that he saw as the essence of modern politics (Orwell 1952, 4:137).

Midge Decter, director of the neoconservative Committee for the Free World, said in support of the Committee's founding in 1981 to combat the ideas of American leftist intellectuals: "Anti-democratic ideas have seeped into the culture at every point, corrupting thought and debasing language almost exactly term for term, as George Orwell predicted" (Goldstein 1982, 1). The Leftists promptly responded with observations about the Orwellian overtones in the choice of the committee's first major effort, with an ad in the *New York Times* in April 1981 which defended the Reagan administration's support of the junta in El Salvador, widely regarded as one of the world's bloodiest regimes (B-7). The previous year, Bertram Gross's book *Friendly Fascism* claimed that neoconservatives and other members of the New Right establishment like Decter had surpassed *Nineteen Eighty-Four* in propagating "triplespeak" (Gross 1980, 19). On the other side, Arnold Beichman's book *Nine Lies about America* cited the facile application to America of the word "fascism" by Gross (in an earlier article) and other leftists of that period as a classic case of Orwellian corruption of language (Beichman 1972, 36–38).

Us vs. Them—Different Sides, Similar Arguments

Not only in their citations of Orwell against each other, but on every issue, each side attributes total righteousness to its own causes and total iniquity to its opponents. To be a regular reader of journals like *The Nation, The Village Voice,* and *In These Times* on the left, and *Commentary, National Review,* and *American Spectator* on the right, is to be constantly reminded of the inelegant but profound folk saying, "Everybody shits, but your own doesn't stink."

Each side constantly accuses the other of a double standard in judging the left and the right, worldwide and domestically. Jeane Kirkpatrick's famous 1979 *Commentary* article, "Dictatorship and Double Standards," which prompted President Reagan to appoint her Ambassador to the United Nations, charged that the United States under the Carter administration's human rights policies exacted a stricter standard from friendly, right-wing dictatorships than from Communist ones or from terroristic insurgents. Leftists countered by accusing Kirkpatrick of Orwellian semantic gymnastics in distinguishing merely "authoritarian" right-wing dictatorships from "totalitarian" Communist ones and in euphemistically describing the former as "moderately repressive" and ruled by "moderate autocrats." Noam Chomsky and Edward Herman (1979) pointed to the American right's double standard in using the word "terrorism" only in reference to leftist insurgents. Herman (1982) wrote in *The Real Terror Network:*

> We have been living not only in an age of escalating "terrorism" but in an age of Orwell, where words are managed and propaganda and scholarship are organized so that terror *means* the lesser ter-

ror—the greater terror is defined out of existence and given little attention. With the accession to power of Reagan, Haig, and Kirkpatrick we have entered the *post*-Orwellian era. Claiming a new dedication to fighting "terrorism," this administration has rushed to the support of the world's leading terrorists, including the rulers of the most torture-prone NSSs [National Security States] and assorted other right-wing governments with a proclivity to violence. (13)

The game on both sides is not just tu quoque but tu solus. Each portrays the other side's forces—the domestic ones, not simply their foreign connections—as the implacable, exclusive enemies of freedom and democracy, and its own forces as their pristine, sole defenders. Each views its own side as feeble, dispersed, and persecuted by the Other, which is always portrayed as all-powerful; lavishly financed; intricately coordinated (if not conspiratorial); in tyrannical control of the government, mass media, schools, universities, and think tanks. The other side's personalities and ideas are always "trendy" and "fashionable," and always get circulated at cocktail parties. (No one on Our side ever, ever goes to a cocktail party, or would be caught dead having a fashionable idea.) Our journalists are pillars of integrity and independence who write "exposés" and "make revelations"—Theirs are propagandists and secret agents whose writings are made up of "smears" and "innuendo." Each accuses the other alternately of elitism and of debasing elite standards; of effete intellectualism and of anti-intellectualism.

Each side also considers itself the exclusive guardian of intellectual, moral and aesthetic standards—which are under constant siege from the other guys. Robert Moss, co-author of *The Spike,* a trashy right-wing propaganda novel, became arbiter of literary taste in reviewing *Assassination on Embassy Row,* by John Dinges and Saul Landau, for *National Review.* (The book under review was an account of the killing of Chilean politician Orlando Letelier, a case in which neither the book's authors nor Moss were impartial analysts, as we will see.) Undoubtedly taking his cues from left reviews of *The Spike,* Moss described the book as "sloppily written, jargon-loaded, and as well-organized as a mangrove swamp . . . [T]his awesomely bad book . . . [uses] the vocabulary of the political gutter" (Moss 1980, 1147–48). Each side is equally quick to drop its standards and jump into the gutter to savage any opposition work or to uncritically laud any tract that favors its own causes. The uncritical praise by much (though not all) of the left press, for the Costa-Gavras film *Missing,* which presented a leftist bias on the coup in Chile, mirrored the right press's adulatory response to *The Spike.*

Each side's journalists and scholars are predisposed to accept, without challenge, assertions supporting their side whose documentation is dubious or lacking altogether—while simultaneously questioning with scrupulous care, the other side's evidence. Documentation within each side's networks tends to be "symbiotic" (as Ronald Reagan, in a rare lucid insight, once phrased this phenomenon) and authors frequently cite as proof assertions that have previously appeared in allied publications, even if they were unsupported in that source. Thus Edward Jay Epstein revealed how in the late sixties the false claim that twenty-eight Black Panthers had been killed by the police circulated throughout liberal journalistic circles without anyone bothering to check it out (Beichman 1973, 47–51). And Hillel Levin pointed out in *The Nation* (Dec. 6, 1980) that Rael Jean Isaac, author of an article in *Midstream* earlier that year which attacked the leftist Institute for Policy Studies, cited an article by Joseph Shattan in *Commentary* for verification of the contents of an alleged IPS internal memo. Levin checked Shattan's footnote, to find that *his* source was an earlier article on the same subject—by Isaac (Levin 1980, 609).

Each side delights in catching opposition representatives in conflicts of interests, while covering up its own. When either is accused of such conflicts, the first response is to deny them, then when presented with irrefutable proof, to rationalize them. Similarly, with revelations of allies' versus opponents' associations with foreign governments or with U.S. intelligence agencies, each side presumes that such associations by its friends (when they can no longer be suppressed or denied) are aboveboard, altruistic, and justified in the defense of freedom and democracy—while those on the other side represent sinister conspiracies and personal opportunism. All of the following material is based on secondary sources whose own credibility, of course, reiterates the same questions subject to this article.

Left vs. Right—Different Sides, Similar Behavior

Robert Moss's review in *National Review* of *Assassination on Embassy Row* by John Dinges and Saul Landau accuses the authors and other media friends of the Institute for Policy Studies (IPS) of "spiking" (i.e., suppressing) mention of documents found in the briefcase of assassinated Chilean politician Orlando Letelier (Moss 1980, 1148). These documents allegedly linked Letelier and IPS with Russian and Cuban intelligence agencies. (Letelier and Landau were both fellows in the Washington headquarters of IPS and in Moss's *The Spike* a thinly fictionalized IPS is a KGB front.) Moss points out that, while Dinges and Landau do discuss a letter in the briefcase from Salvador Allende's daughter, Beatriz, in which she mentions to Letelier that he was being paid $1,000 a month by the remnants of the Allende government exiled in Cuba, the authors describe Beatriz's husband only as "a Cuban government official" (Dinges and Landau 1980, 15), whereas Moss identifies him as "one of the top officers in Castro's secret service" (Moss 1980, 1148). Moss further notes that Dinges and Landau make no mention of a letter in the briefcase that Letelier was to deliver by hand from Landau to a friend in Cuba, which stated Landau's commitment to "making propaganda for American socialism" (Moss 1980, 1148). Landau later acknowledged (pers. corresp.) that his letter was only a friendly greeting, and that Moss took the quote about propaganda out of its jocular context. Meanwhile, Moss fails to mention a passage in the Dinges-Landau book which says of the charge that Letelier was a Cuban agent, "The FBI found no evidence Letelier was working for any government, either Cuban, Chilean or other." (Dinges and Landau 1980, 371).

Aryah Neier responded to Moss's review with an article entitled "The IPS and Its Enemies" in *The Nation,* December 6, 1980, refuting Moss's interpretation of the Letelier documents as evidence of a Cuban-IPS conspiracy. But Neier does not mention Moss's identification of Beatriz Allende's husband as a Cuban intelligence officer, and he repeats Dinges and Landau's characterization of him as only "a Cuban government official." Nor does Neier reply to Moss's reference to the Landau letter.

On the other hand, Moss's review mentions nothing of his own vested interests in Chile. According to a 1980 article by Fred Landis in the libertarian journal *Inquiry,* when Salvador Allende was President of Chile in the early seventies, Moss worked for a Chilean think tank, the Institute of General Studies, a CIA front that fabricated disinformation based on forged documents linking Allende to Communist plots, and that otherwise conspired to overthrow him. And Landis reports evidence that Moss's pro-Pinochet book *Chile's Marxist Experiment* was secretly financed by the CIA, which chose him to write it, provided the title and outline, and paid for his trip to Chile. Moss later moved on to work for the Somoza regime in Nicaragua, which paid him $40,000 a year as editor of a pro-government newsweekly. Landis notes the Orwellian twist that the conservative organization called Accuracy in Media has designated Moss "the finest investigative reporter of our era" (Landis 1980, 23).

Moss's *National Review* article also says nothing about a passage in the Dinges-Landau book alleging that a week before his assassination, two of Letelier's murderers visited the office of Senator James Buckley (brother of William F. Buckley, editor of *National Review*) to see a cousin of one of them who worked for the senator (Dinges and Landau 1980, 21–22). Another book on Letelier published in 1980, *Death in Washington,* by Donald Freed and Fred Landis, accused William Buckley of being an accessory in Letelier's murder, as well as having a long history of complicity with the CIA and the Chilean and Cuban right wings in both his publications and his covert activities. It *is* a matter of public record, not disputed by Buckley, that he and other *National Review* associates helped form the American-Chilean Council in 1974, against which the Justice Department filed a suit (in 1979) that forced it to register as an agent of the right-wing Pinochet government. Between 1974 and 1979, *National Review* published several articles by William Buckley, Robert Moss and others denying any involvement of the Pinochet government, playing up the briefcase letters to implicate Letelier in spy intrigues, and suggesting, as one article put it, that Letelier may have been killed by a "left-wing Chilean group intent on disrupting Chile's relations with the United States" (Judis 31). Agents of the Pinochet Government's secret police, however, were eventually convicted for the murder of Letelier and an IPS associate, on the confession of one of them—who was also one of the visitors to Senator Buckley's office.

The Freed-Landis book, in turn, provoked a libel suit by the CIA officers it accused of complicity in the Letelier killings. Supported by the Buckleys, the CIA men denounced the book's "absurd charges." A subsequent ad in *The Nation* (October 3, 1981) for the Donald Freed Defense League attributed this suit to part of a campaign, pushed by the Reagan administration, "to stifle further voices that dissent to police state organizations and their activities. Nineteen eighty-one counts down to 1984" (311). The libel suit against Freed was eventually dismissed in court.

Will the *real* Big Brother please stand up?

Any Escape from the Hall of Mirrors?

Is there any way out of this Orwellian hall of mirrors? It would apparently be too much to expect either side to make the modest concession that its own shit does on occasion stink; to admit that it is predisposed to the equal and opposite patterns of bias it accuses the other side of. And yet, what sensible person could deny the applicability to all political polemics today of E.P. Thompson's observations about the opposing sides in the nuclear arms race?

> Each bloc is at pains to deny and conceal its own areas of greatest military strength, and to advertise a pretense to strength in areas where it is weak. The intelligence agencies that report on each other's resources are themselves an interest group, with high ideological motivation, and on occasion they deliberately manufacture alarmist reports . . . The name of the game, on both sides, is mendacity. (18)

One possible form of semantic depollutant might be a journal or regular TV or radio program either based on a debate format (such as the magazine *Skeptic,* which unfortunately did not gain enough circulation to survive) or serving a similar function to Albert Camus's idea, never realized, for a "control newspaper" regularly investigating the accuracy of reports in other media of all political persuasions. Such a journal would take as its point of departure the assumption that all political factions are subject to their distinct patterns of bias and conflicts of interest, and would serve as a referee, investigating and weighing the opposing claims of each accordingly, perhaps with an editorial staff drawn equally from the various sides. Another possible antidote would be for the public to demand that government officials—from the President on down—and other politicians, as well as journalists, scholars and teachers, be regularly required to debate opponents face to face, rather than being allowed to make unchallenged edicts.

Pending the establishment of such a referee journal, the temptation must be resisted to lapse into the cynical assumption that all sides lie equally and that the truth is entirely a matter of subjective perception—precisely the doctrine of The Party in *Nineteen Eighty-Four.* Even if no one side has the total or constant claim to the truth each habitually assumes it has, and even when the rhetorical patterns of two sides mirror each other, one may still be right and the other wrong on any given issue and, on balance, in general. Unremitting judgments must be made, according to our best lights, if we are to save our sanity and keep from being pulled fatally into the labyrinth of doublethink.

Works Cited

Beichman, Arnold. *Nine Lies About America.* New York: Pocket Books, 1972.

Chomsky, Noam, and Edward Herman. "The Semantics of Terror and Violence." In *The Washington Connection and Third World Fascism.* Boston: South End Press, 1979.

"David Atlee Phillips v. Donald Freed et al." *The Nation,* 3 Oct. 1981: 311.

deBorchgrave, Arnaud, and Robert Moss. *The Spike*. New York: Crown, 1980.

Deckter, Midge. Quoted in Richard Goldstein, "The War for the American Mind." *The Village Voice*, 8 June 1982: 1.

Dinges, John, and Saul Landau. *Assassination on Embassy Row*. New York: Pantheon, 1980.

Empson, William. *Some Versions of Pastoral*, 58. New York: New Directions, 1960.

Freed, Donald, with Fred Landis. *Death in Washington: The Murder of Orlando Letelier*. Westport, Conn.: Lawrence Hill, 1980.

Gross, Bertram. *Friendly Fascism: The New Face of Power in America*. M. Evans, 1980.

Herman, Edward. *The* Real *Terror Network*. Boston: South End Press, 1982.

Howe, Irving, ed. *Nineteen Eighty-Four: Texts, Sources, Criticism*. New York: Harcourt Brace Jovanovich, 1982.

Judis, John. "William F. Buckley, Jr.: The Consummate Conservative." *The Progressive* 45 (September 1981): 25–33.

Kirkpatrick, Jeane. "Dictatorship and Double Standards." *Commentary* 68, no. 5 (1979): 34–45.

Landis, Fred. "The Best-Selling Lies of 1980." *Inquiry*, 29 Dec. 1980: 17–23.

Lasky, Victor. *It Didn't Start with Watergate*. New York: Dell, 1977.

Levin, Hillel. "Disinformation Please." *The Nation*, 6 Dec. 1980: 609.

Mackenzie, Angus. "Sabotaging the Dissident Press." *Columbia Journalism Review* (March-April 1981): 57, 59–60, 62–63.

Moss, Robert. "The Spike." *National Review* 32, no. 19 (1980): 1147–49.

Neier, Aryeh. "The I.P.S. and Its Enemies." *The Nation*, 6 Dec. 1980: 605–8.

Nobile, Philip. *Intellectual Skywriting*. New York: Charterhouse, 1974.

Orwell, George. *Nineteen Eighty-Four*. New York: New American Library, 1949.

———. "Politics and the English Language." In *In Front of Your Nose (1945–50)*, (127–40). Vol. 4 of *The Collected Essays, Journalism and Criticism of George Orwell*. Edited by Sonia Orwell and Ian Angus. 4 Vols. New York: Harcourt, Brace & World, 1952.

Porter, William E. "Plant a Column." *Assault on the Media: The Nixon Years*. Ann Arbor: University of Michigan Press, 1976: 271–73.

Schell, Jonathan. *The Time of Illusion*. New York: Knopf, 1976.

Thompson, E.P., and Dan Smith, eds. *Protest and Survive*. New York: Penguin, 1980.

"We—a group of intellectuals and religious leaders—applaud American policy in El Salvador." Advertisement. *New York Times*, 6 April 1981: B-7.

9 Worldthink

Richard Ohmann
Wesleyan University

Mainstream representations of the world—my subject in this essay—are rich in ideological words, concepts, and images that a gradual historical process has familiarized for most people in this society. Reagan's gladiators could send up new extravagancies of word and thought (*freedom fighters* as a term for right-wing murderers and mercenaries), but they did so within a semantic field already bent and smeared, over decades of imperial rhetoric. In my view, the accepted language of U.S. foreign policy is even more corrupt and dangerous than the crass jingoism of the particular Reagan moment.

Not that it's unimportant to expose and ridicule the blatant distortions, euphemisms, and lies. Critical intellectuals, who do have at least a small public voice, have thereby a responsibility to resist every new act of linguistic cynicism or legerdemain. To fix on some nuclear examples: we should make a disrespectful noise when the Emperor of the Free World decides to call the MX missile system the *Peacekeeper,* no question. But the world doesn't need us to keep watch over such murderous tomfoolery: a hundred journalists and politicians will cry halt, and the new usage will go the way of the late fifties coinage, *clean bomb,* with its radiation measured in *Sunshine Units*—laughed out of the lexicon. In front of me as I write is Nicole Hollander's comic strip, "Sylvia," a neat example:

> The Reagan Administration announced that since the renaming of the MX missile "Peacekeeper" has proved acceptable to the American public, it will now refer to unemployment figures as "worker vacation statistics," and to the recession as "doing the hokey pokey."[1]

A widely read book like *Nukespeak,*[2] simply by assembling a collection of these terms, can discredit them. To read through the tough-casual

Copyright © 1987 by Richard Ohmann. Reprinted by permission of Wesleyan University Press.

lexicon of *megadeaths, nuclear umbrellas, clean surgical strikes,* cities as *bargaining chips,* and so on, is to perceive this as a code facilitating the zany death games of smartasses from Rand and the Pentagon and Harvard; boys who have somehow graduated from fraternity pranks to a deadly and irresponsible preeminence without growing up. Or a fine piece of reportage like Robert Scheer's *With Enough Shovels*[3] can provoke a healthy terror mainly by quoting the night thoughts of those who have the power to end all our lives.

The limit on this remedy is that it promotes a vision of our leaders as Dr. Strangeloves, and hence a hope that we might regain sanity in public discourse merely by turning out of office a particular group of maniacs. But any new set of leaders, short of a government genuinely oriented toward peace, would inherit the death machine and the generals and the lobbyists, as well as the accumulated legacy of concept and language that has been left us by forty years of carrying on daily life with the bomb in our midst, and of learning not only to think the unthinkable but to forget that it *is* unthinkable. The language of military policy is a structure of quiet, deadly euphemisms beneath the veneer of blatant, deadly euphemisms like "Peacekeeper." Conservatives and liberals, doves and hawks alike, wear this vocabulary like a comfortable old hat. Getting rid of the Reagan administration, with its policies drawn from the lunatic Right, would not purify this deeper stratum of language and thought.

Thus, it is easy to mock a supposedly reassuring term like *nuclear exchange,* and insist on substituting the more blunt *nuclear war*—yet *war* itself soothes and deceives in this context: A war is a military conflict between nations through the engagement of their armed forces, with civilians pretty freely killed along the way, and with territory and power to be won or lost. That's bad enough, but in no significant way does the definition apply to the events that would take place were the Soviet Union and the United States to cut loose with their missiles. This would not be a *conflict,* but a technological spasm beyond the control of either side. It would not be *between nations,* but would annihilate all nations, at least in the Northern Hemisphere. The *armed forces* of the U.S. and U.S.S.R. would never *engage* with each other. The very distinction between *civilians* and "armed forces" would vanish, except that some of the higher ranking military men, ten stories underground, would probably survive for a while longer than any civilians. No nation could retain its identity as a society, much less *win;* none would be able to occupy the uninhabitable *territory* of another, and no *power* of human institutions, including government, would remain. The term *war* masks all this, and makes the unprecedented and abominable seem routinely horrible.[4]

Likewise, nuclear weapons are not weapons (you can't use them to fight, or wage a battle).[5] *Strategic* nuclear missiles could implement no strategy, if fired, and in fact would obliterate the very relationship of means to ends that makes strategy a meaningful concept. The word *defense,* already a sick joke for other reasons in the phrase, "Department of Defense," implies in a nuclear context something that cannot be the case, for there is no defense against missiles carrying nuclear bombs. (The fond hope that there might be, a hope latent in the misused word, has helped make the Strategic Defense Initiative politically viable though almost all scientists think it technically absurd.) *Security,* as in "national security" and "collective security," refers to a condition of mortal danger. And *disarmament,* as used by the negotiating "teams," refers to a process by which the two superpowers would retain enough bombs to destroy each other and everyone in between.

How do the illusions and lies behind terms like these escape serious challenge? In part because they fit easily into a conception of our world that is thoroughly familiar. In this conception, good and evil stand opposed across an iron curtain that girdles the globe—two systems of belief and two eschatologies that can unstably coexist but never change: One or the other must finally rule. So high are the stakes in this transhistorical opposition that it requires weapons and strategies that might end history. Our defense is not the defense of people and a productive system and a set of human interests, but of an eternal principle: A war which almost no one survived could still be a victory, if evil were itself destroyed. Naturally, in a battle of such proportions ordinary citizens have nothing to contribute; they must deed over their futures to a handful of leaders grown godlike through the power they command. Naturally, too, societies on the margins of this confrontation have no standing except as they can be deployed in the positional jockeying of good and evil; their people do not exist as beings with their own history and needs, but only in relation to the Manichaean struggle. To be sure, few see the world in just this way—or see it this way all the time—but because the picture is there as a ready referent in political debate, those who would contest it are forced to begin by examining it as if it were a rational construct.

This picture connects the semantics of nuclear confrontation to those of more mundane discourse about foreign policy. Take a little thing, like the names of countries. When Alexander Haig said (while still secretary of state), "more help to El Salvador is needed," what could *El Salvador* possibly have meant? The Junta, of course,[6] and its military cadres of the right, who had killed 15,000 to 20,000 citizens of the country in the previous two years. And when Haig went on to say, "they're going to continue to need security support"[7] plainly his pronoun did not refer to the opposition in this civil war, or to the peasants, for whom U.S. "security support" means only the secure knowledge that there will be more bodies to bury tomorrow morning. Yet his use of the name "El Salvador" reassures us that we are helping a whole people, rather than helping one faction—and a faction, at that, which by all accounts has set some kind of record for viciousness, even among our authoritarian friends. The deception is possible only because it accords with a world picture that constitutes El Salvador and other nations as counters in a transcendent moral opposition,[8] so that what goes on inside the country really doesn't matter as long as the rulers are on "our" side.

The semantics work the same way when our government wishes to harm, not help: Haig once referred to Libya as "a cancer that has to be removed."[9] Does this not encourage his hearers to think beyond opposing the Quaddafi government, and imagine with equanimity some rather wholesale destruction of Libyan society? (By what means could one "remove" a whole country? Only, one assumes, by one of those "surgical strikes.") And when a country is beyond both harm and help, its name may cease to refer to its government *or* to the majority of its people, as when an unnamed U.S. official said, "Barring a miracle, Nicaragua is a lost cause."[10] Lost to whom? And did we lose it in the same place we lost Vietnam? (These small countries are apparently easy to misplace.) The lost cause was not Nicaragua, but what our government took as its right to control the future of that society—though it must be added that a year later our leaders have not given up on finding Nicaragua again, through support of the same bloody killers who used to run it.

In each of these instances a U.S. official appropriates the name of a country, along with the feelings most of us have about whole peoples and sovereign nations, attaching the name and the feelings to some construct which answers only to the needs of the U.S. government as its policymakers see them. In this lexicon, societies disappear, to be replaced by tallies on some global score sheet.[11] This inverted, telescopic view of other societies, incidentally, permits a close connection between intervention and nuclear force. Thus Richard Perle, Assistant Secretary of Defense for International Security Policy, commented on the "effect that the nuclear balance has on our willingness to take risks in local situations." He meant that if the Soviets are more afraid of us than we are of them, we can more cheerfully mine the harbors or assassinate the leaders of small societies—indeed, invade them outright if the war of good and evil calls for that. The term *local situations* derives its meaning from the global struggle, not from the wishes of local human beings. Needless to say, this attitude makes the bomb an implement of routine foreign policy, in its use as a standing threat to any power that would impede our imperial will by supporting popular revolutions.

If the humble names of countries serve so readily the imperial outlook of the evangelists, abstractions are understandably more pliable. President Reagan said to the International Monetary Fund, "We who live in free market societies believe that growth, prosperity, and ultimately, human fulfillment, are created from the bottom up, not the government down." One who considers the U.S. a free market society will naturally see no contradiction in going on to say, "Unless a nation puts its own financial house in order, no amount of aid will produce progress."[12] Just how are nations to do this, unless their governments intervene in the operations of the market (with the benign aid of the International Monetary Fund or the World Bank), to starve their citizens? *Free market* is a term without a referent in the real world, but with a heavy freight of value in the system of polarities that constitutes the apocalyptic world image. It may be applied as one wishes, usually to advance the freedom of large corporations in making markets and people unfree.

Again, *terrorism* used to be a handy word, meaning, roughly, the advancement of political aims by the threat or use of indiscriminate violence. I don't know what it means any more: our officials apply it not only to IRA or PLO street bombings, but also to a range of events from sabotage, to mob rampages, to assassination of political enemies—but not to similar actions by right wing governments or paramilitary death squads. And our media accepts without comment Menachem Begin's practice of referring always to the PLO (and indeed the whole Palestinian people) as "terrorists," even at times when his own government is destroying refugee camps and killing thousands of civilians. The word floats free, a bundle of affects to be attached wherever those with access to the media can slap them.

Ditto for *human rights*. The administration has found that these do, after all, count for something in circles like Congress and the court of world opinion. So a State Department memo, approved by Secretary Haig, declared that "human rights is at the core of our foreign policy because it is central to what America is and stands for."[13] (America?) Whatever human rights are, they must have been flourishing at that time in Chile, Argentina, Uruguay, and Paraguay, because our government had recently supported loans to the regimes that presided over these countries, indicating that they measured up to the human rights provisions of the International Financial Institutions Act of 1977.[14]

Fortunately, Haig has given us a map to this part of the semantic field by defining the one word in terms of the other: "International terrorism . . . is the ultimate abuse of human rights."[15] Nothing remains of meaning here, other than a moral polarity which may be applied in whichever way the purposes of the great demand. And indeed, the main administrative use of all these terms in foreign policy discourse is to destroy their referential meaning, saving the moral feeling that used to accompany it for opportunistic purposes of the moment. Of course any vocabulary is a battleground. The opposition can always contest or try to rehabilitate the heavily freighted words, as I am doing now. But virtually the whole public debate is carried on in this debased verbal coinage, while a few intellectuals buzz away in books or journals with at most a few thousand readers.

This is the crux. For if the world picture behind U.S. foreign policy were the sudden, Machiavellian invention of a few leaders, they would have little chance of establishing it. Instead, it has evolved through a complex process of interaction among leaders, intellectuals, media professionals, and millions of ordinary citizens. One can see the power dynamics of the process more nakedly by looking back at an earlier stage, when the image of the United States as bearer of righteousness among nations was not broadly accepted, and when leaders like Theodore Roosevelt had to argue for it openly:

> The simple truth is that there is nothing even remotely resembling "imperialism" or "militarism" involved in the development of that policy of expansion which has been part of the history of America from the day she became a nation. The word means absolutely nothing as applied to our present policy in the Philippines: for this policy is only imperialistic in the sense that Jefferson's policy in Louisiana was imperialistic; only military in the sense that Jackson's policy toward the Seminoles or Custer's toward the Sioux embodied militarism.[16]

Plain expression of sentiments like these, today, would stamp the writer as a racist and a hypocrite. Yet the discourse of world politics that I have been discussing has slowly naturalized and neutralized these same premises—except that *expansion* no longer entails the formal annexation of territory by our government. The terms and meanings of that discourse gain wide circulation, of course, through the media, and I now return to that subject.

The boundary between Pentagon-talk and news reportage is naturally permeable: journalists must report what important officials say. But in what ways do they mediate its transmission? They may hold a new usage up for analysis, even object to it. They may blankly convey it within quotation marks. Or they may, as it were, remove the quotation marks and ease the term from novel speech into routine language. Just as the mainstream journalists refused to swallow "Peacekeeper" for the MX missile, most of them kept a critical distance between themselves and the Reagan usage of "freedom fighters." Yet there is a tendency for Pentagon-talk to become media language over a period of time.

A personal experience will illustrate the point. Sometime around 1968 I complained in writing to the *New York Times* about that paper's repeated use of the word *enemy*, in news reporting, to refer to the Vietnamese National Liberation Front. A staff member actually troubled to write back, explaining that the *Times* used this word only in a descriptive, not in a pejorative, sense. I suggested to him that the nonpejorative use of "enemy," like that of *kike* or *wop*, was difficult to achieve. That terminated our brief correspondence. The point is that somehow, between perhaps 1964 and 1968, government officials' conception of the South Vietnamese opposition as enemy of the American people had slid comfortably into the standard lexicon of our newspaper of record. Thus did the *Times* help naturalize the war, even while becoming more critical of it on the editorial page.

Journalists' habit of depending on inside sources tends to align their basic conceptions with those of high officials, and make their language porous to official words. The professional doctrine of journalistic objectivity offers no defense against such leakage over time. And other journalistic routines and attitudes abet the distortion of international news as they do that of domestic politics. For instance, television's requirement that each news segment take the shape of a "story" urges correspondents toward narrative closure. In coverage of international events, this drive toward resolution, even when no actual resolution is in sight, tends to return a story at its end to the perspective of American policy makers, whose plans and ideas serve as a bulwark against disorder. Again, the demand for exciting visual images to hold viewers' attention increases the likelihood that when foreigners turn up on the screen they will appear marching or demonstrating or conducting guerilla attacks or enduring them or being bombed or holding hostages. Foreigners, by pictorial definition, are violent and irrational, quite different from us.

It is worth mentioning three other ways in which the exigencies of TV journalism foster worldthink. Whatever else it is, the news must be habit-forming entertainment, to keep ratings and revenues up. Producers of the news, as of other shows, work toward this end partly by staying with dependably popular subjects. Happenings in other countries are not normally among those subjects. Daily coverage of Brazil or

India does not appeal to mass audiences, so news divisions hold foreign coverage down to a barely respectable minimum—except when events abroad impinge on the stability of the world order as perceived by U.S. leaders. News is, by definition, that which disturbs the status quo. For that reason, and because networks don't have the staff or the air time to cover the slow unfolding of the social process in other parts of the world, Iranians, Palestinians, Filipinos, and so on appear on our screens mainly when they become unruly, when they threaten "collective security," when they do something unwelcome to the authorities. After the disruption ends, they recede back into nonexistence.

Second, because TV news sells itself as "right up to the minute," it feeds on what is happening *now,* and tries to hold its audience by presenting brief, dramatic segments of event. Thus, it virtually excludes history, which appears only as hastily assembled "background" for a current outrage. (Perhaps the most egregious example in recent years was the pathetic attempt of newspeople to remedy their ignorance about Grenada when it suddenly became news in the Fall of 1983.) We do not see on our screens the long infusion of multinational capital into third world countries, the gradual development of expectations and grievances, the rise of indigenous movements, or the evolution of local politics—nothing that would humanize the mob on the screen and make its actions predictable or comprehensible.

Finally, like other shows, the news organizes reality around famous persons. Consider how the image of domestic politics is mostly narrowed to the doings of a few candidates and officeholders. Likewise, the news tends to present a handful of leaders—Arafat, Khomeini, Castro, Walesa, Aquino—as synechdoches for their entire societies. History, economics, politics, the complex struggles of a people, all dissolve into personality and celebrity.

In all of these ways the institutions and people who picture the world for television watchers create a systematic ignorance of Latin America, Asia, Africa, and the Middle East. These parts of the rest of the world are supposed to stay out of sight, and in fact not exist, other than as a field for the normal cultivation of U.S. projects and a stable weight in the balance of good and evil. Think of the way Latin American societies appear and disappear: Nicaragua exists on the screen at the moment for obvious reasons, though its realities run a poor second to talking heads from our government fitting Nicaragua into *their* reality. El Salvador has receded into the shadows, now that things are going "well" there. Honduras is only a place where Contras hang out and where U.S. forces maneuver. Panama is just one name in the list of "Contadora nations." Belize is a total blank. And so on.[17] In addition, the homogenizing process I have described blends these societies together, and indeed tends to make them indistinguishable from Arab societies, African societies (South Africa excepted), and the rest. All merge into a general type of *the other*.

If that is correct, it helps explain why public rage over the taking of hostages in Iran was so undifferentiated. I remember vividly the sight (on TV) of a spontaneous demonstration on the streets of Washington, soon after the hostages were taken. A man was shouting repeatedly, "We're *tired* of other countries telling us what to do," and then he led the crowd in a wholehearted rendition of "God Bless America." (Given the last thirty years of U.S.-Iranian relations, I wonder how Iranian viewers would have responded to this scene, and what in particular they would have thought to see a black man venting such sentiments.) The United States is the only society that really exists as a society—however distorted—on television. The way Americans experience it, of course, depends in good part on subordination of other societies, but we can't see that process and the dominated are not available to be perceived, except as people who suddenly, incomprehensibly, and irrationally appear on the screen, cause some trouble, are eventually taken care of, and recede back into nonbeing. This is one of the forms hegemony takes, mediated by the peculiarly complex social relations of the consciousness industry.

Capitalism is indeed the most opaque of all social forms, and far more opaque today than when Marx made this observation. In it, human beings and whole societies vanish behind market relations and market culture. We cannot know our interdependence. Exploitation appears as freedom; conflict, as an abnormality rather than as the engine of history. The discourse of foreign affairs takes place in a near-vacuum of knowledge and understanding, where other peoples, their histories, and their aspirations are momentary distractions.

To sum up these reflections, I suggest that the deeper and more dangerous lies implicit in this discourse derive from and support a picture of the world as organized around two great moral forces. This picture expresses in a broad way the interests of those with power. When it is generally accepted or only weakly challenged, it gives legitimacy to their projects by making their interests seem the interests of "us" all. The words, concepts, and images I've discussed can seem valid only from a perspective of power, from which most people and their needs appear as problems to be solved. And this perspective is inseparable from a flagrantly undemocratic structure of communication,[18] which endows a few with the power to speak, and casts the others as masses to be spoken about and to.[19] Yet the structure of domination persists not because our ruling class uses the media that some of its members own as organs of propaganda, but because its hegemony saturates the practices and beliefs and feelings of most Americans, including those who staff the media.

If I am generally right in this analysis, the world picture and the language that accompanies it will change significantly only when the power of the rulers is challenged by broad social movements, when new voices are admitted to the central arena of discourse, and when the majority of the people become leading actors in the historical process. Until that happens, however—and to help *make* it happen—critical intellectuals have a responsibility to expose and attack the underlying concepts and images of foreign policy discourse.

Notes

1. Hollander, Nicole. "Sylvia." *In These Times*, 22 Dec.–13 Jan. 1983.

2. Bell, Richard C., Stephen Hilgartner, and Rory O'Connor. *Nukespeak: Nuclear Language, Visions, and Mindset*. San Francisco: Sierra Club Books, 1982.

3. Sheer, Robert. *With Enough Shovels: Reagan, Bush and Nuclear War*. New York: Random House, 1982.

4. Noting this anomaly, John Somerville proposed the alternate term *omnicide*, in a letter to *Monthly Review* 34, no. 2 (1982): 61–2.

5. As this phrase stretches the meaning of "weapons," the implements that used to be called weapons (and a lot more besides) have come to be designated "conventional" weapons, with a corresponding reduction of disgust at the idea of fragmentation bombs, napalm, agent orange, and other cruel innovations which would have been thought barbarous in the age of the rack and wheel.

6. A much longer history lies behind this way of using the names of countries than behind the semantics of thermonuclear talk. But the two converge in our leaders' current picture of the world, which subordinates all peoples and all social process to the great battle of East and West.

7. *New York Times*, 6 Nov. 1981: 13-A.

8. It is interesting to note that Congress, in a pathetic attempt to impede our government's murderous El Salvador policy, has exacted a biannual certification (from that same government, of course) that the Salvadoran regime is making "progress" in human rights, as a condition of further military aid. This reassurance is apparently necessary in order to maintain the claim that our side is that of the angels. Naturally the certification dependably issues forth.

9. *Counterspy*, Nov. 1981-Jan. 1982: 31.

10. *Newsweek*, 16 Nov. 1981: 59.

11. There may be a parallel usage among Soviet leaders. They at least make a distinction between a government and its subjects, but perhaps in their lexicon the phrase, "the people," constitutes a similar subordination of social complexity to ideology.

12. *In These Times*, 21–27 Oct. 1981: 11.

13. *New York Times*, 8 Nov. 1981: E-2.

14. Derian, Patricia. "Some of Our Best Friends Are Authoritarians." *The Nation* 7 (Nov. 1981): 469.

15. Derian 469.

16. The editors of *Monthly Review* dug up this quotation, and printed it on p.9 of the Dec. 1982 issue. It is from *The Works of Theodore Roosevelt*, National Edition. Edited by Hermann Hagedorn (New York, 1926) 14: 368; and originally from a letter accepting the vice-presidential nomination, 15 Sept. 1900.

17. Of course there are excellent journalistic sources of fuller and more accurate information, such as *AMPO: Japan-Asia Quarterly Review, TCLSAC Reports* (on Southern Africa), and *NACLA Report on the Americas.* But these reach only a tiny readership. And even such weak, if courageous, opposition may draw heavy artillery fire from the establishment, as in the "60 Minutes" attack (23 Jan. 1983) on the World Council of Churches and other religious social action groups, one of which has given NACLA financial support.

18. Raymond Williams has often pointed out that the word "communication" itself implies a false claim, in most usage, since it refers to messages that go in one direction only.

19. It is inseparable, too, from the more basic structure of capitalism, which casts ordinary people as material whose labor is a commodity, and as masses of consumers who must be mobilized to buy what they have produced—but that's another story.

10 "Bullets Hurt, Corpses Stink": George Orwell and the Language of Warfare

Harry Brent
Baruch College
City University of New York

Although most educated people in the United States can claim some familiarity with George Orwell's *Nineteen Eighty-Four*, many of them are probably unaware that Big Brother, The Ministry of Truth, and Newspeak are not abstractions chiefly associated, as the Left would have it, with Hitler or, as the Right would have it, with Stalin. More important in Orwell's experience than either the German or the Georgian was the Spaniard, Generalissimo Franco. The dynamics of *Nineteen Eighty-Four* have their roots in Orwell's actual experience, specifically in his service to the Republican cause during the Spanish Civil War.

This essay will explore some of the connections that Orwell began to make in Spain between language and warfare, connections we see in *Homage to Catalonia*. I believe that Orwell's experiences in Spain not only helped lay the groundwork for *Nineteen Eighty-Four*, but also made him especially aware of the necessity for language to reflect reality accurately, a principle that was to guide the rest of his writing and his life.

In 1942, in his essay entitled "Looking Back on the Spanish War," Orwell asked

> How will the history of the Spanish war be written? If Franco remains in power his nominees will write the history books. . . .
> . . . If the Leader says of such and such an event, "It never happened"—well, it never happened. If he says that two and two are five—well, two and two are five. This prospect frightens me much more than bombs. (2:258–59)

Here we see some of the roots of *Nineteen Eighty-Four* in Orwell's fears for the emergence of a system of political engineering in which history would become whatever the ruler wanted it to be.

The Spanish Civil War was significant for Orwell because he participated in the frontline fighting against the Fascists. It was in Spain that Orwell came close to death (he was wounded in the neck by a bullet) and where he experienced day-to-day hardships which, unlike those recorded in *Down and Out in Paris and London,* he could not leave at will. The daily experience of being close to immediate death prompted Orwell to use language with great precision. In Spain he learned the truth of war firsthand, that "a louse is a louse and a bomb a bomb," and that "bullets hurt, corpses stink" (2:250).

Orwell recorded his experiences in Spain in *Homage to Catalonia.* The book is the story of his military service with the Republican cause in 1937 on the Zaragoza front in Catalonia (the northeastern region of Spain) and his unlucky adventures in Barcelona, where he found himself enlisted by sheer accident as part of the minority in the internecine strife that characterized life on the Republican side.

Let us begin at the end of *Homage to Catalonia.* Orwell has just left Spain by way of the French border and has reached the seaside town of Banyuls.

Banyuls is not a particularly friendly town. Located in the extreme south of France, it is the last place of any importance before the Spanish border. Hunted by the leadership of his own Republican side, Orwell stopped there, glad to be out of the fighting and wanting a rest. In *Homage to Catalonia* he remarks that "the little town seemed solidly pro-Franco," that the waiter in the local café, aware of Orwell's Republican associations, glowered at him, and that he and his wife remarked to each other that they wished they were back in Spain (229).

What is striking about the passage is an evident nostalgia for danger. What may not be as evident is that Banyuls, for Orwell, is much less sharply defined than the Barcelona he has just left. Orwell says of his entry into France that "With every mile that you went northward France grew greener and softer." He contrasts France with Spain, remarking that in Spain things seemed clearer, more well-defined. The softness of the French landscape leads him to comment on the nature of perception itself: "It is difficult to be certain of anything except what you have seen with your own eyes" (230–31). Orwell warned his readers to "beware of my partisanship, my mistakes of fact and the distortion inevitably caused by my having seen only one corner of events" (211). It is as if his leaving Spain, where "mountain and vine" clearly defined the landscape, gave Orwell cause to question his own vision. The soft focus of the French landscape made him wonder about the accuracy of his perceptions and the possibilities for precision in language. It is almost as if Orwell is telling us that one must go to Spain, or at least have an experience like "Spain" to talk about life in a sharply defined way.

Orwell was forever going places, to Burma in his first attempt at a profession, to Paris to write about being "down and out," and to Spain to fight for a cause he believed in. Part of his motive for these journeys was to see to the essence of things: the roots of poverty in Paris, the roots of war in Spain. Orwell's need for direct experience is reflected in his preference for direct language. Though possessed of great ironic perception, he was not a man of much verbal irony, a characteristic that cost him a greater literary reputation. This point is illustrated by one of his encounters with Henry Miller.

Miller gave Orwell a corduroy jacket when Orwell, on his way to Spain, visited him in Paris. To push the gift on Orwell, Miller jestingly told him that it was a contribution to the Republican cause. Later, however, Miller remarked that he would still have given Orwell the jacket had he been going to help the Fascists (Perles 1955, 156–59). Orwell refers to this meeting in his essay, "Inside the Whale," which includes a critique of Miller's *Tropic of Cancer:*

> I first met Miller at the end of 1936, when I was passing through Paris on my way to Spain. What most intrigued me about him was to find that he felt no interest in the Spanish war whatever. He merely told me in forcible terms that to go to Spain at that moment was the act of an idiot. He could understand anyone going there from purely selfish motives, out of curiosity, for instance, but to mix oneself up in such things *from a sense of obligation* was sheer stupidity. In any case my ideas about combating Fascism, defending democracy, etc etc were all baloney. (519)

Orwell's criticism of Henry Miller is very much like his criticism of Miller's novel:

> Miller's outlook is deeply akin to that of Whitman, and nearly everyone who has read him has remarked on this. *Tropic of Cancer* ends with an especially Whitmanesque passage, in which, after the lecheries, the swindles, the fights, the drinking bouts and the imbecilities, he simply sits down and watches the Seine flowing past, in a mystical acceptance of the thing-as-it-is. Only, what is he accepting? In the first place, not America, but the ancient bone-heap of Europe, where every grain of soil has passed through innumerable human bodies. Secondly, not an epoch of expansion and liberty, but an epoch of fear, tyranny and regimentation. To say "I accept" in an age like ours is to say that you accept concentration camps, rubber truncheons, Hitler, Stalin, bombs, aeroplanes, tinned food, machine guns, putsches, purges, slogans. (1968, 1:499)

Perhaps those who looked down on Orwell in the Fifties, who noted his lack of verbal irony, dismissed these words as pseudo-Marxist cant. No doubt many of those same people also dismissed Miller for prurient opportunism. I suggest, however, that ironically, the attitude Orwell exhibits here has something very much in common with Miller, and, by extension, with Whitman; i.e., an appreciation of simplicity and directness in language cultivated through a keen eye to see "the thing-as-it-is" and to call it such. Perhaps Orwell's great failing was his reluctance or inability to use verbal irony, to get himself perceived as a possessor of "wit." He fails to comment with "wit" about Miller's gesture of the coat or about the language of *Tropic of Cancer*. Orwell's "failure" resides in either his inability or his refusal to use the language of indirection. Certainly his great success (as was true of Miller) was to see through obfuscation in language, through the talk that covers up. Orwell's concern for directness and honesty in language cannot be easily separated from his admiration of these virtues in life.

Long before *Nineteen Eighty-Four* or "Politics and the English Language," Orwell began to hone a hatred of obfuscation. The language of *Burmese Days* and *Down and Out in Paris and London* already marked him as a writer who cultivated simplicity and directness; however, it was in *Homage to Catalonia* that tensions between directness and honesty, on the one hand, and complexity and untruth on the other, received more constant attention. Perhaps it was the experience of war, of almost being killed, that gave Orwell the extra push that was to make him the twentieth century's champion of stylistic clarity. It is hard to sound witty and truthful at the same time when recounting such experiences. Whatever the case, *Homage to Catalonia* shows that warfare provided him with the arena to take language to its bones.

In the opening passage of *Homage to Catalonia*, Orwell speaks of his encounter with an Italian volunteer who had also come to aid the Republican side:

> He was a tough-looking youth of twenty-five or six, with reddish-yellow hair and powerful shoulders. His peaked leather cap was pulled fiercely over one eye. He was standing in profile to me, his chin on his breast, gazing with a puzzled frown at a map which one of the officers had open on the table. Something in his face deeply moved me. It was the face of a man who would commit murder and throw away his life for a friend—the kind of face you would expect in an Anarchist, though as likely as not he was a Communist. There were both candor and ferocity in it; also the pathetic reverence that illiterate people have for their supposed superiors. Obviously he could not make head or tail of the map; obviously he regarded map-reading as a stupendous intellectual feat. I hardly know why, but I have seldom seen anyone—any man, I mean—to whom I have taken such an immediate liking. While they were talking round the table some remark brought it out that I was a foreigner. The Italian raised his head and said quickly:
> "Italiano?"
> I answered in my bad Spanish:

> "No, Ingles. Y tu?"
> "Italiano."
> As we went out he stepped across the room and gripped my hand
> very hard. Queer, the affection you can feel for a stranger. . . .
> One was always making contacts of that kind in Spain. (1–2)

In the Eighties, this is not the way to start a good book. Orwell's sensibility as reflected here lacks the irony and ambiguity that literary criticism of our age associates with complexity of thought. As Orwell chose to be on that "other" side in the Spanish Civil War, he also chose that great otherness of a writer who uses the language of direction at the expense of irony and ambiguity: he speaks with simplicity and truth. This is why Orwell is generally seen as a sort of second-rate novelist by the critics of our time. It is also why we instinctively regard him as *the* great critic of language in our age.

Orwell was aware of his place in the twentieth century literary tradition, and if he was able to endure condescension, he was also capable of meting out his own rather harsh literary judgments. In "Inside the Whale" Orwell has some unkind words for the intellectuals of his day who, in his frame of reference, had abandoned their independence for the security of larger movements, such as the Communist Party and the Roman Catholic Church. His few good words are for T.S. Eliot, whose acceptance of Anglo as opposed to Roman Catholicism, "embraced the ecclesiastical equivalent of Trotskyism" (515). An ardent internationalist, Orwell was nonetheless wed in his heart to his native land. Perhaps this is why he could spare the Anglican Eliot. He showed no such mercy to W. H. Auden.

As the subject of "Inside the Whale," Auden was initially selected for praise. Orwell quotes an extract from his poem, "Spain," calling it "one of the few decent things that have been written about the Spanish War":

> Tomorrow for the young, the poets exploding
>   like bombs,
> The walks by the lake, the weeks of perfect
>   communion;
>   Tomorrow the bicycle races
> Through the suburbs on summer evenings. But
>   today the struggle.
>
> Today the deliberate increase in the chances
>   of death,
> The conscious acceptance of guilt in the
>   necessary murder;
>   Today the expending of powers
> On the flat ephemeral pamphlet and the boring
>   meeting. (516)

Halfway through his evaluation of Auden's poem, however, praise suddenly changes to invective, as if a sudden truth had caught Orwell and spun him one hundred-eighty degrees in midsentence:

> The second stanza is intended as a sort of thumbnail sketch of a day in the life of a "good party man." In the morning a couple of political murders, a ten-minutes' interlude to stifle "bourgeois" remorse, and then a hurried luncheon and a busy afternoon and evening chalking walls and distributing leaflets. All very edifying. But notice the phrase "necessary murder." It could only be written by a person to whom murder is at most a *word*. (516)

Orwell goes on at some length to castigate "Mr. Auden's brand of amoralism."

Although Orwell is being unfair to Auden (there is sufficient ambiguity in the poem to lead to many supportable conclusions about the meaning of "necessary murder"; indeed, Auden revised the poem several times), what is most remarkable is that Orwell begins by using Auden's poem to buttress his own criticism of the political timidity of twentieth-century writers and then—in the process of making that argument—he changes it into an attack on Auden's use of language. Orwell seems comfortable enough with Auden's ideas until Auden uses language to misrepresent reality, horrible reality. What Orwell objects to is the phrasing. He has a mind directed to language.

But there is more to it than that. Through language, Orwell is able to sense that Auden, in the very act of criticizing the same people as does Orwell himself, obliquely identifies with murderers and thereby apologizes for murder itself. Orwell is not one to talk about ambiguity, but about truths, central truths, even where they exist in ambiguous contexts. And Orwell, always one to speak in plain terms, has no patience with abstract ambiguities that predicate a necessity for murder. It is a strange line that Orwell treads, between the tunnel vision of "party men" and the "multiple perspectives" of new critics. Orwell, it seems, is too much interested in truth and it is his contempt for language misused, for "necessary" murder, that prods him toward the allegorical truth of *Nineteen Eighty-Four*.

Perhaps Orwell's attack upon Auden was prompted by Auden's use of Spain as the background metaphor in his poem. There is a certain universal distaste for those who write about real tragedy from the vantage of comfort, and this is felt most acutely by those who have seen or experienced the same tragedy firsthand. Orwell was no stranger to the things Auden was writing about, and it must have galled him that this young, intellectual poet and sometime political activist would dare to write in such a judgmental way about something that Orwell had actually experienced.

Homage to Catalonia is the antithesis of Auden's "Spain." A record of Orwell's experiences in the Spanish Civil War, its perspective and tone show Orwell's deep regard for the direct, the immediate and the real. There is virtually no hypothesizing in his book. From time to time, Orwell gives brief explanations of the political background that turned one Republican faction against another, but for the most part the book is a narrative of his day-to-day experiences as a volunteer—experiences that included several brushes with death, and that threw into high relief the ordinary things of life; experiences that helped Orwell to develop that clarity of style which marks his later writings. It is a book with little speculation and much direct talk.

Homage to Catalonia is not a good book to read to get an idea of the history of the Spanish Civil War. Orwell was somewhat confused about the general political divisions of even the Republican side. His enlistment on the side of the vaguely Trotskyist but mostly anarchist P.O.U.M. (*Partido Obrera Unificación Marxista*—Party of Marxist Unification) happened by chance, Orwell having brought to the Spanish front a letter of introduction from an English friend with connections to it. Indeed, when the P.O.U.M. was suppressed by the Communists and Orwell found himself fired upon by former comrades, he was somewhat at a loss to understand why.

From the very beginning of *Homage to Catalonia,* Orwell concentrates on those details of daily life in the barracks and trenches that evoke our response to the humanity, or lack of it, inherent in the situation of war. His attention to detail in the reality he saw, his horror in the little things and his recognition that humans can put up with such horror, paved the way for similar details in the world of *Nineteen Eighty-Four.*

From the very first chapter of *Homage to Catalonia* Orwell seems to assume that his readers will know what the Civil War is about. He gives no introduction to the politics of the situation; no general overview of the military positions of the two sides. What interests Orwell is that the post he reports to had once been a riding school, that the parade field is covered with gravel, and that "the whole place still smelt of horse-piss and rotten oats" (7). Orwell is concerned with the changing position of women in the revolution, but instead of discussing the issue abstractly, he tells us that on his arrival the militiamen laughed at women at drill, while "a few months earlier no one would have seen anything comic in a woman handling a gun" (7). He always chooses the illustration over the abstraction.

Orwell's attention to the truth of detail forms a web of coherence for the entire narrative. Early in the story, he comments about lice:

> The human louse somewhat resembles a tiny lobster, and he lives chiefly in your trousers. Short of burning all your clothes there is no known way of getting rid of him. Down the seams of your trousers he lays his glittering white eggs, like tiny grains of rice, which hatch out and breed families of their own at horrible speed. I think the pacifists might find it helpful to illustrate their pamphlets with enlarged photographs of lice. Glory of war, indeed! In war *all* soldiers are lousy, at least when it is warm enough. The men who fought at Verdun, at Waterloo, at Flodden, at Senlac, at Thermopylae—every one of them had lice crawling over his testicles. (76)

Orwell mistakenly attributes ovaries to male lice, but in all other respects his description is essentially accurate; an accuracy that most people writing about war tend to miss. All through the book, his focus is on the small details that tell us the truth of war as accurately as the photographs of Cappa, or (as with the lice) with greater accuracy than any photograph is capable. Even when recounting the very complex factional warfare in Barcelona, Orwell notes that he was glad to buy some goat's cheese and that behind the barricades "men were frying eggs" (127).

Orwell writes with much the same attitude as Robert Graves in *Goodbye to All That,* an autobiography centered on the First World War in which it is assumed that the reader knows the essence of the conflict, at least from the Allied side. Both authors also focus on one-to-one encounters with the enemy. Graves, while on duty as a sniper, tells us that he just could not pull the trigger on a German soldier taking a bath (164). Orwell, however, seems the harder man; at least the language he uses and the picture he paints with it has harder edges. After he and his comrades breached the Spanish line, Orwell found himself chasing one of the defenders through a communications trench:

> He was bareheaded and seemed to have nothing on except a blanket which he was clutching round his shoulders. . . . [M]y mind leapt backwards twenty years, to our boxing instructor at school, showing me in vivid pantomime how he had bayoneted a Turk at the Dardanelles. I gripped my rifle by the small of the butt and lunged at the man's back. He was just out of my reach. And for a little distance we proceeded like this, he rushing up the trench and I after him on the ground above, prodding at his shoulderblades and never quite getting there—a comic memory for me to look back upon, though I suppose it seemed less comic to him. (92)

If the retrospective irony here is uncharacteristic of Orwell, his attention to detail is not. For Orwell, the language of warfare eschews any specifically military terminology, or even any abstract terminology. It is simple and direct, the language of everyday life. What makes the foregoing passage so eerie is that Orwell describes his trying to bayonet a man to death with the same kind of tone he might use to describe an athletic exercise like trying to row a boat. The man who called Auden out for abstractly predicating a necessity for murder now speaks with a strangely detached enthusiasm about almost having committed a "necessary murder" himself. Orwell reports the facts even when they are inconsistent with his vision of himself.

Later in the novel, when fighting has broken out among various factions in Barcelona, Orwell finds himself confronting one of his former comrades (erroneously identified by Orwell as a Civil Guard) across the rooftops. Orwell trains his rifle on the man he thinks is about to begin shooting at him. They exchange words. The "civil guard" explains that he was not going to shoot at Orwell but at a third individual who had fired on him first. Orwell then asks, "Have you got any more beer left?" His tentative comrade answers: "No, it's all gone" (133). Even in life-threatening situations, Orwell focuses on the little things. Ironies in his works come not from his imagination, but from his eyes and his ears. Orwell does not usually write like Hemingway. It is only when he is faced with life and death situations that "the ordinary" takes over, in his syntax and in his reports. In *Homage to Catalonia*, we see the ordinary as special because death is always just at hand.

Even the passage in which Orwell is shot through the neck is simple and direct. Without the speculation on ultimate matters one might expect in a description of such a moment, Orwell speaks of the event almost as if he is recounting a minor skiing accident:

> Roughly speaking it was the sensation of being *at the centre* of an explosion. There seemed to be a loud bang and a blinding flash of light all round me, and I felt a tremendous shock—no pain, only a violent shock, such as you get from an electric terminal. . . . I fancy you would feel the same way if you were hit by lightening. (185)

Warfare is simple, stark, real. The language of warfare avoids embellishment and apology. It is not the language of Auden.

The starkness and simplicity of his language reflects the simple bravery of Orwell's action on the battlefield. Bernard Crick, Orwell's biographer, records the reminiscences of Bob Edwards regarding Orwell:

> He was absolutely fearless. About seven hundred yards from our
> lines and very close to a Fascist machine-gun post was a huge crop
> of potatoes. The war had interfered with the harvesting and there
> were these lovely potatoes. Orwell worked it out that a man, crawl-
> ing on his stomach, could just not be hit by machine-gunners at that
> distance. With a sack—about three times a week, yes—he'd say,
> "I'm out for potatoes" and I'd say "For goodness sake, you know,
> it's not worth the risk." He said, "They can't hit me, I've already
> proved it." And they shot at him, you know, every time he went out
> for potatoes, they were shooting all the time. But he'd worked it out
> that they just couldn't hit a man at this distance. (Crick 1980, 325)

In *Homage to Catalonia,* Orwell modestly implies that he was not the
only one who went for potatoes:

> We discovered another patch farther on, where there was prac-
> tically no cover and you had to lift the potatoes lying on your
> belly—a fatiguing job. If their machine-gunners spotted you, you
> had to flatten yourself out like a rat when it squirms under a door,
> with the bullets cutting up the clods a few yards behind you. It
> seemed worth it at the time. Potatoes were getting very scarce. If
> you got a sackful you could take them down to the cook-house and
> swap them for a water-bottleful of coffee. (74)

It is hard to question the sincerity or the simplicity of a man who risks
machinegun fire to gather potatoes. Yet, as with all abstractions, Orwell
was beyond "sincerity." In a world that talked a lot about action, he
simply acted. In the world of language, he simply spoke the truth,
whether about being hit by a bullet or about trying to bayonet a man to
death.

If Orwell could be brave for necessity—to gather potatoes—he
could also kill for the same reason (his criticism of Auden notwith-
standing), as we saw in his account of the bayonet chase. At another
point in *Homage to Catalonia* the Fascists launch an earnest attack on the
P.O.U.M. position. Orwell and his comrades respond with grenades:

> I flung it and threw myself on my face. By one of those strokes of
> luck that happen about once in a year I had managed to drop the
> bomb almost exactly where the rifle had flashed. There was the
> roar of the explosion and then, instantly, a diabolical outcry of
> screams and groans. *We* had got one of them, anyway; I don't know
> whether he was killed, but certainly he was badly hurt. Poor
> wretch! I felt a vague sorrow as I heard him screaming. (97)

For Orwell, action and language existed on the same plane of reality.
His objection to Auden was not so much that Auden countenanced
political killing, but that he used mere language to apologize for it, or
to make it seem understandable from the perspective of the political

activist in the poem. As we have seen in the episodes of the grenade and the bayonet, Orwell himself was capable of killing for his own political beliefs. The difference between him and the character Auden created is that Orwell would talk about his actions from experience.

One should not get the impression that Orwell was some kind of cold-blooded killer who tried to justify the taking of life simply by owning up to the deed in straightforward language. If he was capable of killing in battle, he still felt the reluctance and repugnance associated with such an action. In "Looking Back at the Spanish Civil War," he mentions that at one point he had an easy shot at an enemy:

> At this moment a man, presumably carrying a message to an officer, jumped out of the [Fascist] trench and ran along the top of the parapet in full view. He was half-dressed and was holding up his trousers with both hands as he ran. I refrained from shooting at him. It is true that I am a poor shot and unlikely to hit a running man at a hundred yards, and also that I was thinking chiefly about getting back to our trench while the Fascists had their attention fixed on the aeroplanes. Still, I did not shoot partly because of that detail about the trousers. I had come here to shoot at Fascists; but a man who is holding up his trousers isn't a Fascist, he is visibly a fellow creature, similar to yourself, and you don't feel like shooting at him. (2:254)

Details matter to Orwell; details like the trousers. He tells the simple truth, whether it be about his attempt to use a bayonet on another human being, or about his reluctance to shoot an enemy holding up his pants, or about gathering potatoes under fire. The ambiguity for Orwell is in the heart, never in the words. The words simply and truthfully tell what happened.

Perhaps the final word on Orwell's experiences in Spain, and on his use of language in relation to warfare, is that his concern for simple and immediate truth transcended whatever larger political commitments he held. We know that Orwell was against Fascism, but what of his attitude toward the Fascists themselves? In *Homage to Catalonia* he says:

> In trench warfare five things are important: firewood, food, tobacco, candles and the enemy. In winter on the Zaragoza front they were important in that order, with the enemy a bad last. . . . The real preoccupation of both armies was trying to keep warm. (23)

Slightly later, he explains that the Republicans frequently aimed propaganda at the Fascist lines by shouting revolutionary messages. One of them was especially interesting to Orwell:

> Sometimes, instead of shouting revolutionary slogans he simply
> told the Fascists how much better we were fed than they were. His
> account of the Government rations was apt to be a little imagina-
> tive. "Buttered toast!"—you could hear his voice echoing across the
> lonely valley—"We're just sitting down to buttered toast over here!
> Lovely slices of buttered toast!" (43)

As Orwell himself points out, neither he nor the man shouting had
tasted butter in weeks. Yet for Orwell this small lie contained one of the
greatest truths of the war; that Fascist or Communist, men know that
bullets hurt, that corpses stink, and that in cold, wet trenches buttered
toast tastes good.

Works Cited

Crick, Bernard. *George Orwell: A Life.* Boston: Little, Brown, 1980.

Graves, Robert. *Good-Bye to All That.* New York: Jonathan Cape & Harrison
Smith, 1930.

Happenstall, Rayner. "George Orwell: A Programme of Recorded Reminiscences." BBC, London, 20 Aug. 1960.

Orwell, George. *Burmese Days.* London: Secker & Warburg, 1949.

———. *Down and Out in Paris and London.* London: Secker & Warburg, 1951.

———. *Homage to Catalonia.* New York: Harcourt, Brace & World, 1952.

———. "Looking Back on the Spanish Civil War." In *My Country Right or Left
(1940–43)*, 249–67. Vol. 2 of *The Collected Essays, Journalism and Letters of
George Orwell.* Edited by Sonia Orwell and Ian Angus. 4 vol. New York:
Harcourt, Brace & World, 1968.

———. "Inside the Whale." In *An Age Like This (1920–40)*, 493–527. Vol. 1 of
The Collected Essays, Journalism and Letters of George Orwell. Edited by Sonia
Orwell and Ian Angus. 4 vol. New York: Harcourt, Brace & World, 1968.

———. "Politics and the English Language." In *In Front of Your Nose (1945–50)*,
127–40. Vol. 4 of *The Collected Essays, Journalism and Letters of George Orwell.*
Edited by Sonia Orwell and Ian Angus. 4 vol. New York: Harcourt, Brace &
World, 1968.

Perles, Alfred. *My Friend Henry Miller.* London: Neville Spearman, 1955.

11 Political Language: The Art of Saying Nothing

Dan F. Hahn
Queens College
City University of New York

The "hot air" quotient of political rhetoric is so high that even casual observers of the political scene cannot help but notice it. So perhaps it is relatively unnecessary to prove that the rhetorical devices identified here—euphemism, simplification, generalization—mean that politicians often say nothing. Yet it is necessary to demonstrate why and how the "art" is practiced.

The electorate hold differing opinions on issues, personalities, government—and a politician who advocates any one position alienates those who disagree. Yet politicians cannot remain quiet. They must make the "rubber chicken" circuit. They must talk. So they rely on the technique of saying nothing.

Everyone wants a New Deal, a Fair Deal, a part in settling the New Frontier, a chance to live in a Great Society, a Kinder and Gentler Nation. People who have thought about our society know what they would do to achieve the promise of these catchphrases. Politicians who enunciate such contentless locutions do the voters the great service of allowing them to keep their dreams and, indeed, to vote for them.

Consider, for instance, the "Grand Vision" for the "flowering of the Atlantic civilization" enunciated by Barry Goldwater as he accepted the Republican presidential nomination in 1964. This Atlantic civilization was to be effected by the joining of all Atlantic Ocean countries; then—with the United States as the central pillar—linking the Atlantic civilization to the Pacific. The entire complex was to be used to achieve peace and guide emerging nations. It was, to say the least, a nationally egocentric dream not dissimilar to the "March of the Flag" expansionist vision proclaimed seventy years earlier by Senator Albert Beveridge. And it was just so much "hot air"; in fact, Goldwater never mentioned it again in the remainder of his campaign.

Regardless of ideology, the politician must be for hard work, God and country, and against the "military-industrial complex," "lawless

111

crime," and "deceit in high places." The politician who uses this language of the public thereby demonstrates an identification with the public which is properly middle-of-the-road. Such mediocrity wins elections. The politician hasn't said anything, but has demonstrated the right attitudes. The electorate can vote for this person, who is one of them.

The calming influence of political rhetoric, then, reinforces the comfort provided by political symbolism as found, for instance, in patriotic celebrations. The animals in Orwell's *Animal Farm,* we recall,

> found it comforting to be reminded that, after all, they were truly their own masters and that the work they did was for their own benefit. So that, what with the songs, the processions, Squealer's list of figures, the thunder of the gun, the crowing of the cockerel, and the fluttering of the flag, they were able to forget that their bellies were empty, at least part of the time. (127)

Why, then, if all these rhetorical and symbolic mechanisms work to soothe the public and encourage them to accept the status quo, is such a large portion of that public disenchanted with the contemporary political world? Why did confidence in government fall to the 30% level? (Etzioni 1978, 17) Why are the indices of political participation—voting, party membership, political club affiliation—at all-time lows? (*New York Times* A-12)

I do not mean to suggest that all of the political ennui can be traced to political language. Euphemisms did not make inflation intractable; simplifications did not create the unemployment lines; generalizations did not infuse bewildering complexity into formerly simple social systems. But neither do I believe that political language is blameless. Specifically, in what follows I will argue that the language of politicians has been of central importance in the following ways:

1. Euphemisms make situations that are intolerable seem tolerable, thus lessening our inclination to act to change them.

2. Problems are explained too simply, leading us to adopt oversimplified solutions.

3. Euphemistic inaccuracies lead to inappropriate solutions.

4. Simplifying matters by identifying solutions with leaders leads us to believe that removing the leaders will solve the problems.

5. Generalizations lead us to think politicians agree with us when, indeed, they have other policies in mind.

6. Generalizations allow leaders to manipulate us through an anxiety-reassurance cycle (although we have come to believe only one part of that cycle—nothing really reassures, everything creates anxiety).

The cumulative effect of these "contributions" is that they undermine the political decision-making process, short-circuit the reasoning process, and contribute to the adoption of anemic political policies.

Yet even as I condemn contemporary political language, and the politicians who employ it, I realize that they have little choice. Our two-party, nonideological system forces politicians to try to appeal to all of us because a breadth of appeal is necessary to get elected. Thus, the electoral restraints demand a political language as broad as the electorate. Euphemisms, simplifications and generalizations, then, become the primary forms of language for politicians. It is, obviously, a chicken-and-egg problem: It makes little sense to call for politicians to change their language as long as it is working for them. My hope is that the following analysis will help convince both politicians and citizens that the short-term advantages of such language are not worth the long-term dangers.

Euphemisms

Euphemisms, words which mask reality by giving it a better face, function to make things sound better than they are. There is, of course, a sense in which all language is necessarily euphemistic, because the world which we attempt to depict with words is chaotic and ambiguous while, by comparison, language is systematic and orderly (Gibson 1974, 4). How we perceive the world is determined by the language used to describe it. We can perceive only what our language allows us to perceive, so we cannot "tell it like it is." The best we can do is to tell it "like we see it."

Not only is our language by nature euphemistic, but we are by nature in need of euphemisms; our humanness impels us to mask reality. We all desire to bathe ourselves in a more glorious light than we probably deserve. None of us likes to consider ourselves ugly, or mean, or any of a hundred other things which we doubtless are at one time or another. The point, of course, is that all of us engage in euphemisms. We do so because we desire to put our "best face" forward.

Why, then, be concerned about how euphemisms function in the language of politics? The problem is that euphemisms are inherently inaccurate, but inaccuracy is not inherently dangerous. An inaccuracy which leads us to act more humanely may be beneficial, while one that leads to an inappropriate solution is obviously harmful.

An innocuous example of a euphemism which uplifts humanity without creating any obvious danger is renaming garbage collectors *sanitation engineers*. While it may be rather strange semantics, the renaming brings with it no moral or ideological destructiveness.

But not all euphemisms are so innocuous. A clear example of a potentially dangerous euphemism relates to the specific brand of killing referred to by the term "war." The euphemisms of the Vietnam War were particularly disturbing. American Air Force personnel, for example, took "suburbia" to Vietnam.

> When they brought a lot of bombers from Guam, 2,500 miles away, and dropped huge supplies of bombs from 40,000 feet, enough to wipe out a whole valley, they called it a *carpet raid*. Vietnamese huts were *barbecued* by American firepower. To kill people with machine guns from the air was to *hose* them. With cluster-bomb units, a pilot could *lawn-mower* an area, destroying everyone in a long path several hundred feet wide. (Gibson 1974, 20)

Daisy cutters were bombs used to destroy rice paddies; killing civilians in open areas came to be known as *rabbit shooting* (Slater 1976, 43).

Understand, however, that while these euphemisms are considered destructive by many, their use allowed the participants to overcome moral repulsion to killing and get on with the job at hand. Calling war a lawn-mower job makes it easier to do. When there is a necessity for war, the euphemisms are necessary, too. But the Vietnam War was considered by many to be unnecessary and they were able to see through the genocidal implications of euphemisms like *rooting out the infrastructure*, used to mask the indiscriminate killing of civilians along with military opponents (Slater 1976, 44).

But most euphemisms are neither totally destructive nor totally uplifting. For example, it is more humane to call someone *culturally deprived* than "poor." However, such a euphemism takes the blood out of the problem; "culturally deprived" takes the hunger out of poverty. Euphemisms may make problems more manageable (like the Air Force pilot, we may need euphemisms in order to act; it is difficult to deal with the overwhelming implications of hunger so we underwhelm with "culturally deprived") but defining the suffering out of a situation may also make the problem more tolerable, thus lessening our inclination to act.

Simplifications

We Americans like things simple. We like our Bic to light with a flick, our lawnmowers to start first time, every time. We want to push a button and smell good all day. We want one-step photography and instant mashed potatoes.

We also want our politicians to talk simply. "With an American, the suspicion of the glib talker is almost an act of conscience" (Hall 1973, 66–67). We do not like big words—small is beautiful—and the people who utter big words are suspect.

Politicians play upon this desire for simplicity. "When politicians speak, they like to make things as easy as possible, to make things understandable for, as they say, 'all men of good will.' They would like to be geniuses of simplification" (Heer 1971, 66). And if problems need to be simple, then solutions to those problems have to be presented in simplified form as well.

Political Slogans

The point at which consumers and producers of political rhetoric most clearly demonstrate their preference for simplification—is in the political slogan. Of all political rhetoric, the slogan is the simplest, emptiest, most popular, and most insidious. For slogans do strange things to us, or we do strange things to ourselves through our slogans. We use them as shorthand for defining our beliefs. But often the slogans come to define us. Consider the process: a group of people want to live peacefully, undisturbed, naturally. So they select a flower, the simple daisy, as their nonverbal slogan; one they think captures many complicated thoughts and encapsulates them in simple terms. Having selected their slogan, they come to think of themselves as flower children. The slogan started out to define their beliefs; it ended defining them.

While slogans begin as simplifications of our beliefs, repeated often enough, they come to be our beliefs. The slogan *America—Love It or Leave It* originated in reaction to criticism of the country. But as the slogan was repeated again and again, it became a statement with which to taunt the critics. Beliefs about the country were forgotten; what was left was a shouted alternative. The slogan ceased to express any beliefs about the goodness of the country and came, itself, to be a belief.[1]

But slogans are only extreme cases of this self-reflexive tendency. Processes nearly identical are at work in all political simplification.

Politicians respond to their public's and their own desires for simplicity and often come to believe their own simplifications.

Finally, slogans—simplifications of reality—bring varying ideological positions under one roof. *Peace Now* was the slogan adopted by those who saw war itself as immoral, as well as by those who merely believed the Vietnam War was immoral.

Identifying Problems with Incumbents

Beyond slogans, the political world is simplified by identifying problems with incumbents, thus saving the public the trouble of attempting to understand their policies: "leaders may be displaced as a reaction to strong aversion for their policies, as Johnson and Nixon were, but the policies themselves need not be displaced" (Edelman 1975, 23). Policies are simplified by being associated with leaders. But the association soon becomes a confusion, and the reelection or rejection of the leader becomes all-important—the policy be damned.

Simplifying Issues

Even when we do not identify problems with politicians, we still simplify the issues. Take, for example, the whole area of "law and order."

> The slogan crystallizes a sense of individual and social disorder, of a center that is not holding; yet it allows one to maintain that the solution must come from within the eye of the storm rather than from the external forces that brewed the storm in the first place. (Robertson 1970, 3)

In other words, when we identify a problem as a law and order issue, we are prompted by that label to look for the solution within the legal system. Thus we find crime being blamed on "softheaded judges" or "mollycoddlers." While such persons might contribute in some way to the problem, it is doubtful that too many criminals ever selected a life of crime because a searching analysis of society revealed that certain judges and "do-gooders" would take pity on them when they got caught. Be that as it may, the point is that when we simplify an issue we may lead ourselves into an incorrect diagnosis and an unworkable solution.

The problem, of course, is that reality is complex. Politicians select a portion of reality they perceive as a problem and give it a name, perhaps using a euphemism. Next, they describe the problem in a logical language so simplified that almost effortlessly, everyone can understand it. So it is easy to become convinced that, indeed, it is a simple problem, solvable by simple solutions. Finally, when the solution to the problem does not work, the fault must be with the person who proposed the solution and not with the solution itself. Throughout this process, the demand for simplicity is preeminent and precludes any realistic attempts to solve problems.

Generalizations

Both euphemisms and simplifications generalize, but there are additional functions of generalizations:

1. They complement our all-encompassing two-party system
2. They endanger the creation of meaningful distinctions
3. They are dangerous to individualism
4. They allow leaders to manipulate us through an anxiety-reassurance cycle

1. *The two-party system requires generalizations.* Unlike most countries, America has political parties that are nonideological. In order to appeal to the broad electorate, party politicians state their positions in generalities. Unfortunately, this generalization process is often self-defeating for the official who has achieved office, because policy decisions are much more specific than the campaign rhetoric implied. Take, as an example, Nixon's 1968 "Plan for Peace" in Vietnam. He refused to identify the content of his plan during the campaign. Once elected, however, he had to implement specific policies—and those specifics could not please as many people as had his rhetorical generalizations. Those who had read their own preferred solutions into his campaign generalizations felt they had been misled. Thus, the generalizations which had helped Nixon gain office made it difficult for him to govern. Generalization is required by the necessity for appealing to a diverse audience; disillusionment is necessitated by the implementing of specific policy.

2. *Generalizations endanger the creation of meaningful distinctions.* The world of advertising offers this example:

> As everything becomes inflated and *tremendous*, the word loses its currency. What is normal becomes tremendous. What used to be large is now "giant king size" and we have reached the point of no return. (Berger 1974, 240)

Analogously, when *national security* is so broadened as to encompass burglary, wiretapping, surveillance, invasions of privacy, and even assault, "national security" and *national interest* become synonymous. We are led to believe that national security is the totality of "national interest," forgetting that one of the most compelling facets of American national interest is freedom. "National security" is the "giant economy size" of contemporary politics.

3. *Generalizations are dangerous to individualism.* To take all of the poor and lump them together into the category of *culturally disadvantaged* is to generalize away their individuality. Some people are poor because they are culturally disadvantaged. Some have had home lives that denied them cultural values. Some are lazy. Some are frozen out of the economic system by racism. Some are stupid. Some are the victims of unethical or illegal business practices. But only one attribute of their lives—their poverty—is used to define them.

American technology supports the tendency toward sameness. In an earlier, more natural existence, differences in nature and individual idiosyncracies were taken as positive attributes. "Glory be to God for dappled things,"—but Gerard Manley Hopkins wrote in an earlier age in his poem "Pied Beauty." But as technology exerts more and more influence, sameness replaces uniqueness as the operant value. There is security in the identical blandness of McDonald's hamburgers, assembly line educations, and mass-produced politicians.

4. *Generalizations allow our leaders to engage in a drama of suspense and solution that ensures our allegiance as it befuddles our minds.*

> [E]very regime both encourages public anxiety and placates it through rhetoric and reassuring gestures. We are constantly told that the Russians are ahead of us in this or that weapon system or that some trouble spot threatens peace or American interests. At the same time we are reassured that American military power is massive and leaders are acting with maximal effectiveness. The cycle of anxiety and reassurance provides a supportive following. (Edelman 1975, 22)

Lacking the knowledge to challenge either the extent of the threat or the efficacy of the reassuring counter-measures, the public is dangled on generalized rhetorical strings manipulated by its leaders. Betrayed by generalizations, the public hangs there—washing cars, mowing lawns, reelecting leaders.

While the political Art of Saying Nothing is not a new phenomenon, it does seem reasonable to hypothesize that it is newly dangerous. When the crises that face us are increasingly dangerous, the results of miscalculation in a nuclear age are increasingly serious. When the need for clarity is thus increasingly demanding, continued reliance upon euphemisms may paralyze our ability and willingness to act.

When the problems we face increase in complexity, the continued use of simplifications in both problem-description and solution-seeking becomes not just banal, but dishonest and stupid. When over 50 percent of those who voted for Proposition 13 in California thought it would not mean any diminution in government services, it became obvious that over-simplification had become a real enemy.

Generalizations Provoke Distrust

When the population increasingly distrusts politicians to such an extent that the whole governmental system is distrusted, we know that generalizations are creating too many governing liabilities to be continued, despite their positive influence in persuading voter decisions at the polls.

Lest I, too, be accused of oversimplifying, I should point out that this distrust extends beyond government to big business and big labor, to "bigness" in general. Hence the current popularity of the "smaller is better" syndrome. Much of that distrust, I would argue, comes from the "biggies" who "talk down" to the citizens, distorting the world to make it understandable. But simplified and generalized descriptions from the powerful just do not describe the world that people inhabit.

And despite the complaints of the citizens (requests to "tell it like it is," grumbles about how "nobody can be trusted" and "all politicians are liars"), all they get is more of the same. So, quite rationally, the people have come to expect less. A continuation of the discredited rhetoric of big government, big business, and big labor will continue to feed this decline in expectations.

In a less complicated and dangerous age we could afford the political art of saying nothing, and even find an occasional Senatorial windbag charming and quaint. But that day has passed. Albeit sophisticated and slick rather than quaint, the windbags are still with us—and will stay as long as their rhetorical products can be sold to the consumers.

Our only hope, it seems, is to educate those consumers to want a better rhetorical product. It may be a long shot, but it may also be the only race in town. How that education should proceed I cannot say, but I suspect we could do worse than starting with the truths in this story told by an ancient wiseman:[2]

A Chinese sage of the distant past was once asked by his disciples what he would do first if he were given power to set right the affairs of the country. He answered: "I certainly should see to it that language is used correctly." The disciples looked perplexed. "Surely," they said, "this is a trivial matter. Why should you deem it so important?" And the Master replied: "If the language is not used correctly, then what is said is not what is meant; if what is said is not what is meant, then what ought to be done remains undone; if this remains undone, morals and art will be corrupted; if morals and art are corrupted, justice will go astray; if justice goes astray, the people will stand about in helpless confusion."

Notes

1. I trace the preceding two arguments to Frank D. McConnell, "Toward a Lexicon of Slogans," *Midwest Quarterly* 13, no. 1 (1971): 72–73, especially to this line: "The individual believer, then, in choosing to let himself be defined by the attitudes of the slogan, recapitulates the collective choice which effectively creates the ideological community to which he belongs."

2. Thomas S. Szasz, "Language and Humanism," *The Humanist* (January-February 1974): 29.

Works Cited

Berger, Arthur. "Hot Language and Cool Lives." *Language Awareness.* New York: St. Martin's Press, 1974.

Edelman, Murray. "On Policies that Fail." *The Progressive* 39, no. 5 (1975): 22–23.

Etzioni, Amitai. "America's New Split Personality." *Psychology Today,* October 1978: 17–18.

Gibson, Walker. "Euphemisms." *Harper Studies in Language and Literature.* New York: Harper, 1974.

Hall, Elizabeth. "The Freakish Passion: A Conversation with George Steiner." *Psychology Today,* Feb. 1973: 56–68.

Heer, Friedrich. "Man's Three Languages." *The Center Magazine* 4, no. 6 (1971): 66–70.

McConnell, Frank. "Toward a Lexicon of Slogans." *Midwest Quarterly* 13, no. 1 (1971): 69–80.

"The Non-Voters." *The New York Times,* 5 Nov. 1978: A-12.

Orwell, George. *Animal Farm.* New York: Harcourt Brace & World, 1946.

Robertson, John A. "The Costs of Overcriminalization." *Psychiatry and Social Science Review* 3, 1970.

Slater, Philip. *The Pursuit of Loneliness: American Culture at the Breaking Point.* Boston: Beacon 1976.

Szsaz, Thomas S. "Language and Humanism." *The Humanist* 33, no. 1 (1974): 25–30.

12 Fiddle-Faddle, Flapdoodle, and Balderdash: Some Thoughts about Jargon

Frank J. D'Angelo
Arizona State University

It goes by various names: medicalese, legalese, businessese, Pentagonese, bureaucratese, and officialese. No segment of public language is immune to its virulent effects. Once contracted, it has a tendency to spread, transmitting its harmful and corrupting influence. Like any disease, it may be considered from the standpoint of its diagnosis, its treatment, prevention, and control. I am, of course, talking not about a rare, communicable physical disease, but about jargon, that social disease whose effects are no less upsetting to health and public order. For in the minds of many critics, characterized more by dis-ease than disease, the English language is ailing, and in this paper I would like to attempt a diagnosis and offer a remedy.

Undoubtedly there have always been speakers and writers who have resorted to fiddle-faddle, flapdoodle, and balderdash—to meaningless, incoherent, and nonsensical gibberish, characterized by abstract and pretentious language and doublespeak. But in recent years, jargon seems to have spread like an abscess, tainting and infecting the health of the language.

For example, in an article entitled "Telling It Like It Is in the Tower of Babel," the prominent literary critic Cleanth Brooks exclaims:

> Ours is a time in which cant is spoken and heard everywhere. It is a time of inflamed rhetoric. Moreover, it is time in which language is systematically manipulated by politicians, advertisers, and publicity [people] as it has probably never before been manipulated. I am concerned with what is happening to our language. But I am, of course, even more deeply concerned with what is happening to ourselves. The two concerns cannot, in fact, be separated. If you debauch a language, you run a grave risk of debauching the minds of the people who use it. (84)

Douglas Bush, writing in *The American Scholar,* reinforces Brooks' claim: "People who have a conscience about language, who see the far-

121

reaching consequences of linguistic corruption, have continued to express concern, because corruption continues to spread not merely in everyday speech and writing but in public utterances on war and peace, indeed in all areas and on all levels" (240). The writer Jean Stafford, in an article in the *Saturday Review World,* is even more assertive:

> [U]pon its stooped and aching back it [the American Language] carries an astounding burden of lumber piled on by the sociologists and the psychologists and the psychosociologists, the Pentagon, the ad[agents]. . . . The prognosis for the ailing language is not good. I predict that it will not die in my lifetime, but I fear that it will be assailed by countless cerebral accidents and massive strokes and gross insults to the brain and finally will no longer be able to sit up in bed and take nourishment by mouth. (14)

An article in *Time* magazine titled "Can't Anyone Here Speak English?" declares that "it takes no schoolmaster's prissiness to recognize that in various major and minor ways, the American language is being brutalized" (35). Melvin Maddocks, in "The Limitations of Language," puts it more forcefully: "With frightening perversity—the evidence mounts daily—words now seem to cut off and isolate, to cause more misunderstanding than they prevent" (20).

Almost no profession or occupation is immune to the bombast, babble, jargon, and jabber of modern prose. Incoherent and meaningless talk and writing seem to have no boundaries. Even the highly respected medical profession has its gibberish. Michael Crichton, author of *The Andromeda Strain* and other popular novels and a doctor, has taken a close look at the writing in medical journals, particularly at back issues of the *New England Journal of Medicine.* His findings? Too many words, too many abstractions, unnecessary complexity, redundancy, repetition, and a poor flow of ideas. An article in *Time* magazine on "Doctor's Jargon" quotes Crichton as offering these examples:

> **Redundancy:** The most common form is paired words, for example, "interest and concern," when one would serve nicely.
>
> **Wrong words:** "Purely" for "only."
>
> **Too many abstractions:** "Improvement in health care is based to an important extent, on the viability of the biomedical research enterprise, whose success, in turn, depends."
>
> **Ambiguity:** "Corticosteroids, antimalarial drugs and other agents may impede degranulation, because of their ability to prevent granule membranes from rupturing, to inhibit ingestion or to interfere with the degranulation mechanism per se."
>
> **Unnecessary qualifications:** "Many, but not all, of the agents also have valuable analgesic effects. . . . It is usually wise, *unless there is good reason to the contrary.*" (35, my emphasis)

In an interview with a reporter for United Press International, Crichton stated that the style of most medical prose is

> as dense, impressive and forbidden as possible. Even the simplest concepts are restated in unrevealing forms. The stance of the authors seems designed to astound and mystify the reader with a dazzling display of knowledge and scientific acumen. (B-11)

Medical prose is not the only kind of writing that exhibits an impairment of language. Legal prose, which in its contaminated form is known as "legalese," also at times displays symptoms of disorder and decay. According to Richard Falk, in an article entitled "Legal Language as Semantic Fog":

> Law, as a general system of social control, and the participants in the legal decision-making process, such as legislators, judges, and lawyers, manifest a psychopathic alienation from external reality. This alienation is masked as a mystique allegedly made necessary by the complexity of the data in the field of law. On closer examination, we discover that legal technicalities are devices used to permit high-level abstraction and therefore to cloak the manipulative and self-manipulative forces imbedded deeply in the language of law. (227)

According to an article in *The New York Times,* lawyers and judges "are beginning to worry about how often they have been misunderstood, and they are discovering that sometimes they cannot even understand each other" (B-3). Here are a few examples. In a routine dispute between a tenant and a landlord, the controversy is referred to in legal terms as being between the *petitioner-landlord-appellant* and the *respondent-tenant-respondent.* "All the more" is changed to *hereinbefore.* Legal phrases such as *voir dire, res ipsa loquitur* and *Rule in Shelley's Case* abound.

> "Law schools blame colleges, colleges blame secondary schools and secondary schools blame primary schools," said Justin A. Stanley, the president of the American Bar Association. "I see a lot of writing that is at best careless. Rules of grammar are disregarded, if in fact they are known. I'd like to have every young lawyer pass a grammar test." (B-3)

Like medicalese and legalese, businessese is a disease that afflicts letters, reports, and articles. Business makes extensive use of the passive voice. In *Is Anybody Listening?* William H. Whyte points out that in business, "Nobody ever does anything. Things *happen*—and the author of the action is only barely implied . . . while prices may rise, nobody *raises* them" (48). Carl Goeller, in his book on clear writing, says that business makes widespread use of stock phrases: *please be advised; in reference to your letter of January 13; we wish to call your attention to the fact that; this letter is in reference to; please feel free to contact me at your earliest convenience* (61). Businessese uses big words, long, involved sentences, and stilted expressions. The antidote? A good dose of brevity, clarity, and simplicity.

Pentagonese flourishes on clichés, euphemisms, and abstract diction. In the Pentagon, a rifle does not merely fire. That's much too simple. Rather it has "the capability of firing." Stefan Kanfer, writing in *Time* magazine, reported that during the Vietnam War a U.S. Air Force colonel grumbled to reporters: "You always write it's bombing, bombing, bombing. It's not bombing. It's air support" (35). This memorable statement would receive the first Doublespeak Award to be given by the NCTE Committee on Public Doublespeak. Israel Shenker reported other euphemisms that came out of the Vietnam war: *advisors* for troops, *wasted* for murdered, and *termination with extreme prejudice* for assassination (21).

Almost as unhealthy as the clichés and euphemisms in Pentagonese is the use of abstract and Latinate diction to obscure clear communication. There are such memorable examples as *infrastructure; defoliation; escalation; routine, limited-duration, protective-reaction air strikes; limited air interdiction,* and *area denial.*

According to the *Washington Post,* Defense Department documents revealed that a California research company, financed by the Pentagon, is studying ways to "determine the nuclear weapon employment strategy that would eliminate the U.S.S.R. as a functioning national entity" (A-2). Another consulting firm, also financed by the Pentagon, is exploring "the viability of employing strategic nuclear weapons to achieve regionalization of the Soviet Union" (A-2). Asked to explain what this means, a Defense Department official said that this is an attack "that would destroy regional areas that support the present Soviet government" and "unleash forces of separatism" (A-2). This same consulting firm is also looking at ways to "paralyze, disrupt or dismember" the Russian government by wiping out its top officials. This process goes by the name of "strategic targeting against Soviet leadership" (A-2). Said one official who has been involved in all of these Defense Department projects: "We are trying to see in the ultimate nuclear exchange, what should we be trying to do other than just flatten their industry?" (A-2).

One last example of Pentagonese comes from an interview with then Secretary of State Alexander Haig published in *Time* magazine. Haig was asked: Has El Salvador been overblown as a foreign policy issue? He replied:

> I am concerned that with modern communications there is a penchant for episodic emphasis. It always includes the risk that we will lose sight of the forest for preoccupation with the trees. (24)

Haig was then asked if he favored conducting human rights diplomacy privately rather than through Congress. He responded:

> [W]e must continue to be deeply concerned about abuses to human rights wherever they occur; but, there are such questions as whether amelioration of those abuses is best achieved under the glare of public criticism and animosity and confrontation, or whether it is best achieved in a quieter dialogue between states with a healthy relationship. (24)

Like the other infirmities of language, Pentagonese is an attempt to control the reactions of the public by avoiding language that creates verbal pictures or language that has negative connotations and by substituting a more neutral or abstract language. But such language is not the sole possession of the Defense Department. Continuous exposure to this pestilence of language almost inevitably results in the patient's passing along its symptoms to others. Even presidents are not immune to the virulent effects of jargon. When President Gerald Ford was a guest lecturer at Yale University, he was asked which former president he admired the most. According to Donna Woolfolk Cross, his reply was: "I identify affirmatively with Harry Truman" (46).

The language of former President Ford exhibited symptoms of that malady of language known as bureaucratese. Bureaucratese is the kind of forbidding prose used by government officials and politicians in Washington and in state and city governments. Maury Maverick, a former congressman from Texas, called this kind of writing "gobbledygook." (Chase 1954, 249) Gobbledygook, Maverick maintained, is that polysyllabic language used by the people in Washington. It uses extremely long sentences and pretentious and abstract language. In the *Power of Words*, Stuart Chase gives a number of amusing examples of gobbledygook:

> A New Zealand official made the following report after surveying a plot of ground for an athletic field:
>> It is obvious from the difference in elevation with relation to the short depth of the property that the contour is such as to preclude any reasonable developmental potential for active recreation.
> Seems the plot was too steep.

An office manager sent this memo to his chief:

> Verbal contact with Mr. Blank regarding the attached notifica-
> tion of promotion has elicited the attached representation inti-
> mating that he prefers to decline the assignment.

Seems Mr. Blank didn't want the job. (250)

My favorite example of gobbledygook is taken from a story told by
Stuart Chase about the Bureau of Standards in Washington:

> A New York plumber wrote the Bureau that he had found hydro-
> chloric acid fine for cleaning drains, and was it harmless? Wash-
> ington replied: "The efficacy of hydrochloric acid is indisputable,
> but the chlorine residue is incompatible with metallic perma-
> nence."
>
> The plumber wrote back that he was mighty glad the Bureau
> agreed with him. The Bureau replied with a note of alarm: "We
> cannot assume responsibility for the production of toxic and nox-
> ious residue with hydrochloric acid, and suggest that you use an
> alternate procedure." The plumber was happy to learn that the
> Bureau still agreed with him.
>
> Whereupon Washington exploded: "Don't use hydrochloric
> acid; it eats hell out of the pipes!" (259)

Perhaps it is inaccurate to create a separate category of jargon for
officialese, as distinct from bureaucratese or Pentagonese. But what I
mean by officialese is the kind of language used by public officials other
than government bureaucrats to cover up the clumsy mishandling of
public affairs. For instance, Donna Woolfolk Cross reports that the
investigating panel that reported on the collapse of the Teton Dome in
Idaho, which killed fourteen people, concluded that "an unfortunate
choice of design measures together with less than conventional precau-
tions" caused the calamity (31). The *Public Doublespeak Newsletter* noted
in its January 1979 issue that an airline reported to its stockholders that
the airline had picked up more than $1.5 million in profits after taxes
in 1978 thanks to the "recent involuntary conversion of a 727 aircraft"
(3). The "involuntary conversion" was the crash of a plane in Florida in
which three passengers died: the airline made more money on insurance than the plane actually was worth. An airline official defended the
use of the circumlocution, commenting that the phrase was "a widely
used accounting term" (3).

A more humorous, but still ominous, example of officialese is that of
Colorado State Representative, A. J. Spano, who is reported in the
January 1980 issue of the *Public Doublespeak Newsletter* as having introduced a bill in the Colorado legislature to downplay Denver's reputation as the city with the second dirtiest air in the nation. He proposed a
new rating scale so that the level of pollutants called "hazardous" by the

Federal government would carry the more innocuous label *poor,* "dangerous" would become *acceptable,* "very unhealthful" would become *fair,* "unhealthful" would become *good,* and "moderate" would become *very good* (2).

Corporations and other large organizations are extremely sensitive about their relationship with the public. They do not wish to offend any group, nor do they wish to make any public pronouncements that will prejudice their self-interests. Consequently, they develop a language of doublespeak to issue policy announcements, a language that is carefully selected in content and form. Such language is used either to withhold information or to present it in a disguised manner. Seldom does it present a clear statement of facts to the public.

The danger in using officialese is that it oversimplifies or blurs complex situations. By calming anxiety and anger, it may lull people into a false sense of security, make bureaucratic bungling seem harmless, and seriously interfere with people's perceptions of reality. When abstract language and euphemisms are substituted for more accurate terms, people may mistakenly believe that public officials have identified a cause and that a remedy will follow. But their words are often nothing more than meaningless abstractions used to evade responsibility for their actions.

The examples of jargon from various professions, occupations, and disciplines could go on forever. The essential question is, Why do speakers and writers use jargon? Some writers use jargon to obscure the truth. Others use it to sound impressive, to give the user status. Still others use it to conceal a lack of ideas or to give weak ideas authority. In *Death in the Afternoon,* Ernest Hemingway decried this lack of clarity in language:

> If a man writes clearly enough anyone can see if he fakes. If he mystifies to avoid a straight statement, which is very different from breaking so-called rules of syntax or grammar to make an effect which can be obtained in no other way, the writer takes a longer time to be known as a fake. . . . True mysticism should not be confused with incompetence in writing which seeks to mystify when there is no mystery but is really only the necessity to take to cover lack of knowledge or the inability to state clearly. (54)

At the beginning of my essay, I said that I wanted to do two things: to attempt a diagnosis of the use of jargon and to offer a remedy. Although in the course of this essay, I have given a diagnosis of sorts, by presenting examples of jargon from medicine, law, business, and government, I would now like to isolate more specifically the main features of jargon, make a few qualifying comments about each, and then conclude with a remedy that may contain effective advice for the novice writer.

Jargon is characterized by the following:

1. Using several words when one word will do:

exhibits a tendency	→	tends
in an efficient manner	→	efficiently
make inquiry regarding	→	inquire
resembling in nature	→	like
reach a decision	→	decide
avail oneself of	→	use
render operative	→	fix
causative factor	→	cause
a long period of time	→	long time

2. A preference for abstract nouns ending in *-tion, -ity, -ment, -ness, -ance, -ative, -ate, -ous, -cy, -ist,* and the like:

utilization	dentition
nullity	pertinacity
apportionment	exigency
credulousness	diplomatist
discountenance	parsimonious

3. Excessive use of words with Latin or Greek prefixes:

abnegation	debriefing
circumspect	upgrade
contravene	antitechnology
nonpreferential	bioelemetric
intrazonal	dishabituate

4. The use of stock phrases:

in the final analysis
other things being equal
from the point of view of
within the framework of
in the event that

5. The substitution of euphemisms for less explicit inoffensive terms:

terminal living	→	dying
defensive maneuver	→	retreat
mild irregularity	→	constipation
bathroom tissue	→	toilet paper

encore telecast	→	rerun
senior citizens	→	old people
underprivileged	→	delinquent
substandard housing	→	slum

6. The overabundant use of clichés:

lock, stock, and barrel	one and all
null and void	as thick as thieves
pick and choose	a grievous error
safe and sound	all to the good
fair and square	blank amazement

7. The extensive use of the passive voice, rather than the use of the more direct active voice:

Passive: Job opportunities may be increased by higher education.
Competitive activities should be avoided.
The report has been solicited by the committee.
Unpredictable elements must be anticipated.

Active: Higher education may increase job opportunities.
Avoid competitive activities.
The committee has solicited the report.
Anticipate the unpredictable.

8. The extensive use of noun strings:

human factors engineering support
host area crisis shelter production
     planning workbook
management information system plan
Congress refugee panel visit ban

Almost all of these characteristics of jargon, of course, need qualifying. Occasionally a long phrase such as "along the lines of" might be more appropriate than "like." Abstract nouns are not always to be avoided, especially if they can take the place of a long phrase. Latin and Greek prefixes often add flexibility to the language, enabling us to coin new words. Stock phrases such as "inasmuch as" and "with reference to" sometimes enable our thoughts to flow more smoothly than single words. And surely euphemisms are not always to be avoided. One can think of certain social situations, dealing with death or bodily functions, for example, when a euphemism might be used to avoid unpleasant associations. And like euphemisms, clichés also have a place in the language. Is it always more effective in speech or writing to say "cold" rather than "as cold as ice"? Some clichés add intensity to the language.

There are times when the passive voice cannot be avoided, especially when we don't always know the agent in our sentences. There are also times when the passive voice may be preferred, as in the description of a scientific process, when the writer wants to put the emphasis on the process and not on the agent. Finally, noun strings can sometimes add flexibility to the language. Short noun strings abound in the written and spoken language—e.g., pressure cooker, life style, case study.

So much for the diagnosis. Now for some remedies:

1. Punctuate long sentences so that they give the effect of a series of shorter sentences and so that they are more easily read.
2. Prefer the single word to the circumlocution.
3. Replace abstract and general words with concrete and specific words.
4. Avoid using too many words with Latin or Greek prefixes and suffixes.
5. Avoid euphemisms.
6. Avoid clichés and stock phrases.
7. Prefer the active voice to the passive.
8. Rewrite noun strings as prepositional phrases or relative clauses.

Clearly, all of these guidelines must be modified in relation to the writer's purpose, his or her audience, and the occasion. The kind of style I am advocating is the so-called plain style, a style that emphasizes economy of language, useful for much public discourse, but there are other styles that might be more appropriate for particular situations.

I began this paper by using medical metaphors of sickness and remedy, disease and cure, talking about language as if it were an organism like the human body, which over the years has become corrupted and defiled. But these analogies, like all analogies, must be accepted with reservations, for as Ronald Gross says in his article "On Language Pollution":

> The job of the critic of language today calls for diligence as well as intelligence. Wholesale denunciations of the state of the tongue are of limited usefulness. It is more courageous to call one prominent [person] a liar than to proclaim that the entire language is become debased. Not language, but this [person's] words: not the whole tongue, but this party's evasions and obfuscations must become targets. This is unremitting, unpretentious work, to be undertaken by many hands whose impact will only be collective. (58–59)

Works Cited

Brooks, Cleanth. "Telling It Like It Is in the Tower of Babel." *The Intellectual Digest* 2, no. 5 (1972): 84–86.

Bush, Douglas. "Polluting Our Language." *The American Scholar* 41 (1972): 238–47.

"Can't Anyone Here Speak English?" *Time*, 25 Aug. 1975: 34–36.

Chase, Stuart and Marian Tyler Chase. *Power of Words*. New York: Harcourt, Brace, 1954.

Cross, Donna Woolfolk. *Word Abuse*. New York: Coward, McCann, & Geoghegan, 1979.

"Doctor's Jargon." *Time*, 12 Jan. 1976: 35.

Falk, Richard A. "Legal Language As Semantic Fog." *ETC: A Review of General Semantics* 17, no. 2 (1959–60): 227–32.

Goeller, Carl. *Writing to Communicate*. New York: New American Library, 1975.

Gross, Ronald. "On Language Pollution." *Coming to Terms with Language*. Edited by Raymond D. Liedlich. New York: Wiley, 1973.

Hemingway, Ernest. *Death in the Afternoon*. New York: Scribner's, 1932.

"An Interview with Haig." *Time*, 16 March 1981: 24.

Kanfer, Stefan. "Words from Watergate." *Time*, 13 Aug. 1973: 20.

"Lawyers Admit Problems Understanding Each Other." *The Arizona Republic*, 9 April 1977: B-3. Condensed from *The New York Times*.

Maddocks, Melvin. "The Limitations of Language." *Coming to Terms with Language*. Edited by Raymond D. Liedlich. New York: Wiley, 1973.

"Muddy Medical Prose Is Styled to Dazzle Readers, Writer Says" *The Arizona Republic*, 29 Dec. 1975: B-11.

"1978 Doublespeak Award." *Public Doublespeak Newsletter* 4, no. 2 (1979): 3.

"1979 Doublespeak and Orwell Awards." *Public Doublespeak Newsletter* 5, no. 2 (1980): 2.

Shenker, Israel. "Zieglerrata." *The Arizona Republic*, 13 (April 1974): 21–23.

Stafford, Jean. "Plight of the American Language." *Saturday Review World*, 4 Dec. 1973: 14–18.

"Studies Target Soviet Destruction." *The Arizona Republic*, 13 Feb. 1979: A-2. Quoted from *The Washington Post*.

Whyte, Jr., William H. *Is Anybody Listening?* New York: Simon and Schuster, 1952.

13 How to Read an Ad: Learning to Read between the Lies

D. G. Kehl
Arizona State University

"Why do you spend money for that which is not bread, and the fruit of your labor for that which does not meet your needs?" This question, as timely as one's latest trip to the supermarket or political rally, is also timeless, for it was posed not by Vance Packard or David Horowitz or Joe McGinnis but by the prophet Isaiah over 2,600 years ago. The implicit answer in the eighth century B.C. may have been: "Because you are dim of sight, dull of hearing, and slow of wit." For the modern buyer the answer might simply be: "Because a fool and his money are soon parted." Or it might be phrased as follows: "You spend your hard-earned money on illusory commercial promises just as you 'buy' deceptive political propaganda because you are functionally illiterate, never having learned to 'read' an ad."

"The public buys its opinions as it buys its meat or takes its milk, on the principle that it is cheaper to do this than to keep a cow," Samuel Butler wrote. "So it is," he concluded, "but the milk is more likely to be watered" (Keynes and Hill 1951, 221–22). In order to avoid getting watered milk or unwholesome bread substitutes, it may be impossible to keep a cow or flour mill and bakery. The solution lies rather in learning to read and discern so as to counter the manipulative effects of Reality Control and Newspeak.

I. A. Richards purported to teach us "how to read a page," John Ciardi "how to read a poem," Mortimer Adler "how to read a book," Caroline Gordon "how to read a novel," Ronald Hayman "how to read a play," and Ezra Pound simply "how to read"—but who has taught us how to read an advertisement?

But who ever reads an ad? Who needs to be told how to read what we never bother to read? Those who respond in this way should be

Reprinted, with changes, from *English Journal* 72 (October 1983) by permission of the author and the publisher.

reminded of Daniel Boorstin's conclusion that "advertisement is our most popular reading, listening, and watching matter" (1962, 223), and of the recent estimate that "average" U.S. adults are exposed to over five hundred advertising messages daily, of which they consciously perceive perhaps around seventy-five (Key 1974, 80). Malcolm Muggeridge has coined the term *newsak* "to characterize this advertisement bombardment that harries one even when one seeks blessed tranquility in the car or bathroom" (1969, 69). The total volume of this propaganda blitz has been estimated conservatively by Alvin Toffler to be ten to twenty thousand words in print and twenty thousand words of radio and television "ingested" daily by the "average" U.S. adult (1971, 166). Wilson Bryan Key has set the total at more than "100,000 carefully edited, slanted, and skillfully composed words—words which sell, propose, and plead for [our] attention, [our] sympathy, [our] loyalty, and most of all, [our] money" (1974, 81).

And yet despite the further estimate that by the age of eighteen the modern American youth has watched 350,000 TV commercials, these young people, as Aldous Huxley pointed out in the late 50s, "are nowhere taught, in any systematic way, to distinguish true from false, or meaningful from meaningless, statements" (1958, 106). Surely one of the great inadvertences of our educational system has been our willingness to subject young people to the onslaughts of advertisement—both commercial and political—without equipping them with the abilities of advertence, that is, the keen awareness of words as symbols, and their persuasive and pervasive power.

In the late 19th century, Samuel Butler noted that "the most important service rendered by the press and magazines is that of educating people to approach printed matter with distrust" (Keynes and Hill 221). Today, nearly a century later, in the lengthening shadow of 1984, the need for such education is even more pronounced, but the press and magazines, apprehensive about loss of subscriptions and advertising revenue, are surely not interested in arousing any distrust in printed matter. The task of teaching how to read an ad, though it is the English teacher's by default, is closely related to our job of teaching how to read a poem, a story, a play, or a novel—and it's about time we got down to the business of getting the job done. As that patron saint of Romantic poetry, William Blake, expressed it in two poems,

> They ever must believe a lie
> Who see with, not through, the eye.[1]

Blake's notion of seeing *through* the eye, of intensely engaging the imagination, is obviously different from Butler's notion of casting a jaundiced eye, of regarding all printed matter skeptically. Yet the two share common ground in their attempts to get through illusion to reality. Similarly, the effective reader of advertisement will not only see through the eye but see through the propaganda; he will become less gullible but not at the cost of becoming totally cynical. It may be true, as someone has said, that perceptive reading is "eye and ass power," but not merely in the sense of training the former and taxing the latter. Reading is eye and ass power also in the sense of sharpening the focus of the eye in order to avoid being made an ass.

Just as there are different kinds of levels of reading, so there are different ways of reading an ad. Charles Walcutt has specified four kinds of reading:

1. *guessing,* that is, making assumptions about meaning of words by looking at pictures;
2. *stumbling,* getting fragmented understanding here and there;
3. *skipping,* getting the gist of meaning only; and
4. *skimming,* making one's way through the material swiftly and getting a general understanding of its meaning. (1962, x)

It seems fair to say that advertisers and their clients benefit most when our reading consists of guessing, stumbling, and skipping, for when we simply make assumptions on the basis of pictures, fragmented understanding, and general "gists" of meanings, the door is wide open for the subtleties of associations, diversion, and subliminal seduction.

Mortimer Adler's four levels of reading are perhaps even more apropos of advertisements (1967, 16ff.). The first level is *elementary, rudimentary, basic,* or *initial* reading, perhaps a combination of Walcutt's "guessing" and "stumbling." Even otherwise highly-educated, sophisticated individuals may read ads in this way simply because of lack of time or refusal to devote time to careful reading of ads as one peruses a magazine or newspaper. This kind of rudimentary reading suits the advertiser's purpose of communicating false generalizations, half truths, and appeals to the subconscious mind.

Adler's second level, *inspectional* reading, is generally the equivalent of Walcutt's "stumbling" and "skimming." The reader, conscious of limited time, seeks to answer questions prompted largely by curiosity, questions which are typically general and superficial, such as "What is this ad about?" or "Why is that seductive girl staring at me from this page?"

The third level of reading according to Adler, the *analytical,* involves a careful, systematic analysis of the entire book (or ad) and its symbols, with the reader asking many pertinent questions.

The fourth and highest level of reading Adler calls *syntopical* or *comparative* reading, which, when applied to advertisements, would involve not only an analysis of the ad and its parts, but also a comparison-contrast of the ad and its symbols with other ads and their use of symbols.

At this point there can undoubtedly be heard a round of demurrers expressing something like this: "Surely you don't think anybody actually reads ads analytically or syntopically or even inspectionally, except maybe ad writers or people who write papers about ads. And surely you aren't suggesting anything so preposterous and impracticable as the notion that we *should* take time to read ads in such a sophisticated way and teach students to do so, are you?"

A suitable response might be: "Yes, we have no bananas today, but, no, we do have some very nice carrots." They are electric carrots dangling out there in front of us on sticks, for as J.B. Priestley put it, "Admass is a consumer's race with donkeys chasing an electric carrot" (1957, 219).

It is obvious that most people read ads only on Walcutt's elementary, cursory levels of guessing and stumbling, as evidenced by the fact that advertising in North America is a flourishing $27 billion a year business. The ad writer wants us to "read" the ad, but only on a superficial level. Sometimes the writer even admonishes us to "Read This," as an ad for Korbel brandy does, just as one friendly hometown mortuary urges us to "Read this and a very difficult thing may become a little less difficult." It is unlikely, however, that *read* in such cases is intended in the sense of the Old English source of the term—*raeden:* to consider carefully; to discern, peruse, inspect, deliberate, interpret. (Few people realize that one of the obsolete denotations of "read" was the fourth stomach of ruminant.) In this connection, it may be pertinent to paraphrase Francis Bacon's famous statement about tasting some books, swallowing others, and chewing and digesting some few others. All ads are to be tested, none to be simply swallowed, some to be chewed and spit out, and some few to be ruminated.

Meticulous reading of any material demands time and effort, but once a workable strategy is developed, both time and effort can be minimized. Such a strategy must be based on certain deliberate assumptions, whether one is reading commercial, social, or political propaganda. (Hitler in *Mein Kampf,* we should remember, defined propaganda as "political advertising" [1942, 193]. The methodology of the two is strikingly similar.)

The first basic assumption takes the form of a prerequisite condition to be met by the reader. Just as the reading of literature requires a willing suspension of disbelief, so a perceptive reading of advertisement requires a willed suspension of belief. Both the belletrist and the ad writer are fabricators; the significant difference is that whereas the former presents heightened truth through the openly acknowledged illusion of art, the latter often misrepresents as truth what is subtly concealed illusion—for nakedly commercial purposes. Readers must therefore devise what someone has called a "system of discounts"—not a blanket cynicism but a discriminating analysis that enables one to discount half-truths, innuendoes, and blatant falsehoods.

Other basic assumptions essential to the perceptive reading of ads involve the recognition of certain dichotomies almost always present in advertisement ipso facto. One set of dichotomies is that of the projected voice and the real one, the ostensible purpose and the real one. Perhaps the most common pseudovoice in advertisement is that of the avuncular public servant personally concerned about the welfare of each one of us. Such a voice conveys the common ostensible purpose of improving our lives, meeting all our needs, assuring our comfort and security, and making us perfectly happy and content. How could one possibly question such honorific motivation when we hear from "The Good Guys at Kalil Bottling Company," or from "Farmer's Insurance Group—with good guys to look after" us or when we're told that "Metropolitan really stands by" us and that we're "in good hands with Allstate"; that United States Steel is "helping to rebuild the American Dream," that Buick Opel is "dedicated to the free spirit" in all of us and Oldsmobile Omega wants to build one "just for us" while Jack Daniels in the homey hills of Tennessee lovingly, patiently charcoal-mellows whiskey "drop by drop" and Juan Valdez in Colombia picks out the very finest coffee beans just for us? Lane Furniture tells us, "We're made with love"; a commercial for a dental clinic assures us in song, "The difference, my friend—we care about you"; Gerber products come to us with "fifty years of caring" and Pampers are made with "tender, loving care." Failure to resist this avuncular voice may result in our forgetting that the real motivation is, after all, Mammon.

Another common pseudovoice in advertisement is that of eternal youth, either in the form of seductive femininity or male machismo. Such archetypes are widely used for purposes of *adverting*, that is, drawing or turning the reader's attention from the real business at hand (a sale) by associating the product with an illusion. Many ads for health spas and automobiles, for example, advert(ise) the illusion; not the product. At other times, the pseudovoice takes the form of a testimonial from a popular entertainment figure or sports idol. The disparity lies, of course, in the fact that success and popularity in one field do not necessarily qualify one as an expert in another; moreover, many celebrities very likely have never even used the products that they are paid so handsomely to endorse.

Besides pseudopurpose and pseudovoice, there is pseudologic: the dichotomy between specious reasoning and valid, sound logic, or between irrational propaganda and the pseudorational guise in which it is presented. Consider the *fabulous,* the *sensational Mark Eden Mark II Bust Developer with IVR,* an ad which appeared in a recent issue of *Mademoiselle.*

> Now with IVR, no matter what your bust problem—whether you are flat-chested and want to quickly add 3, 4, 5, 6, or more shapely inches—or whether you want to firm up, fill out your cup size and develop rounded shape and glorious high cleavage—only Mark II does it all—the world's most totally effective bust developer! . . . Now a woman can actually see her bust become rounder and fuller before her very eyes. First a gentle flush across the bosom and then, incredibly enough, inches actually added to the bust from the very first day. . . . The ultimate bustline with IVR.

The reader might well imagine that "IVR" is an amazing new scientific elixir, perhaps resembling that which Hawthorne's Aylmer concocted to remove a birthmark from his wife's cheek. But in small print at the bottom we are told that IVR—"exclusive with Mark Eden Mark II," stands for *Infinitely Variable Resistance.* The discerning reader might well say, "What a bust!"—and turn the page, richer by at least $10.95 and considerably wiser.

Perhaps the greatest dichotomy in advertisement is that between language and reality. In his book *The Theatre of the Absurd,* Martin Esslin alludes to the "trend of the times in the workaday world of the man in the street." Esslin writes:

> Exposed to the incessant, and inexorably loquacious, onslaught of the mass media, the press, and advertising, the man in the street becomes more and more skeptical toward the language he is exposed to. The citizens of totalitarian countries know full well that most of what they are told is doubletalk, devoid of real meaning. They become adept at reading between the lines; that is, at guessing at the reality the language conceals rather than reveals. In the West, euphemisms and circumlocutions fill the press or resound from the pulpits. And advertising, by its constant use of superlatives, has succeeded in devaluing language to a point where it is a generally accepted axiom that most of the words one sees displayed on billboards or in the colored pages of magazine advertising are as meaningless as the jingles of television commercials. A yawning gulf has opened between language and reality. (359)

Similarly, Leo Spitzer, in an essay entitled "American Advertisement Explained as Popular Art," notes that "the public accepts willingly the hypocrisy" of the commercial artist (1962, 253). And in regard to political advertisement, poet John Berryman said: "From public officials we expect lies, and we get them in profusion" (Kostelanetz 344). The evidence surely indicates that Esslin, Spitzer, and Berryman are correct about the disparity between the language of propaganda and reality, between words and referents.

But perhaps they overestimate the perception and sophistication of the "average" U. S. reader of ads. Wasn't it H. L. Mencken who said somewhere that nobody ever went broke underestimating the intelligence of the American public? It may be true, as Spitzer says, that "the advertiser does not ask that his words be taken completely at face value" (253). But it is also true that he knows full well that the success of his ad depends upon its being read just superficially enough to permit its seductive, associative archetypes to lodge in the subconscious and its illusory promises to appeal sufficiently to one or more of the Seven Deadly Sins to bear the desired fruit of Mammon. As Aldous Huxley noted in his essay "The Arts of Selling," advertisement "depends for its effectiveness on a general failure to understand the nature of symbols" (1958, 50).

It is necessary, then, for the reader to approach an ad with the basic assumption that the copywriter uses language less to *express* than to *impress*, less to *illuminate* than to *manipulate*, less to *win* with *reason* than to *baffle* with *bull*. Like the perceptive reader of belleslettres, the reader must read not only the declarations but also the implications; not only the denotations but also the connotations. The reader must be alert not only to what the "voice" means to say but also to what the voice says without meaning to—and to what is left unsaid. The reader must assume that more often than not the voice, the persona, the narrator is unreliable. To echo Will Rogers, the copywriter is, in a sense, archetypal con artist persuading readers to buy something they don't need with money they don't have.

Perhaps the most effective counterstrategy—which, in a sense, is what reading an ad entails—is to pose a series of pointed questions, as Adler has for evaluating books, and then attempt to answer them.[2] For advertisements, think VAPID—an acronym formed by the following questions about the voice, audience, purpose, idea and devices of any ad we read:

Voice

What *voice* is speaking in this ad? Is it an authentic, credible and creditable one?

Audience

What *audience* is the ad directed toward? And why?

Does the ad writer take unfair advantage of the reader or viewer, as in the case of print ads and commercials, especially those for cereals, directed toward children? Another kind of ad with special appeal to a particular audience—and by reverse psychology making an appeal to those not in the category explicitly addressed—is the cigarette or liquor ad which assures smokers and drinkers that it is perfectly acceptable to indulge, as long as it's *their* product. An ad for Vantage cigarettes is addressed

> to the 56,000,000 people who smoke cigarettes. A lot of people have been telling you not to smoke, especially cigarettes with high "tar" and nicotine. But smoking provides you with a pleasure you don't want to give up. . . . But there is one overriding fact that transcends whether you should or shouldn't smoke and that fact is that you do smoke, and what are they going to do about that?

Purpose

What is the *purpose* of the ad—both the ostensible one and the real one?

The question is especially pertinent, for example, in relation to ads that purport to have great humanitarian concern; a concern that is undercut by the product itself or by the company's unscrupulous activity. What *really* is the purpose of this ad from the Distilled Spirits Council of the U.S.?

> It's all right to offer someone a drink. It's all wrong to insist. If you choose to drink, drink responsibly.

Or what about the so-called "public service" ads by gas companies in relation to the energy crisis, or the propaganda for nuclear energy, or an ad from the American Electric Power Company assuring us that America's coal resources "won't come near short supply for over 500 years"?

Idea

What is the central *idea* of the ad, its thesis or hypothesis, its focus—both ostensible and real?

Ordinarily the central focus can be analyzed in terms of the appeal to one or more of the Seven Deadly Sins: pride, covetousness, lust, anger, gluttony, envy, and sloth. If we were not motivated by silly vanity, vainglory, and conceit, would such ads as this one for Volvo be effective? *Drive a car that impresses people who aren't easily impressed.*

Further understanding of advertisement's central appeal is conveyed in:

The Advertiser's Decalogue

1. Thou shalt indulge thyself and never feel guilty.
2. Thou shalt take unto thee graven images of standard brands and be taken in by their promises of gratification and glory.
3. In the name of independence thou shalt do thine own thing, eschewing all authority and restriction.
4. Remember popular opinion, taste, and current fads to serve them wholly.
5. Seven days a week shalt thou demand instant ease, relief, satisfaction and luxury, eschewing any discomfort as evil.
6. Honor Scientism as Savior, that thy days may be long and prosperous in the land which advertising hath made the wealthiest on earth.
7. Thou shalt pursue happiness, pleasure, and thrills as the ultimate end of life.
8. Thou shalt seek to live by bread alone, for man's life consisteth in the abundance of Mammon.
9. Thou shalt live wholly for the here and now.
10. Thou shalt covet thy neighbor's possessions and satisfy thy animal urges at any cost.

And the common appeals of advertisement can be summarized in:

The Advertiser's 23rd

The Adman is my Shepherd,
I shall ever want.
He maketh me to walk a mile for a Camel;
He leadeth me beside Crystal Waters in the
    High Country of Coors.
He restoreth my soul with Perrier.
He guideth me in Marlboro Country
For Mammon's sake.
Yea, though I walk through the Valley of the
    Jolly Green Giant,
In the shadow of B.O., halitosis,
    indigestion, headache pain, and
    hemorrhoidal tissue,
I will fear no evil,
For I am in Good Hands with Allstate;
Thy Arid, Scope, Tums, Tylenol, and
    Preparation H—
They comfort me.
Stouffer's preparest a table before the TV
In the presence of all my Appetites;
Thou anointest my head with Brylcream;

My Decaffeinated Cup runneth over.
Surely surfeit and security shall follow me
All the days of Metropolitan Life,
And I shall dwell in a Continental Home
With a mortgage for ever and ever.

Devices

Having asked and answered questions about voice, audience, purpose, and key idea or appeal, one is then ready to pose what is perhaps the most important question of all: What are the specific *devices* or techniques used? This question can, in turn, be broken down into the following categories.

- What is the overall design or structure of the ad?
- What "adverting" or attention-getting ploys are used?
- What place do nonverbal symbols play?
- What information is provided and support given?
- What does the language convey denotatively? Connotatively? Objectively? Subjectively?
- What kind of rhetoric does the ad employ?

The Rhetoric of Cow and Bull

The rhetoric of advertisement can be analyzed according to two general categories: the rhetoric of *cow* and the rhetoric of *bull*.[3] Ads that present "cow" are those which list impressive-sounding data, scientific or pseudoscientific facts, and all the latest "test evidence"—but with no indication of contexts, frames of reference, and points of observation which necessarily determine the origin, nature, meaning, and relevance of the facts. There is no indication of control factors, applicability, or relevance.

Ads that present "bull," on the other hand, are those which discourse *generally* but with no factual data.

The copywriters of Cow are the shysters, attempting to cow the reader, to overawe or intimidate with technical-sounding data from the sacred cow of Scientism. They parade their *advanced, new, improved breakthroughs,* their *ultra-advanced, new, double-protection formula,* and their unpronounceable, cryptic "active ingredients" like *sodium monofluorophosphate* and *monosodium glutamate, nonoxynal 9* and *Superorb 7.* Or they provide irrelevant personal data as in this ad for Dewar's Scotch:

Sharon Miller
Home: Salmon, Idaho
Age: 36
Profession: White-water guide
Hobbies: Skiing, kayaking, horseback riding, yoga
Most Memorable Book: *Thomas Wolfe's Letters to His Mother*
Scotch: Dewar's White Label

The details are apparently intended to convince us, by association, to buy Dewar's because such a wholesome, all-American, clean-cut, adventuresome woman like Sharon Miller prefers White Label.

The copywriter of Bull is the bullster, attempting to persuade through bluster, bluff, and blather. The common method is overstatement; the popular form, the superlative. One of the greatest bullsters in the Southwest is "Tex" Earnhardt, "Arizona's Largest Ford Dealer," whose print ads announce "No bull since 1951" and whose TV commercials, featuring Tex straddling a Brahma bull, conclude with the statement, "And that ain't no bull." Bullsters, it seems, typically feel the need to insist that they are *not* bulling us.

The shysters of Cow have recently adopted new strategies using "health fears," misinformation, and innuendoes to confuse and mislead the public by claiming that one product is "safer" than another. For example, one popular soft drink is advertised as being caffeine-free with the strong suggestion that the substance is unhealthful, a conclusion that has not been borne out by scientific studies, according to the American Council on Science and Health. Similar fear tactics intended to cow us are used in advertising decaffeinated coffee despite the fact that it has been proven that such coffees contain only a little less caffeine than do regular coffees. Similarly, ads for filter cigarettes have engaged in cowing with their claims of low tar and nicotine, but what they do not say—and what studies presented at the 55th Scientific Session of the American Heart Association have shown—is that filter cigarettes are no better at reducing carbon monoxide, a substance linked to heart disease, than nonfilter cigarettes.

Still other cowing (fear) tactics concern the use of artificial sweeteners despite the fact that new research has shown that normal use of the sweeteners does not cause cancer as previously reported. Further, some food company advertisers talk out of both sides of their mouths, in true doublespeak fashion, in claiming that some of the products contain no preservatives or other chemicals while, at the same time, advertising other products that *do* contain them. Similarly, advertisers for one brand of mayonnaise warn prospective purchasers not to buy any products "with ingredients you can't pronounce" but fail to mention that their brand of mayonnaise contains *phosphatidyl cholines and glycerol esters of linoleic acid.* That nicens little boy named Baby Tuckoo had better watch out for the moocow coming down the road!

Occasionally the cow and the bull get together in the same ad and produce either a variant of the all-too-familiar cock-and-bull or yet another Golden Calf venerated in modern America no less fervently than was its ancient prototype. If the Israelites needed to learn to read and heed what was written on those tablets of stone, modern Americans need to learn to read not only those ancient precepts but also what is written in ubiquitous ads. For if we fail to master the eye and ass power of discriminating reading, we are likely to be cowed and bulled until we find ourselves asses chasing electric carrots.

Notes

1. The two poems are "Auguries of Innocence" and "The Everlasting Gospel." Perhaps Blake was influenced by Plato's *Theaetetus,* in which Socrates asks the question, "Which is more correct, to say that we see or hear with the eyes or the ears, or *through* the eyes or ears?" and to which Plato responded: "I should say *through,* Socrates, rather than *with.*"

2. Adler has suggested these four questions one must ask about any book: (1) What is the book about as a whole? (2) What is being said, in detail, and how? (3) Is the book true, in whole or part? (4) What of it?

3. The terminology is borrowed from William G. Perry's essay "Examsmanship and the Liberal Arts: A Study in Educational Epistemology." In *Examining in Harvard College: A Collection of Essays by Members of the Harvard Faculty.* Cambridge: Faculty of Arts and Sciences, 1963: 125–135. See my essay "The Rhetoric of Cow and the Rhetoric of Bull" *Rhetoric Society Quarterly* 14 (Summer-Fall 1984): 129–38.

Works Cited

Adler, Mortimer. *How to Read a Book.* New York: Simon and Schuster, 1967.

Boorstin, Daniel. *The Image, or What Happened to the American Dream.* New York: Atheneum, 1962.

Ciardi, John. *How Does a Poem Mean?* New York: Houghton Mifflin, 1989.

Esslin, Martin. *The Theatre of the Absurd.* Garden City, N.Y.: Doubleday, 1961.

Gordon, Caroline. *How to Read a Novel.* New York: Viking, 1964.

Hitler, Adolf. *Mein Kampf.* Munich: Müller and Son, 1942.

Huxley, Aldous. *Brave New World Revisited.* New York: Harper, 1958.

Key, Wilson Bryan. *Subliminal Seduction.* New York: Signet, 1974.

Keynes, Geoffrey and Brian Hill, eds. *Samuel Butler's Notebooks.* New York: E. P. Dutton, 1951.

Kostelanetz, Richard. "Conversation with Berryman." *Massachusetts Review* 11, no. 2 (1970): 340–347.

Muggeridge, Malcolm. *Jesus Rediscovered.* New York: Doubleday, 1969.

Pound, Ezra. *How to Read.* New York: Hasnell House, 1971.

Priestley, J. B. "The Writer in a Changing World." *Thoughts in the Wilderness.* New York: Harper, 1957.

Richards, I. A. *How to Read a Page.* Boston: Beacon, 1973.

Spitzer, Leo. *Essays on English and American Literature.* Princeton: Princeton University Press, 1962.

Toffler, Alvin. *Future Shock.* New York: Bantam, 1971.

Walcutt, Charles. *An Anatomy of Prose.* New York: Macmillan, 1962.

14 Subliminal Chainings: Metonymical Doublespeak in Advertising

Don L. F. Nilsen
Arizona State University

A number of years ago, George Lakoff delivered a series of lectures proposing a linguistic model which he called "Gestalt Linguistics." This model investigated the cultural facts we need to know in order to interpret a sentence. As an example, he asked us to make believe we had come to America from a foreign country and came across the phrase "topless legislation." This expression would be totally meaningless to the foreigner who did not share something of American culture, for the legislation is indeed not topless. In fact, anyone attempting to interpret this sentence is required to go through a series of metonymical chainings in order to arrive at a cultural gestalt that makes the phrase understandable:

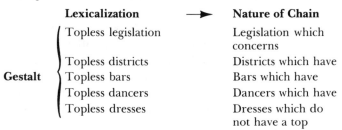

	Lexicalization	→	**Nature of Chain**
	Topless legislation		Legislation which concerns
	Topless districts		Districts which have
Gestalt	Topless bars		Bars which have
	Topless dancers		Dancers which have
	Topless dresses		Dresses which do not have a top

This chain provides our English language with five expressions, none of which can be understood without subliminally developing the chain. "Topless legislation" is not topless. A "topless district" is not topless. A "topless bar" is not topless. And a "topless dancer" is certainly not topless. In this entire chain, it is only the dress which is topless. The chaining is so significant in our culture that we are not even allowed to call a bar with no roof a "topless bar," since that expression would be very misleading.

This chaining process in language is the rule rather than the exception; for every expression we hear, our minds are trained to investigate the various culturally compatible chainings and settle on the particular

147

chaining that is most appropriate and sensible for the context in question. Thus a "cement truck" is not a truck made out of cement, but a truck for hauling cement; and a "greenhouse" is not a house which is green but rather a house that contains green things; and a "slam dunk" is something which happens on a basketball court rather than in a coffee shop.

Effective advertisers must know three things. They must know their product; they must know the culture; and they must know their potential customer. Furthermore, they must know enough about language to use their knowledge about the product, the culture, and the customer to persuade the customer to buy the product.

But there is an added complication: customers don't necessarily want to buy the product, and at any rate they don't trust the advertiser, who doesn't necessarily have the customer's best interest at heart. Customers realize that it is the function of the advertiser to sell the product (get the money to change hands), and it is therefore the function of customers to resist buying the product (get the money to stay put). If customers realize they are being advertised at, they will quickly build their defenses, and the ad will thereby be rendered ineffective. Advertisers must therefore communicate, "Buy my product" at a level where customers don't realize they are being affected. This is called subliminal advertising.

In his books *Subliminal Seduction, Media Sexploitation,* and *Clam Plate Orgy,* Wilson Bryan Key has investigated some of the techniques of subliminal communication which advertisers use to sell their products. They airbrush barely detectable words and symbols into clouds, ice cubes, smoke, flowing hair, and other free forms. If you point out to ad readers that these messages are there, and ask them if they saw or were affected by these messages, they will respond, "Certainly not." And that's exactly what the advertising people want them to say and think, but the advertising people have done numerous studies (the results of which are not generally available to the public) which provide strong evidence that such subliminal messages are indeed understood at some subliminal level, and are indeed affecting the buying behavior of the customers.

The subliminal messages which Wilson Bryan Key is studying are typically one-word or one-symbol messages. They are made subliminal by being airbrushed or otherwise blended into the environment so that they are barely visible. On the other hand, the subliminal messages of the present article always involve more than one word, because here it is not the word itself which is subliminal, but rather the relationship between one word and another. The problem with talking about this relationship is that the audience will first see no relationship at all, and then, once they see the relationship they will say, "But that's obvious." The only way to make them aware of the subliminal effects of the word associations is to give them just the two associated words and force them to attempt to develop the relationship by themselves.

I once gave another linguist the expression *Midas Mufflers* and asked him to try to figure out the nature of the relationship between the two words. He immediately saw the alliteration of the *M*'s, but then he said, "Let's see, Midas was a King."

I agreed and told him that the Midas Muffler company had even dotted their *i* with a crown to help ad readers make that association.

He said, "King Midas had the golden touch."

I agreed, but asked, "What does a king have to do with mufflers, and what is the relevance of the golden touch?"

He said, "Well, mufflers don't make any noise."

I said, "That's right, they're silent." And then but only then could he make the connection: *Silence is golden.*

At this point I got a reaction similar to what I get when I tell a joke involving a pun—a sort of smiling groan. He thought a while and said, "But maybe 'silence is golden' is not the bridge; maybe the bridge is simply that gold is valuable and Midas Mufflers are equally valuable."

I responded, "Well, yes, that too."

This linguist is the first person I've talked with who has been able to develop the complete chain on a conscious level. But we are all able to understand more than we are able to communicate. We are like the child who asked if a certain building was made out of "alunimum." When his father responded, "Yes, it *is* made out of aluminum," the child angrily retorted, "not *aluminum, alunimum.*" The child could hear but could not reproduce the difference.

Somehow, we all sort-of but not-quite make the connection of Midas and mufflers across the proverb, "Silence is golden." Some people make the connection more than others, and nobody makes it all the way—at least on a conscious level. We are a great deal smarter than we think we are about making these chainings because this is necessarily a well-developed skill of language-possessing humans. At the same time we are a great deal more naïve than we think we are about the effects that these chainings have on our lives, because they happen subliminally.

There used to be a television commercial for *Vanquish* (a headache medicine) where a person holds up two fingers and sings three short notes and one long note. This simple commercial had seven different meanings:

1. The *V* stands for Vanquish,
2. the fingers are held in a sign of *V* for Victory—victory over pain,
3. this *V* sign is also used as a Peace Symbol—peace and quiet,
4. the *V* symbol is linked to the Roman Number V standing for five,
5. this linking is reinforced by the fact that the person is singing the first four notes of Beethoven's Fifth Symphony,
6. which is reinforced by the fact that the Morse Code for *V* is three dots and a dash,
7. and since the music is played upbeat, we are reminded not only of Beethoven's Fifth, but also of its modern counterpart, "A Fifth of Beethoven" which
8. provides a whole new set of chainings.

Now you might say, "But I studied Morse Code thirty-five years ago."

I would respond, "Aha, that shows you how subliminal it is."

You might say, "But I never studied Morse Code at all."

I would respond, "Well, six out of seven ain't all that bad."

This ad is like any good examination; everybody gets some of it right, and nobody gets all of it right.

Suppose a new product comes onto the market and the company decides to call it *Mr. Pibb.* Is it merely coincidence that this product is the same color as *Dr. Pepper,* and that it has a similar offbeat taste? Is it coincidence that *Mr.* and *Dr.* are both titles of people (i.e., personification), and that their pronunciation is similar? Or that their letter configuration—going from a capital letter to an *r* to a period—are both like going down a mountain? Is it coincidence that both products begin with *P,* followed by a lax front unrounded vowel, followed by a bilabial stop? And is it coincidence that both use a double letter at the end of the first syllable (*bb* and *pp*), or that a *bb* is simply an upside down *pp*? I suggest that there are too many similarities here for them all to be the result of coincidence.

At one time I was so naïve as to think that *Arby's* restaurants were named after a person by the name of "Arby." Then my daughter, Nicolette, told me that Arby is merely the pronunciation of the letters *R* and *B,* which stand for "Roast Beef." Arby's later unsublimated their ad with a jingle that refers to "America's Roast Beef, Yes Sir."

There are a number of interesting chainings relating to pantyhose. *Ugly Duckling* pantyhose is an allusion to a Hans Christian Andersen fairy tale; *Turtles* pantyhose are called that because "Turtles never run." Another pantyhose name is *Shenanigans* because "Girls who get into Shenanigans have more fun." Then there is *Sheer Energy Pantyhose* "with all-day massage." Think of the associations of "sheer," of "energy" of "pantyhose" and of "massage." Contrast this with an equally descriptive phrase like "Old Ladies' Support Stockings."

But none of these chainings are as effective as those of the product *L'Eggs*. This product is chained to the package (egg), and to its location (leg). The "L" plus apostrophe plus "Eggs" is very French in appearance—glamorous. "L'eggs" seems to have the same French morphological structure as does the actual French word, *L'oeuf*. And that may be the end of this particular chain; however, there is another chain based on the same French word, "l'oeuf." It relates to a score in tennis—*love* which is derived from the French l'oeuf—the egg. The metaphor is exactly the same as the other metaphor meaning zero—goose egg, and is based on shape resemblance. Notice here that I did not attempt to relate the tennis metaphor to the pantyhose metaphor. The chain from L'Eggs to L'Oeuf to Love is an unconscious and nonreinforcing chain. If the chaining does affect the product, it affects it in a negative way, similar to the way the Spanish *No va* affects the American car name, "Nova." I suspect that these unconscious and potentially damaging chainings form an area of needed research in the advertising industry.

A final type of chaining is from product to product. If a particular product has waged an expensive and successful advertising campaign, then another product may attempt to take advantage of the first product's advertising by somehow disguising itself as the first product. We saw this with Mr. Pibb and Dr. Pepper. We see it whenever the word "Cola" is written in exactly the same style as the Cola of Coca-Cola. We see it when a vegetable drink with eight juices tries to take advantage of the advertising campaign of Ford Motor Company by calling it *V–8 Vegetable Juice*. (Here, the shape-metaphor of the V–8 engine is changed to the initialism of the V–8 juice.) We see it when a company that sells car stereo systems tells you to "Midasize your Stereo." We see it when Wheaties establishes the slogan "Breakfast of Champions," and then Quaker Oats comes along with a diet product and calls it "Breakfast of Losers." We see it when Greyhound advertises "Leave the Driving to Us," and then a hotel chain advertises "Let Greyhound do the Driving, and leave the *Rest* to us."

These subtle and sophisticated chainings, and the resultant gestalts which they develop, are powerful influences in our lives. The fact that we have to develop the gestalt by ourselves produces a great deal of tension that we fight desperately to resolve. To convince you of the amount of tension developed in chainings and the resultant incomplete gestalts, I'm going to quote from Charles Hockett's *The View from Language, Selected Essays: 1948–1974:*

> Edward Lear, the Victorian poet
> Wrote lim'ricks, though not so's you'd know it.
> His plots were so terse
> As to need no fifth verse.

Works Cited

Hockett, Charles. *The View from Language: Selected Essays, 1948–1974*, 279. Athens, Ga.: University of Georgia Press, 1977.

Key, Wilson Bryan. *Subliminal Seduction*. New York: Signet, 1974.

———. *Media Sexploitation*. Englewood Cliffs, N.J.: Prentice-Hall, 1976.

———. *Clam Plate Orgy and Other Subliminals the Media Use to Manipulate Your Behavior*. Englewood Cliffs, N.J.: Prentice-Hall, 1980.

15 Doublespeak
and the Polemics
of Technology

Scott Buechler
Martin Marietta Energy Systems

> One of the most critical issues facing problem-solvers and decision-makers is whom to trust.
> —Edward E. David, Jr.

Deceptive language is common throughout our society: we see it in business, industry, sports, and even the university. One would not, therefore, expect the polemics of technology to be free of it either. My purpose in this essay is to analyze the language of the engineer and author Samuel Florman specifically for examples of doublespeak. Both of his books, *The Existential Pleasures of Engineering* and *Blaming Technology: The Irrational Search for Scapegoats,* discuss the philosophy of technology for the benefit of a general audience.

The Complexities of Technology

Etymologically, *technology* means the systematic study of an art or craft. However, while we still discuss the technology of various crafts such as weaving, wood stove construction, carving, and so forth, the word has assumed a more specific meaning. Currently, "technology" is an abbreviated form of *high technology,* the application of advanced scientific knowledge to the creation of such complex products as airplanes, spacecraft, computers, and advanced weapons systems. Some scholars, however, provide a broader definition of the term:

> In brief, technology can be characterized as that form of cultural activity devoted to the production or transformation of material objects, or the creation of procedural systems, in order to expand the realm of practical human possibility. (Hannay and McGinn 27)

Such a definition recognizes not only the physical but also the social aspects of technology, and indicates the range and complexity of the subject. Writing as he was for a general audience, Florman may have

153

fallen initially into error by trying to oversimplify it, for technology is not easily understood, even in a society which is, for all practical purposes, based on it.

In the early 1970s, Samuel Florman noticed that technology was receiving a bad press. To combat this problem, he wrote *The Existential Pleasures of Engineering*, in which he defended the role of the technologist par excellence—the engineer—against the attacks of a number of writers.

Florman's highly readable book was timely, for it addressed an issue that had become heatedly discussed, the philosophical aspects of the technological pursuit. As a result, he and other spokespeople have been invited to speak at conferences and to write for such periodicals as *Harpers*.

The style of Florman's book is admirable. Its wording is clear, direct and sometimes even moving. The purpose behind his book is also commendable; to reaffirm technologists' pride in their work. Unfortunately, the rhetorical means to which Florman resorts invalidates many of his arguments, for they often rely on one form or another of doublespeak. Occasionally the problem is a semantic distortion, occasionally it is a complex logical contortion, and occasionally it is a combination of the two. Some of the logical or semantic slips are more serious than others, but each illustrates doublespeak at work.

I point out these various forms of doublespeak for two reasons. First, they illustrate its various disguises, its camouflage that enables such deceptions to lurk in seemingly clear language. Second, we are part of a highly technological culture; therefore, discussions of technology are discussions of ourselves. It follows, then, that if we wish to discuss ourselves accurately, we need to discuss technology with equal accuracy. In my essay I hope to show where such discussions can go astray.

The Language of "Existential Pleasures"

Defending the engineer against the attacks of Jacques Ellul, René Dubos, Louis Mumford, Theodore Roszak, and Charles A. Reich, Samuel Florman categorized these writers as "antitechnologists." While admitting that they are "masters of prose and intellectual finesse" (58), he attempted singlehandedly (and singlemindedly) to play St. George to the antitechnological dragons and to slay them with his words. However, the weapon Florman used—the written word— harms his own arguments at least as much as it harms those of his opponents. Within the compass of this little book we find name-calling (the antitechnologists become "dyspeptic philosophers" who resort to "false descriptions" and "demonology") question-begging, unsupported accusations, and doublespeak in the form of semantic and logical distortions.

Semantic Distortion

In his attempt to refute one of the antitechnologist's major arguments—that "technology is a 'thing' or a force that has escaped from human control and is spoiling our lives" (53)—Florman writes:

> The first antitechnological dogma to be confronted is the treatment of technology as something that has escaped from human control. It is understandable that sometimes anxiety and frustration can make us feel this way. But sober thought reveals that technology is not an independent force, much less a thing, but merely one of the types of activities in which people engage. Furthermore, it is an activity in which people engage because they choose to do so. The choice may sometimes be foolish or unconsidered. The choice may be forced upon some members of society by others. But this is very different from the concept of technology *itself* misleading or enslaving the populace. (58)

Although Florman confronts a question of genuine importance— do we control our technology or does it control us—his treatment of this issue is troubling. To begin with, he simplifies the issue by attributing concern over technology to "anxiety and frustration"—words connoting weakness. In fact, however, concern over technology results from sober and informed thought. (See, for example, *Daedalus* 109 [1980] which is devoted to the question, "Modern Technology: Program or Opportunity?")

Equally troubling is his general statement, "Furthermore, it is an activity in which people engage because they choose to do so." *Which* people choose to do so? Everyone who engages in it? Or only those who can afford to acquire the education and knowledge needed in order to gain command over advanced technology?

Most troubling of all, is the following line of reasoning: "The choice may be forced upon some members of society by others." But this is very different from the concept of technology *itself* "misleading or enslaving the populace." This is a clear case of semantic distortion, of attaching to a word or phrase a meaning different from (or even contrary to) its established meaning. Claiming that a choice may be forced upon some members of society by others bleeds the word *choice* of its meaning. After all, a choice cannot be forced upon someone and remain a choice.

Logical Distortion

Semantic distortions are not the only form of doublespeak in Florman's arguments. Running throughout the book is a type of logical distortion characterized by a subtle change in focus in the middle of a paragraph or a discussion that results in the logic of an argument appearing more sound than, in fact, it is. Consider the passage below, in which Florman addresses a common concern about technology and citizens' privacy: electronic surveillance and the uses to which it might be put by the government. He describes this concern as the fear "that advances in technology have been helpful to the Establishment in increasing its power over the masses" (63). Florman reviews that fear and calls it bogus:

> In fact, the evidence is all the other way. In technologically advanced societies there is more freedom for the average citizen than there was in earlier ages. There has been continuing apprehension that new technological achievements *might* make it possible for governments to tyrannize the citizenry with Big Brother techniques. But, in spite of all the newest gadgetry, governments are scarcely able to prevent the antisocial actions of criminals, much less control every act of every citizen. Hijacking, technically ingenious robberies, computer-aided embezzlements, and the like, are evidence that the outlaw is able to turn technology to his own advantage, often more adroitly than the government. The FBI has admitted that young revolutionaries are almost impossible to find once they go "underground." The rebellious individual is more than holding his own. (64)

What Florman says about "the rebellious individual" may well be true. However, the issue is not how cleverly rebellious individuals use technology to outmaneuver the government. The question is whether our government, using such technological instruments as electronic surveillance and inaccessible data banks, poses a threat to "the average citizen." In effect, Florman has blurred this distinction, thereby also blurring the distinction between offender and victim. "Hijacking, technically ingenious robberies, computer-aided embezzlements, and the like" are offenses committed by people whose intention it is to gain what they can by victimizing others. Since the average citizen has no such intention in mind, Florman's a fortiori argument is meaningless. It does have instructional value, however, in that it exemplifies another form of doublespeak.

The Language of "Blaming Technology"

In 1981 Florman published a sequel to *The Existential Pleasures of Engineering,* entitled *Blaming Technology: The Irrational Search for Scapegoats.* As its title suggests, this book, too, is polemical. However, while its tone remains contentious, *Blaming Technology* presents a more balanced treatment of the issues raised. This is not to say, however, that Florman has completely avoided the pitfalls that characterize the original book. In *Blaming Technology,* again we find some of the same linguistic and argumentative solecisms that marked, and marred, *The Existential Pleasures of Engineering.*

One of the most complicated examples occurs in a chapter titled "Hired Scapegoats," in which Florman attempts to vindicate the U.S. Army Corps of Engineers, an organization that he believes has been unjustly maligned. Toward the middle of the chapter, Florman sings the praises of the corps:

> Far from being an intransigent bureaucracy, the corps appears to have evolved as an instrument exquisitely tuned to work the will of the people. (46)

Ironically, Florman himself had previously cited several articles exposing the apparent callousness of the corps, and thus his claim about its "exquisite" tuning seems badly skewed.

Florman, undaunted, proceeds:

> All right, critics of the corps might concede, but which people? (46)

Whether or not one "concedes" the point that Florman claims having made, the question he raises is a good one, and his answer is revealing:

> Corps projects traditionally come into being when some local citizens' group gains the political support of a Congressman and the technical approval of the local corps district engineer. Typically, the local group is a Chamber of Commerce or some other representative of monied interest. (46)

The people, then, might in fact be "representatives of monied interest." However, such a definition is obviously too restrictive and makes one wonder why groups or individuals outside of the monied interests are not also categorized as "the people." Florman continues:

> Yet even if many projects are conceived in greed, sponsored under slightly unsavory circumstances, the entire local community often benefits from increased employment and a prospering business climate. (46)

The implication here is that the end justifies the means; or, to put the idea in more modern terms, "the benefits justify the costs." But I wish I knew exactly what was meant by *slightly* (how slight?), *often* (how often?), *unsavory circumstances,* and *the entire local community.* An example would help here but none is forthcoming. On the next page we read:

> Wilderness areas have been flooded, rural families uprooted, archeological sites inundated, and important caves damaged, not because these were objectives of the Corps of Engineers, but because commercial development was mandated by the citizenry. (47)

Archeologists, rural families, wilderness residents and visitors, then, are not among "the people" for whose will the corps works? Flooding, uprooting, inundating, and damaging are all actions showing how exquisitely the corps is attuned to the will of the people? Those classified as "critics of the corps" are therefore not part of "the citizenry"? Finally, when Florman ends with the claim that

> engineering is not anti-environmental. Environmentalism itself is a branch of engineering (49)

we have become too aware of the doublespeak to be fooled.

Pseudorealities

One other problem that Florman's book presents is the use of language to create a "pseudoreality." The root of any written message is the word. Words frequently categorize the things or people or actions to which they refer. Categorizing things, people, and actions without giving a reasoned basis for that categorization can lead to inaccurate conclusions which can, in turn, distort a part of reality. Florman, for example, calls Rachel Carson and Barry Commoner "persuasive alarmists" whose writings have "oversensitized" the public to environmental issues (6). Do these words accurately describe the facts of the matter? Are the connotations of "alarmist" and "oversensitized" really appropriate? Reading the news over the last decade leads me to say, No. Elsewhere, fear of technology is classified as a "phobia," an irrational response, and thereby conveniently dismissed. While this type of linguistic categorization may not exactly be doublespeak, it does show language creating a deceptive reality, a situation that seems somewhat out of keeping with the facts.

A more complex example of pseudoreality, one involving an argument from definition, occurs when Florman argues against the notion that we in the United States live in a technocracy. The anti-technologists, says Florman, decry the "technocratic state," a form of government that, Florman stipulates, can mean only rule by technologists. He points out, however, that engineers and scientists (the technologists) are in fact politically weak figures who simply serve the interests of their community and their profession. Since the only true technocrat would be a technologist with political power, it follows, says Florman, that the fear of rampant technocracy—of government by the technologists—is a canard. He writes:

> Only if the term *technocracy* is expanded to signify rule by economists, business managers, lawyers, and accountants, as well as by scientists and engineers, can it be suggested that we are entering a technocratic age. But this stretches the word beyond all reason. (36)

The meaning of the central term, *technocracy*, determines whether or not we are close to, or already living in, a technocratic age. As this passage states, Florman considers "technocracy" to apply only to rule by scientists and engineers. However, is this too narrow a definition? The 1981 edition of *Webster's Third International Dictionary* supports Florman's argument, for it defines technocracy as "management of society by technical experts." Although one of our presidents was a student of nuclear engineering, his successor was a former actor—hardly what one would call a technical expert—and over the last two decades, our presidents have been primarily lawyers and career politicians. Certainly, then, the United States seems not to have been primarily governed by presidents who were scientists and engineers, nor by senators, representatives, or governors who were scientists or engineers.

Elected officials, however, are in constant need of expert advice, and their advisors—who help in the management of society—frequently come from fields that can be called technical if not technological: political science, economics, military science and the like. That leads us to inquire into the meaning of *technical*, and to ask whether we must limit the meaning of "technical expert" to "technological expert." Another look at *Webster's* shows how complicated this matter can be. "Technical" is first defined as an adjective which denotes:

> having special, usually practical, knowledge, especially of a mechanical or scientific subject.

Although this again lends support to Florman's argument and his use of the word *technocracy*, the next two definitions change the picture, for Webster goes on to define "technical" as:

marked by or characteristic of specialization, [and] of or related to
a particular subject, especially of or relating to a practical subject
that is organized on modern scientific principles.

If we base our discussion on these two definitions of *technical,* we can
conclude that the word denotes specialization and the formal knowledge of the principles of a practical discipline. Now the word *technocracy* begins to mean something else. If technocracy is government by
technical experts, and if "technical" refers to a specialized knowledge
of a particular field or subject, then "technocracy" means government
by specialists, by experts in a field. Since our government comprises
experts from such fields as business, finance, economics, political science, law, diplomacy, and the military, it would seem that it does
indeed show the features of technocracy. But Florman has clearly
anticipated just this argument, and he writes:

> Even if the meaning of technocrat is extravagantly expanded—
> using "technique" as the root instead of "technology"—the place of
> technocracy in our society is far from being established. (36)

Such an expansion is hardly extravagant; in fact, it is invited. Without
it, we cannot recognize the incipient and fully-evolved forms of technocracy within our society.

   Joseph Agassi, in an article titled "Shifting from Physical to Social
Technology," identifies two kinds of technology, the physical and the
social, and writes that:

> technology is in part concerned with machines, in part with hu-
> mans, and only the artificial act of isolation . . . distorts an item of
> technology to look as if it were merely physical technology or
> merely social technology. (199)

Examples of social technology include "planning a school or an educational system, . . . planning a library or an evening of entertainment or
even an industrial concern" (203). In other words, the careful and
systematic planning of human activity is another branch of technology.
If we refer to the definition of technology presented at the beginning
of this essay, we see that technology includes "the creation of procedural systems, in order to expand the realm of practical human possibility." Social technology, then, would involve the creation of
procedural systems and designs by means of which social goals are met.
If we allow the word "technology" to refer to social as well as physical
planning, then we can, in fact, use it as the basis for "technocracy," as
Florman requires, and still conclude that our society does contain the
elements of a technocracy.

We seem to be left with three choices: (1) If we derive *technocracy* from *technology* and restrict the meaning of technology to physical technology—the work of scientists and engineers—then no, we do not live in a technocracy, because we are not primarily governed by scientists and engineers. However, (2) if we extend the meaning of the word *technology* as Agassi and others suggest, and admit within its semantic reach social as well as physical technology, yet continue to require the word *technocracy* to derive from *technology*, then we must conclude that, yes, our society can legitimately be called technocratic. And, finally, (3) if we use *technique* and *technical* as the basis of the word *technocracy*, then we must admit to a substantial technocratic element in our government, for many of our governmental leaders and advisors are technical experts.

Again, we are faced with a complex issue that cannot be resolved without a firm understanding of the meanings of the words used. However, this should not be written off as "just" a matter of semantics because it deals with a question involving a significant part of our reality. So we return to an early statement of Florman's:

> Only if the term *technocracy* is expanded to signify rule by economists, business managers, lawyers, and accountants, as well as by scientists and engineers, can it be suggested that we are entering a technocratic age. But this stretches the word beyond all reason.

In fact there are good reasons for expanding the meaning of the term. In so doing, we also expand the meanings of both *technology* and *technocrat* beyond those used by Florman. And while we cannot conclude that our society is entirely technocratic, the activities of special interest groups, the complex nature of political lobbying, the money required for a political hearing, the power of technological industries—all of these certainly attest to the considerable amount of technocracy at the basis of our current democracy. I think this to be inevitable. We have, after all, a culture based upon both advanced technology and highly specialized, technical knowledge. This must inevitably affect our political system and its operations.

Florman concludes his argument by writing:

> The myth of the technocratic elite is an expression of fear, like a fairy tale about ogres. It springs from an understandable apprehension, but since it has no basis in reality, it has no place in serious discourse. (41)

The simile in the first sentence begs the question, but something even more interesting lies within this passage: The obverse of Florman's statement is that if "the technocratic elite" *does* have some basis in reality, as I think it clearly does, then in fact, it holds a very prominent place in serious discourse, because it has serious implications for the evolution of a technologically advanced democracy. There is no real benefit to ignoring the issue or doublespeaking around it; it would be far better for us to acknowledge our technocratic development and channel it wisely for our own benefit.

Who Can We Trust?

I am left with the feeling that I have "picked on" Florman in this essay, and that does not please me. For one thing, I agree with his basic position that the technological pursuit can be both exciting and ennobling, and can also reflect, as do science and art, the creative capacity of the human mind. Also, I have criticized *only* Florman, but he is not alone among advocates of technology whose arguments reflect problems with the logic of language. Hal Hellmann, for example, includes misleading analogies in his *Technophobia: Getting Out of the Technology Trap*. Florman however, invites discussion because he writes with vigor, and yet his arguments rely heavily on doublespeak. Students of Orwell know that such language cries out for criticism.

In "Politics and the English Language," Orwell described vividly the relationship between thought and language. Arguing that corrupt thought corrupts language, he also pointed out that "if thought corrupts language, language can also corrupt thought" (4:137). The arguments I have analyzed show corruption in both thought and language in a subject which largely defines us as a culture—the pursuit of technology. I have claimed that discussions of technology are discussions of ourselves as a culture and that our descriptions of technology are similarly descriptions of ourselves. It follows, then, that distortions of the subject become distortions of ourselves and of our culture.

Furthermore, inaccurate language can lead to unwise action, for words serve frequently as the basis for action. The misuse of words can therefore lead to abusive action. (An interesting case study is provided by Erica Bates in her article subtitled "The Fatal Consequences of Semantic Ignorance.") Since the effect of technological action is so far-reaching, one would hope that such action would be taken wisely. Such wisdom can come only when the language behind and before the action is also clear and wise.

I began this essay with a quote from Edward E. David, Jr., former science advisor to President Reagan. I wish to end, also, with a quote from him:

> Discussions of technology often seem like discourses on good and
> evil. There are those who see only good in it, who insist that more
> and better technology will resolve most of today's problems.
> Others see only evil; they believe that technology is a principal
> cause of most of society's ills. Arguments along this continuum
> usually end up somewhere in the middle, with a compromise
> solution that seeks to balance costs and benefits. Much is hidden
> within the terms "costs" and "benefits"—for example, at whose cost
> are the benefits achieved and where do they fall? (169)

David is asking two questions here: What meaning do our words
actually have? And what part of our world—both human and natural—are we willing or having to sacrifice to enjoy the very real benefits
of our advanced technology? Knowledge, facts, clear thinking, and
clear language are required to answer those questions. If we add the
equally important need to know "whom to trust," then we can begin to
approach the problem addressed by David in the epigraph to this
essay: we should trust the experts who think, write, and speak clearly
and honestly. Only then do we have a chance of being a productive and
healthy—possibly even a wise—technological culture.

Works Cited

Agassi, Joseph. "Shifting from Physical to Social Technology." *Research in
Philosophy and Technology: An Annual Compilation of Research.* Vol. 1, 199–212.
Edited by Paul T. Durbin. Greenwich, Conn.: JAI Press, 1978.

Bates, Erica M. "The Implications for Semantics of Development in Medical
Technology: The Fatal Consequences of Semantic Ignorance." *ETC.: A
Review of General Semantics* 37, no. 1 (1980): 5–12. (Her analysis is based on
an incident reported in the *Atlantic Monthly,* July, 1979.)

David, Edward E., Jr. "On the Dimensions of the Technology Controversy."
Daedalus 109, no. 1 (1980): 169–77.

Florman, Samuel. *The Existential Pleasures of Engineering.* New York: St.
Martin's Press, 1976.

———. *Blaming Technology: The Irrational Search for Scapegoats.* New York: St.
Martin's Press, 1981.

Hannay, Bruce N., and Robert E. McGinn. "The Anatomy of Modern Technology: Prolegomenon to an Improved Public Policy for the Social Management of Technology." *Daedalus* 109, no. 1 (1980): 25–53.

Hellmann, Hall. *Technophobia: Getting Out of the Technology Trap.* New York: M.
Evans, 1976.

Orwell, George. "Politics and the English Language." In *In Front of Your Nose
(1945–1950),* 127–40. Vol. 4 of *The Collected Essays, Journalism and Letters of
George Orwell.* Edited by Sonia Orwell and Ian Angus. New York: Harcourt,
Brace and World, 1968.

16 Make Money, Not Sense: Keep Academia Green

Julia Penelope

Approximately forty years after Orwell's "Politics and the English Language" appeared, I can observe, without fear of rebuttal, that nothing's changed. In his essay, Orwell observed that "the decline of a language must ultimately have political and economic causes" (169), but he failed to enumerate those causes, whether out of wisdom or timidity I cannot guess. That "something" is seriously amiss with the uses of the English language we hear daily no one would deny. But not even those of us who claim to be "experts" on the subject can agree when it comes to proposing cause-effect relationships between language use and the prevailing social order, identifying which uses of language qualify as bona fide examples of doublespeak, and suggesting ways of actively combatting doublespeak. Taking as my specific case doublespeak in academia, I will argue that academic doublespeak is a response to our social order and to the pressure exerted on universities by those who have some economic and political power in our society or by those who seek such power for themselves.

A similar conclusion was reached by both James Sledd (1972) and D. G. Kehl (1982), although both authors were less generous than I am in their judgments of academics who use doublespeak and, at the same time, more optimistic concerning the likelihood that we are, collectively, capable of reversing the trend. Kehl, for example, offers five causes for what he calls "Educanto":

1. Professional pretensions to wisdom and profundity,
2. the desire to present things as worse or better than they are,
3. the desire to make "simple or nonexistent problems" appear to be complicated (mystification),
4. the need to survive in the academic factory,
5. the need to justify academic institutions as viable, productive organizations during a period of declining enrollments.

165

Likewise, Sledd observed that linguistic interventionists, his particular band of doublespeakers, can hardly be expected to differ ethically from the other men with whom they must wheel and deal.

> Their [middle-class, white linguists] probable motivations include a real desire to do good, some hidden dislike, some fear, and the love of money and status. Foundation men, bureaucrats, and politicians may be expected to share those foibles; and precisely because the whole conglomerate is shaped and moved by the same forces, it cannot move beyond its limits. (448)

While I am willing to grant Kehl's points concerning a general lack of integrity among university faculties, I prefer to emphasize here Sledd's analysis, which, (like Kehl's points four and five), acknowledges social realities within which university professors must try to survive. Rather than wonder why we fail to be more honorable people than the politicians and bureaucrats who financially reward—and punish—our research efforts, I think it's more realistic to understand that we are an embattled profession. That, at least, may give us a basis for weighing, individually, the costs of collusion and co-optation.

The Nature of the Beast

D. G. Kehl's definition of doublespeak comes closest to my own:

> It is the incongruity between what is *said*—or left *unsaid*—and what really *is*, between word and referent, between *seem* and *be*. It is the incongruity between what language is supposed to do—communicate—and what doublespeak does—obfuscate. (152)

The essence of doublespeak is the speaker's refusal to name or describe accurately events and actions; it is the manipulation of vocabulary and syntax in order to omit responsibility for particular actions and events.

In his article, "Doublespeak: Dialectology in the Service of Big Brother," James Sledd suggested a distinction between what he called *New High Bureaucratian* (NHB) and *Somnigraphy*:

> New High Bureaucratian . . . is grammatical and has a meaning but obscures it by jargon. At its best, somnigraphy is neither grammatical nor meaningful; but no sentence can qualify as somnigraphic unless either its meaning or its grammar is somehow deviant. . . . Somnigraphy [is] the art of writing [and speaking] as if one were asleep. (446)

Unfortunately, it is not always possible to distinguish between somnigraphy and New High Bureaucratian; NHB tends to meander into somnigraphy as the writer tries to maintain a high level of obfuscation. The longer one strives to hide meaningfulness in a text, the more likely that text is to become somnigraphic.

The strategies for successful doublespeaking, whether somnigraphy or NHB, are fairly simple, and require a species of lethargic cunning, doubtless traceable to a recessive gene available to just those members of our kind who acquire some measure of power.

1. Speak in a monotone. If you drone long enough, no one will listen anyway, so what you say won't matter.

2. Repeat yourself. Say the same thing over and over, using words you think are related to each other. As long as sound waves continue to bombard the eardrums of your audience, they'll believe you're conveying information.

3. Be innovative. Make up your own words; your audience will believe that it's *their* fault if they don't understand what you're saying.

4. Be creative. Make up your own rules for combining words. Your audience will assume that you're educated if what you say doesn't make any sense.

5. *Never* say what you mean. Someone out there might be listening in spite of rules 1–4.

6. *Never* name names if the guilty belong to your side of an issue.

7. *Always* name names of your opponents. If they're not in power, they're probably guilty of something.

8. *Never* tell the truth. Humankind cannot bear much reality.

The language that serves these strategies is characterized by a similarly short list of features and is highly predictable:

1. Euphemisms abound

2. Human agency is almost always absent; as a result, nominalizations (*the removal, the destruction of*), truncated passives (*Inflation will be halted, A woman was raped*), infinitive constructions (*to speak frankly, to address the issues*), and impersonal sentences (*it is unfortunate, it is often said that*) typify doublespeak

3. Repetition of the same word, or its derivatives and synonyms, occurs frequently

4. Non sequiturs follow one from the other with disconcerting ease

5. Certain cultural metaphors, drawn from sports, disease, sex, and violence, are frequently called forth to enliven the dull and banal.

(See Richard Lanham's *Revising Prose* for a similar list of features that characterize what he calls the "Official Style.")

I have said that we must look to the social and economic forces in our society if we are to understand the development of academic doublespeak. I will hazard a simple bifurcation, and suggest that "political and economic causes" can be described in one of two ways, depending upon how we align ourselves with respect to the status quo: (1) There are some people in the United States who have money, power, or both; and (2) there are other people, and a lot more of them, who have little of either.

Our Edwin Newmans and John Simons have generally (but not wisely) cast their lot with the folks who have money and power, and they have chosen to scapegoat the poor and the oppressed as the perpetrators of "bad English" because, in their efforts to "mainstream" themselves and become "upwardly mobile," the powerless frequently carry their dialects into the job market.

I, on the other hand, have chosen to place the blame on the rich and politically powerful, for two reasons. First, they should know better (the rich and the powerful continue to have access to the "best" educations available in this country); and second, I agree with Orwell: Language is "an instrument which we shape for our own purposes" (1973, 169). (And I hope he would forgive my quoting him out of context. I have not, I believe, perverted his implication.)

The rich and the politically powerful are the shapers of language in our society. We hear their voices replayed daily in the various media dedicated to broadcasting their atrocities and inanities. They write the books that so few people can read, and fewer understand. In a literal sense, the rich and powerful dominate the airwaves and, thereby, the information that reaches our minds.

Those of us who have witnessed the commercialization of academia ("the marketplace of ideas") are also aware of the lack of public support for noncommercial university programs. The traditional anti-intellectualism of the U.S. populace, wed to omnivorous materialism, has transformed American universities into elite preserves in which the most highly subsidized research is concentrated on chemical and bacteriological warfare, the creation of more lethal pesticides, and the invention of less and less nutritious junk foods. That academics with some residue of commitment to the inherent value of ideas should attempt to survive by learning to speak the bureaucratic dialect (however ineptly), makes its own kind of warped sense. Universities are now virtually dependent upon the good will of state legislators and foundations to remain open; university faculties are dependent entirely upon those funds for their salaries.

It is easy to understand why academicians would feel compelled to try to do battle with the ignorant on their own linguistic turf: Nonsense begets nonsense. "Pedagese" is, as Kehl observed, "pretentious and dishonest, seeking less to *express* than to *impress*" (152). Paraphrasing William Carlos Williams, Kehl asserts that the problem goes beyond semantic difficulties:

> To write badly is an offense against higher education since the educational system can never be more than a system of words. Distortion of language is both a symptom and a cause of deeper problems in American education. (152)

While we are placing blame and isolating causes and symptoms, there is something more to be considered: By and large, those people who come to wield economic and political power in this country are trained in American universities.

Where, then, does doublespeak begin? From what sources does it draw its sustenance and longevity? I have suggested "lethargic cunning" only half-seriously. More likely, however, I might as well mention pride, greed, cowardice, fear, arrogance, and malice.

The Beast

It would seem, from the preceding discussion, that we are trapped. Call it what you will: a vicious circle; the horns of a dilemma; Scylla and Charybdis. You will doubtless have noticed that I did not, like the journalistic pedagogues, point an accusing finger at my colleagues, the English professors in the United States. No. I am unwilling to castigate those harmless drudges yet again whose fingers are stenotic with the agonies of arthritis from writing uncounted "awks" in the narrow margins of student papers. It would be utterly unsavory of me to point an accusing finger at the dead and dying, the already moribund. We are the easy targets of those casting about for scapegoats. Because we are professionally committed to trying to teach some variety of "good" language use to our students, we are also held accountable when our efforts go awry.

But I am willing to argue that we are not responsible for the fact that our students do not listen to us when they are in our classes. Nor are they, themselves, entirely to blame. Remember, most of the English they hear and read is doublespeak. To them, we must sound like hopeless fools as we inveigh against the excesses of materialism and ignorance. Furthermore, during a time when departmental budgets and staff have been cut, when English courses for university students have been removed from degree requirements, the ranks of university administrators have been bloated with retired officers from the military and management types from the top of the corporate hierarchy. No. English professors cannot even begin to compete successfully with the administrative progeny of the corporations and the military.

But we do still want to eat; we do still believe that we are entitled to survival, however precarious. The result has been the adoption of that social dialect peculiar to the bureaucratic power structure, a dialect popularized and brought to perfection during the years of Nixon's presidential administration.

Unfortunately, English professors have barely managed to master the rather elementary strategies 1 and 2 for doublespeaking, having been brainwashed by their own English professors to believe that the English language does have a system of rules and that words really do mean things. But droning and repetition have proven to be effective defensive ploys in the classroom and in faculty meetings, situations in which we are fairly certain that no one is listening, as the following examples illustrate. (The italics, unless otherwise stated, are mine.)

1.1 Demand from students is still heaviest in the first 5-week summer session, and so most of you *may wish to prefer that.* [Memo to faculty from English department chair]

1.2 You wind up not only trying to teach them grammar, but trying to *instill into* them some sense of the language. [Faculty member in coffee lounge, English department]

1.3 I plan to go thoroughly with them over it. [Faculty member in elevator, English department]

The very harmlessness of such examples may tempt us to overlook the possibility that, if we are talking to each other in the bureaucratic dialect, we are probably talking that way to our students, thereby perpetuating the dull repetitiveness we urge them to abjure. The practiced obsequiousness of the chair's use of both *wish* and *prefer* in 1.1 couches a warning: If you want the extra money for teaching during the summer, you'd better ask for classes in the first five-week session, because those are the ones that students sign up for. Example 1.2 betrays the teacher's lack of "sense of the language," and 1.3, although intelligible, would sound better if reordered: "I plan to go over it thoroughly with them." While the first sentence indicates that the chair was acquiring some facility with the bureaucratic style, the other two examples, I fear, may only show that influences in the classroom are bidirectional, and these teachers are beginning to talk the way their students write.

Other examples of professional doublespeak suggest that some of us have moved into acquisition of strategy 3 (new words) and are experimenting with innovation:

2.1 We have to decide how we want *to impact* on society. [English professor at committee meeting]

2.2 How is *this impacting* going to take place? [Same English professor, same meeting]

2.3 The AAUP will hold a press conference . . . to respond further to the Regents' refusal *to agenda* the AAUP. [Memo to faculty]

2.4 A proposal that first seems acceptable both to federal EEOC authorities and to state insurance regulators has instead *surfaced a basic conflict* between the two. (TIAA/CREF 1981, l)

The common, but nevertheless obnoxious use of *impact* as a verb probably requires no elaboration here. I include two usages by one English professor to show how thoroughly the noun has been re-categorized as a verb. 2.2 exhibits its derived gerundive form, but the simple noun would suffice, and I suggest that such professional attempts at lexical innovation seem to be the result of experiences with bureaucratic agencies. That is, I think we are trying to learn to talk "their language" in an effort to survive the depredations of administrators.

Dependent upon the beneficence of elected legislators, academics have undertaken to learn how to wield the bureaucratic dialect with some fervor. Frequently, however, it is difficult to ascertain whether the utterances produced by these efforts are legitimate doublespeak or typographical errors. Interpretation and classification depends upon the benevolence of the analyst.

3.1 A staff member may leave the university on December 31, and *the position not filled* until March 1. [Memorandum from Vice-Chancellor for Academic Affairs]

3.2 The dreams and proposals that vitalize a department are presented to and interpreted *by the Dean by the Chairperson*. [Memo from Dean of Arts and Sciences, to faculty of English department]

What is one to make of such infelicities in the writing published by university personnel? Is 3.1 merely a typographical error? Did the secretary who typed the memo accidentally leave out *may* and *be* in the second clause of the sentence? Probably not. Such memos are usually dictated by the administrators and the secretary writes the words down verbatim. More likely, the secretary simply typed the memo as it was dictated. Did the vice-chancellor miss the error when proofreading the memo before signing it, or, perhaps, was it signed without any proof-reading at all? Or is this an example of doublespeak? As it stands, the communication is intended to account for the fact that positions within the university may be vacant for as long as two months, and we are expected to identify with the haplessness of the administrator trapped in bureaucratic red tape, who would like to see vacancies filled immedi-ately, but. . . .

The convolutions of 3.2 are engaging, if mindboggling. Here, the dean, waxing eloquent, apparently got carried away with his own rhetoric while extolling the internal evaluation process for departmen-tal chairpersons. The unfortunate result is an unusual sentence in which the agents of both passivized verbs are piled up at the end of the sentence. Again, it is only fair to ask if anyone took the time to proofread the memo before it was mailed out to the faculty. Moving "by the Chairperson" to a position immediately after "are presented to" might make the statement more intelligible, but no more lovely. But what does the sentence mean? The chairperson *presents* "the dreams and proposals that vitalize a department" to the dean, and the dean *interprets* them. The topicalization of those "dreams and proposals" insinuates that such things do find their way into reality in university departments. But if it is left to the dean to "interpret" them, they are by no means realized unless he approves them. It is possible that place-ment of both agents at the end of the sentence, with "the Chairperson" in sentence focus, sandwiches the agency of the dean as interpreter in such a way that he successfully obscures his authority.

In both of these quotes, the problems I have described can be traced back to deletion of agents, a primary characteristic of the bureaucratic dialect. Things happen; no one is responsible. Even in 3.2, where we are given not one but two successive agents, the overriding authority of "the Dean" is downplayed by its positioning.

The essential feature of bureaucratic structures is the facility with which responsibility for decisions can be "lost" as memos descend from the administration to the faculty. Someone "up there" makes decisions, but tracking them through the swamp of truncated passives and nomi-nalizations is exasperating and tiring. Administrators know this well.

4. This increase is dictated primarily by the fact that the premiums depos-ited have not been sufficient to pay for the claims incurred within our program. [Letter from Board of Regents to university employees]

Ever wonder why your insurance premiums are always becoming more and more expensive? Here's the answer. *Primarily* (there are also some other reasons for raising your insurance premium, but we're not going to tell you what they are, and we're asserting that *this* one is the important one) *this fact* (that all of you are sick too much) *dictates* a higher insurance premium. The administrators, we are to understand, had no choice in the matter; it's the fault of the employees, and that's the "fact." This kind of obfuscation, accomplished by using truncated passives and nominalizations to remove human agency, falls somewhere between the condescension signalled by the fake obsequiousness of several previous examples and the euphemism of the next one.

Euphemism is frequently employed by speakers of the bureaucratic dialect to downplay particularly grisly aspects of their endeavors. Syntactic euphemism, a phenomenon created by the syntactic structures favored by users of the bureaucratic dialect, hides both the logical connections and implications of specific statements. What is more, even "good news" can be stated euphemistically, as the following example illustrates.

5. As a result of *the better than expected mortality experience* for the Optional Group Life Insurance Program . . . during the past policy year, . . . [Letter to university faculty from insurance company]

Good news! Because fewer of the staff died last year than we predicted would, we are *lowering* your insurance premium!

The spookiness of this quotation can be attributed to the fact that the writer has combined simple lexical euphemism with syntactic euphemism to give the statement its eerily impersonal tone. Death has become a *mortality experience* that too few of us sought last year, and the complex syntax of the prenominal modifier, *better than expected,* positioned as an attribute of "mortality experience," confounds us with its implications: "better" compared to *what?* Well, compared to what "someone" expected. *What,* exactly, did that someone expect? We'll never know.

English department chairs, eschewing euphemism, prefer to present bad news *and* good news as unpleasantly as possible. The bureaucratic dialect provides many ways of conveying the more subtle nuances of administrative processes in the midst of a depressed job market.

6.1 I am sorry but our New Appointments Committee was not interested at this time, in pursuing further your inquiry about our advertised position, *which has had to exercise a rigorous selection process.* . . . [Letter from the chair of the English department, to a graduate student applying for a job]

6.2 We place a relatively high percentage of our candidates in good positions; that's because we *handtool them before we turn them out.* [Letter from the graduate chair of the English department to a prospective graduate student]

I did not make up these examples. In 6.1, the chair begins forthrightly enough with "I am sorry." The rest of the sentence is a disaster: You see, our New Appointments Committee is not "interested," (but might be at some unspecified point in the future) in giving your application any more consideration, because the *position* that we advertised has "had to exercise a rigorous selection process." See how simple that was? The position, *not* the committee, was doing the selecting. Watch—no people here!

In contrast, the quotation in 6.2 contains one of the most hideous metaphors I have encountered for describing the learning process at the graduate level. And this person was bragging! Here at our English department factory, where we "turn out" students like some folks make cars, students are blank pieces of tanned leather on which the departmental faculty carve and engrave their abstract designs for posterity. As a result of this imprinting process, our graduates get good jobs. (The queasy and sensitive need not apply.)

Sledd would label the examples I have discussed up to this point Somnigraphy—the art of writing as if one were asleep. As academicians strive to fortify their cubbyholes and salaries against inflation, against increased taxation to fund another "war to end all wars," and against the reality of dwindling enrollments, writers in those disciplines with the most to gain from identifying with the "powers that be" have zealously committed themselves to mastering New High Bureaucratian by obscuring any meaning with jargon—and they have succeeded.

7.1 The *division of* elementary and secondary education is *piloting a process* for the evaluation of teacher education programs based on "Program Approval." *This* means that all of the programs in an institution which lead to endorsement for certification must be *officially* approved by the state education agency. . . . The *state* will use a system of spot-checking transcripts to determine whether or not the institution is operating within the approved program. [Memo from university Department of Education]

7.2 The university, he says, was "faced with some tough personnel decisions. To develop the research and graduate orientation that we felt was necessary, we needed a different set of procedures." Under the new procedures, he says as many as fifty-six full professors are involved in the reviewing. [University administrator]

Careful reading of 7.1 reveals that no human beings will be involved in whatever it is that is going to be done. The "division" will "pilot" the process, and this process will be "based on 'Program Approval.'" What "this" might "mean" remains a mystery.

The speaker of 7.2 is merely a pseudo-agent in the quotation, telling us that "the university"—not its administrators—was "faced with some tough personnel decisions." (Abstract group nouns seem to be having a hard time these days.) We are to be comforted by the fact that the new procedures for making personnel decisions will involve "as many as fifty-six full professors." Why don't I think this gesture of encouraging "faculty input" (as they call it) is going to be an improvement? Yet, the tone of the quotation indicates that the administrator is working hard to present this fact as though the faculty should be grateful.

> 8.1 It is not difficult to see what is wrong in most educational environments, and much has already been done to design materials which make learning as easy as possible and to construct contingencies, in the classroom and elsewhere, which give students powerful reasons for getting an education. (Skinner 1971,156–57)

> 8.2 No geneticist today, I imagine, accepts the hypothesis of the autonomous corpuscular gene; and the genotypic endowment of the individual can only affect the phenotypic resultant through the mediation of innumerable obscure biochemical steps. (Burt 1958, 10)

These passages from the writings of B. F. Skinner and Cyril Burt illustrate the kind of fatuous language that frequently passes for "serious" scholarship and provide evidence for the hypothesis that doublespeak *is* the overt manifestation of doublethink. Reduced to plain English, Skinner asserts that making learning easier gives students "powerful" incentives for going to school, while Burt performs a verbal shrug: the fact is, we don't know anything about the role of genes in producing talented people. The entire phrase, *through the mediation of innumerable obscure biochemical steps,* is throw-away language used to cloak ignorance in indecipherable multisyllabic words. It makes sense, but means only, "I don't know."

Conclusion

This has been a depressing article to write. There have been several times when, faced with the necessity of making some comment on particular examples, I just wanted to throw up my hands and groan. University faculty are in dire straits these days, especially English teachers. We are trapped between the corporate myopia of administrators and cultural myopia of our students. We are trapped by doublespeak, and I see no way to get out of that trap.

We may work and talk and encourage our students *not* to use doublespeak, but even the ones who are listening will remind us that they, too, want to survive. They do not believe they can survive unless they learn how not to say what they mean. I remember one young woman, enrolled in a composition course I was teaching at the University of Georgia, who approached me after class one day and informed me that she had been convinced for most of the quarter that I was crazy. She possessed, however, enough sense of fairness to put to the test my assertions regarding uses of the truncated passive, nominalizations, *be* as a main verb, and prenominal modification. A philosophy course she was taking required a five-page paper, which she'd carefully written in the bureaucratic style I had been inveighing against. She showed me the conclusive evidence: An *A +* from the philosophy professor, who praised her "clarity and insightfulness." She said, "You're right. All anyone expects from us is bullshit."

Unfortunately, the situation also eventually requires them to learn doublethink in order to effectively doublespeak. Although most of them already have doublethink down pat by the time we see them, they do have trouble with the subtleties of doublespeak, and frequently confuse Somnigraphy with NHB. I do my best to help them distinguish between the two dialects.

As this point, I could muster my idealism and integrity (I still have some of both, I believe) and press on my readers the urgency of actively combating doublespeak wherever we find it; of teaching our students to write clearly and succinctly; of watchdogging the writing of our colleagues in other disciplines. Such a conclusion is fairly standard in the literature, and the final sentence of D. G. Kehl's article is typically hortatory:

> If, as Aldous Huxley wrote, "Most of our mistakes are fundamentally grammatical," and if altering our syntax can alter our intellect, as Yeats wrote, then lucid, forceful expression—in what we practice as well as what we teach—is at once a sobering responsibility and a challenging opportunity. (156)

In an atypically optimistic conclusion, James Sledd called the final section of his article "What To Do," and went so far as to list seven "things to do" for the classroom English teacher, but he also prefaced his suggestions with a few words of caution:

> The effect will be best if teachers consciously recognize the frustrations and contradictions which life in a sick world imposes on them

> [schoolchildren]. Because our ruling class is unfit to rule, our standard language lacks authority; and because our society has been corrupted by the profit-seeking of technology run wild, an honest teacher cannot exercise his [sic] normal function of transmitting to the young the knowledge and values of their elders. (455)

I, for one, am no longer "challenged" by the effort of confronting my students' apathy and ignorance, and, although I am willing to accept some measure of responsibility for educating the young, I think it's time we tempered our idealism with recognition of the social realities that surround us and interfere with our best efforts in the classroom. How can we successfully combat the depredations of language when they're so constant? Where will it get us? Something grotesque *has* happened to the English language; somehow the lexical and syntactic rules which used to signal some connection between the speaker, the hearer, and the "world," have become detached from whatever communicative function they might once have served. It's as though the rules which once secured coherence and intelligibility have been torn loose from their roots in the ground of communication.

My students are not interested in learning how to "communicate"; they want me to teach them how to *pretend* to communicate. They think that Ronald Reagan, Alexander Haig, and Howard Cosell make meaning when they speak. They think that B. F. Skinner is right, and that whatever someone in authority says to them must be *true*. They do not yet understand that words create reality; that words have tangible, often long-lasting *effects* on people's lives. As skilled as they are at lying and conning, they do not yet realize that people in authority *also* tell lies.

Furthermore, my own cynicism goes beyond even James Sledd's. I am not committed to teaching my students the "knowledge and values of their elders," because the traditional values and information to which he refers are tainted by misogyny, racism, and classism. Will substituting Plato for Reagan, or Cicero for Alexander Haig, as "authority figures," somehow awaken my students to the dangers inherent in both doublethink and doublespeak? I doubt it. All four men belong to the same prolonged tradition: Protect the status quo; protect the white, male, heterosexual tradition. Women need not apply; blacks need not apply; Third World people need not apply; those "hungry masses yearning to breathe free" need not apply.

But wait! Am I, like Sledd, to be accused of believing "that English teachers can change the world by political action, perhaps by revolution" (455)? I should hope not! Like Sledd, I, too, would "resent the suggestion that I consider English teachers brave enough to start a revolution" (455). As a profession, we are already too stenotropic to compete successfully. Unlike Sledd, I did not always know this; I cannot go on to claim that "I have never entertained such a false and subversive idea in my life" (456). I did once believe that we were not only capable of starting a revolution, but that we would happily see it through to completion. Orwell believed that thinking clearly "is a necessary first step towards political regeneration" (Orwell 1973, 169), and I agree. But I no longer believe that we can take that "first step." The rewards for doublethink/doublespeak are too great; the risks of being "out of order" are too terrifying.

Works Cited

Burt, Cyril. "The Inheritance of Mental Ability."*American Psychologist* 13 (1958): 1–15.

Kehl, D. G. "The Doublespeak of Academia." In *Speaking of Words: A Language Reader*. Edited by James MacKillop and Donna Woolfolk Cross. New York: CBS College Publishing, 1982.

Lanham, Richard. *Revising Prose*. New York: Scribner, 1979.

Orwell, George. "Politics and the English Language." In *Norton Reader*, 168–80. 3rd shorter edition. Edited by Arthur M. Eastman. New York: Norton, 1973.

Sledd, James H. "Doublespeak: Dialectology in the Service of Big Brother." *College English* 33 (January 1972): 439–56.

Skinner, B. F. *Beyond Freedom and Dignity*. New York: Knopf, 1971.

TIAA/CREF. *The Participant*. Newsletter of The Teacher's Insurance and Annuity Association (TIAA) and College Retirement Equities Fund (CREF). March, 1981: 1.

17 Sensationspeak in America

Roy F. Fox
Boise State University

TABLOIDS TERRORIZE SUPERMARKET PSYCHO

Wednesday, May 26—I'm standing in line at the supermarket. The bright, gleaming one with wide aisles, forty-two varieties of cereal, a salad bar, a deli bar, even a candy bar. Now that all of his 116 purchases are bagged and waiting, the shopper in front of me begins fumbling for his checkbook.

I turn to the rack of tabloids beside me. Hmm . . . says right here that Fergie, the "Porky Princess," has been sent to a shrink so she can control her midnight binges on kidney pie. But wait, why doesn't she try the new Tapeworm Diet extolled on another page? These new diet capsules, filled with powdered gelatin and tapeworm eggs, hatch inside your stomach and attach themselves to your intestine. Although they can be uncomfortable, they must never be confused with Oriental Brain Worms, because they are now "The Deadliest Threat Since AIDS." But if Fergie wants the quickest way to thindom, she should follow in the footsteps of the "Woman Swallowed by Escalator." Just as I near the cashier and place my bag of avocados on the counter, I spot another headline: "Yuppies Going Ape Over Shrunken Heads."

WOMAN UNEARTHS ANCIENT CURSE
IN KITCHEN PANTRY
CRAZED NEPHEW LATEST VICTIM

Monday, June 8—Once I recovered from my bout with tabloid trauma, I wondered what old tabloids were like. But stores in four states that

Reprinted from *English Journal* 77 (March 1988) by permission of the author and the publisher.

specialize in old magazines and newspapers do not carry back issues of any tabloids. One clerk gently told me, "Everyone throws them away."

"Is this what you're looking for?" My aunt stands in her kitchen, holding a wrinkled, yellow paper. "I used it to line the bottom shelf in the pantry," she says half apologetically as she hands me the paper, adding, "otherwise I would've thrown it away. . . ."

"Of course . . ." I reply, dazzled at the prospect of an authentic antique, to say nothing of its two-inch headline proclaiming, "Hitler Is Alive" (Turner 1982, 2). I caress the dry newsprint as if it were a vase from the Ming Dynasty. Then I spot the paper's date: July 6, 1982.

ADOLF HITLER—STILL CRAZY AFTER ALL THESE YEARS

> In Pseudocommunication, the Symbol System employed tends toward a confusion of symbols and signs, implying (but not establishing) close relationships between symbol and referent by employing symbols that allow for ambiguity in interpretation.
>
> —Terence P. Moran

Amazing. I thought the old Hitler-is-Alive-and-Well-in-Argentina story went out with Spike Jones and Pinky Lee. Who could possibly put any credence in this line? Then it dawned on me: if George Burns and Ronald Reagan were (and still are) going strong, then why not that lovable ol' Nazi?

According to the article, at the age of ninety-three and "as alert and ruthless as ever," Adolf Hitler, being kept alive by an aide, masterminded Argentina's invasion of the Falklands as well as an outbreak of Middle East fighting. Hitler accomplished this turmoil by "goading" Argentina's right wing junta into occupying the Falklands to "foment world chaos and pave the way for the rebirth of his monstrous Third Reich." How this demonic domino theory is to work is never made clear. But what is made clear by the third paragraph is the tabloid's frame of reference: "[Hitler's] top aide is Dr. Joseph Mengele, the infamous 'Angel of Death' so chillingly portrayed by Gregory Peck in 'The Boys From Brazil.'" The referent here is not history, but Hollywood. And so it goose-steps. . . .

When the paper is opened, the layout of the Hitler scoop blitzkriegs across two pages. More large headlines followed by three exclamation points. One quarter of the first page contains a simple line map of North and South America. A swastika (about half the size of the drawing of South America) appears on the map, and a large arrow points from the swastika to Argentina. The caption under the map states, "HITLER IS HERE—in a Suburb of Buenos Aires." Another quarter of the same page contains a photo of a nondescript man identified as a "Nazi hunter" who is displaying a large photograph identified as Hitler's assistant. But the man in the photo looks much like a young Hitler.

The opposite page of this fascist feature contains three illustrations. The upper right corner of the page is adorned with a photo of Hitler ("at the height of his power") giving the Nazi salute with an outstretched right arm which breaks out of the photo's boundary and stretches halfway across the page. Just under Hitler's outstretched palm is a crude drawing, an *"identikit* drawing specially composed by police," which purports to show Hitler as he looks today. The sketch reveals Hitler as we all know him, only with fewer hairs on his head, a few more crow's feet, and a slightly more sinister expression on his face. But all in all, he remains the same ol' smooth-talkin' panzer-puss.

Below these two illustrations is a photo of one of the psychics mentioned in the article; he holds a long and pointed dagger. The knife is slanting in the same direction as Hitler's saluting, outstretched arm in the photo above. Curiously, the psychic wears what appears to be a military uniform, epaulets and all. This man, too, resembles Hitler. Hence, of the three photos and one sketch in the layout, only one of them is actually Hitler. But they all reek of Adolf.

> In the long run only he will achieve basic results in influencing public opinion who is able to reduce problems to the simplest terms.
>
> —Joseph Goebbels

In keeping with the many illustrations in tabloids, much of the accompanying text stays at a low level of abstraction. Everything must be literalized; everything must be concretized. In one tabloid, even my horoscope, traditionally the most general of seers, states, "Attend a barbecue July 13." In the Hitler article, we are informed that the Führer will not merely continue rooting for the Third Reich for a long time to come, but that he will "live to be 150." Similarly, psychics in this article cannot have fragmented visions or intuitions of an abstract nature. Instead, one psychic's meditation brought a mysterious Nazi dagger in the mail from Argentina—a dagger which "actually touched Hitler's hands within the last two months." These psychics also demonstrated their mental prowess by picking up a pendulum and swinging it over a map. When the pendulum stopped over Argentina, one of the psychics received nothing like an impulse or an unshaped thought, but rather, as he states, "saw swastikas moving past me, then eagles and Iron Crosses." Mercy. Sounds worse than a Driver's Ed training film.

Finally, we are to believe Hitler is thriving because some unidentified folks in West Germany ("a highly respected electronic voice phenomena study group") have the Führer's voice *on tape*. What's more, we are told, the voice is speaking German.

SCIENTIFIC DATA UNCOVERS
THIRD REICH TRANSVESTITE

In this Hitler exposé, the omniscient narrator blends with outside experts—experts, that is, in "private and non-sharable ways of knowing" (Moran 1979, 189). So many psychics float in and out and above this article, that at times it becomes difficult to discern just when the writer is speaking and when a psychic is speaking. In the fog they merge and become one voice.

When it *is* possible to detect the writer's voice, he seems to know things that no human could really know. The author states that "A whole new generation of Nazi fanatics [is] prepared to lay down their lives for him [Hitler]." Really now. Even granting the author some minor concessions—that Adolf *is indeed* at home in an Argentine suburb watching old reruns of "Hogan's Heroes," that Adolf *does indeed* have multitudes of goose-stepping groupies serving him—how can the author speak for *all* members of an entire generation? And how does the author really know if even one neophyte Nazi would lay down his or her life for Aging Adolf, until that moment of truth arrives?

The proof for this article's assertions comes primarily from one psychic corroborating another psychic, and so on. To prove that Hitler's heart still beats for Hamburg, the sequence goes like this: First, two psychics, independent of each other, receive the same message that Hitler is alive. Next, a third psychic, "one of the world's greatest experts on the paranormal," is brought into the action so that he can verify the first two psychics. The way "the world's greatest" accomplishes his assignment is to consult *his own* "specially trained" psychics. Then, an outside expert from Washington University states that

> At 93, you have a very select group of people. . . . The very fact that they have lived so long indicates they are in special mental and physical shape. (Turner 1982, 3)

This expert's statement, "The very fact that they have lived so long," assumes Hitler's existence *for* the reader. But since the expert speaks of "they" and not "he" (Hitler), no lie has really been told. Following this source is the group of people who have tape recorded Hitler's voice.

By article's end, yet another psychic corroborates all the preceding ones and concludes that Hitler is indeed being kept alive "by using hormones from young women." Even assuming that all this "evidence" is correct, what we end up with is the notion that in a tract home somewhere in suburban Buenos Aires, lives a fiendish 93-year-old Führer with breasts.

SPACE ALIENS LED BY JOAN CRAWFORD INVADE SUPERMARKET

According to Abrams (1982), the *National Enquirer* has well over fourteen million readers and an annual revenue of $130 million. The paper's television ad campaign is comparable to Crest and Pepsi-Cola, and its weekly sales are surpassed only by *TV Guide*.

The seeds of this success were sown about twenty years ago when the *Enquirer*'s owner "purged" the tabloid of much of its blood and gore. This mopping up of excess blood helped enable the *Enquirer* to be sold to supermarkets and drugstores, which received 22 percent of the paper's cover price (Abrams 1982, 27). Today, the *Enquirer* and other tabloids can be found in over 170,000 supermarkets and drugstores, usually very near the checkout stands where you can't possibly avoid them while waiting in line. By the time the clerk and the assistant manager explain to the shopper ahead of you that they cannot cash a check from an out-of-state institution called "Steve's Bank and Trust," you have already read the tabloid's first four pages, and you must squelch a desire to buy it so you can find out whether or not the aliens from outer space got a blind date with Vanna White.

Other methods the *Enquirer* reportedly used to enter mainstream America are both sensationally shrewd and tabloid-tacky. For example, the *Enquirer* gave free subscriptions to the wives of food-store executives and big advertisers. The *Enquirer* also made a film, narrated by Chet Huntley, that contained endorsements from Hubert Humphrey, Barry Goldwater, Bob Hope, Billy Graham, and Joan Crawford (Abrams 1982, 29). (I now have a clearer understanding of how, from the late sixties through the seventies, America's foreign and domestic policy was influenced.) I contacted the *Enquirer*'s advertising director to find out if these luminaries were paid for their testimonials. The hostile voice on the other end of the phone said, "They did it for free." To double-check, I contacted Barry Goldwater's office and no one there could confirm or deny the ad director's statement. (Extremism in the defense of extremism is no vice.)

MIRACLE READING DIET
FUELS PSYCHIC'S PERVERTED POWERS

To explain the *Enquirer's* and other similar tabloids' popularity requires just as much speculation as displayed by the gaggle of psychics who figured out the Nazi-inspired Falklands fiasco. Let the pendulum swing.

First, most people would agree that tabloids are marginally amusing and enjoyable. A sugared prescription to break the routine of daily life, maybe the bizarre contents of a tabloid can function not as a mirror of reality, but as an easily digestible substitution for it—at the very least, a morsel of dessert after a bland meal. The workhorse that provides much of the tabloid's appeal—even if that workhorse is Mr. Ed—is the headline. Though often misleading, tabloid headlines are actually mini-stories in themselves because they frequently tell readers how to respond: *Cybill's Secret Nightmare; Jessica Hahn's Shocking Secret.* Also, tabloid headlines can entertain readers by using alliteration and puns: *Terrifying Encounter Turns Trucker into a Whimpering Wreck.* It makes sense then that, like so many of us, tabloid readers get much of their news from television and radio, because news stories transmitted through the electronic media are essentially headlines. A hot-wired nation with a fast-food stomach and a credit-card soul is also likely to have a headline mentality.

Another possible reason for their incredible popularity is that tabloids provide an outlet for our need to snicker at the glamorous and rich and famous who, in whatever escapades of crime and sex, have descended to the same lower station in life as we have. After all, in the unjust world of plain folks, where champagne and cash never flow and klieg lights never glow, doesn't a pound of flesh and a glass of blue-blood really hit the spot? And for only about seventy cents, isn't it comforting to know that even Cosby had trouble controlling his kids? That even Joan Collins has trouble maintaining her marriage?

In addition to this "vindication" that attracts readers, it is possible that we are drawn to tabloid traumas because we need assurance that "things could always be worse" for us. And to maintain this advantage, the worse things get for the average reader, the worse things must necessarily get for the folks within the tabloid pages. If your neighbor has trouble losing weight, he can take solace in Julius Riedler, whose wife stated that he "got so hungry on a sauerkraut diet that he grabbed two fish from our little girl's goldfish bowl and ate them right there in front of her" (Heidt 1987, 23).

At the opposite end of the spectrum, maybe the tabloids attract huge crowds because our society, in many ways, pressures its members to deaden their senses. Isolated in a technological tenement, we take drugs, alcohol, deodorants, creams, and even wear headsets, just so we can stifle or kill any discordant human sense. Maybe we turn to tabloids for relief from a lonely and sanitized world, so that we may vicariously glory in the parading about of *other* people's senses, of *other* people's humanness.

Finally, maybe another reason for the popularity of the tabloid— and its general acceptance—is the benign tone of its language. In a disarmingly simple way, tabloid language assumes from the outset that its readers will have a substantial degree of trust in its words. The tone of its language is personal; famous people are referred to by their first names. Its language is almost always ultimately optimistic. Tabloid readers may believe pretty much all the paper says, or believe only part of what the paper says, or believe none of it. But in any of these cases, readers likely are not worried, for the tone of the language is so harmless, so innocuous, so simple. And, I might venture, if readers do not seriously object to what they perceive to be half-truths or outright lies, the basis has been laid and the climate has been created for a cautious acceptance, for a kind of pseudo-authenticity that could possibly grow into eventual full-fledged belief.

Readers who are conscious of language may figure, "So what? I read nonfiction novels and I watch docudramas on television. And most of all, what used to *sound* like truth from Washington often turns out to be lies. So if I'm gonna be hoodwinked, I might as well be taken in by language I understand the first time I read it—and be entertained to boot. So what's the big deal, huh?"

EUPHEMOIDS BLUDGEON CAMPER IN NATIONAL PARK

Tuesday, July 9—A week ago I abandoned my stack of tabloids to go camping. It is now late afternoon and I am driving on Highway 20 towards Arco, Idaho. In fact, I'm driving through the U.S. Department of Energy's Idaho National Engineering Laboratory (INEL), formerly the National Reactor Testing Station—what locals call "The Site." The area is a flat, 570,000 acres of sagebrush and sand, an arid climate where rivers disappear into lava beds.

In the distance, far off the main road, are groups of nondescript buildings, towers and domes, each complex separated from the next by vast stretches of desert. INEL concerns itself with breeder reactors, nuclear submarines ("naval propulsion," according to INEL's brochure) and "waste management." The INEL brochure also carries a photo of this "waste," which reveals rows upon rows of neatly stacked metal cans. The photo's caption reads, "RWMC Transuranic Storage Area." What am I expecting? That they would caption the photo with "Ten Thousand Cans of Highly Radioactive Stuff We Don't Know What to Do With"? I drive farther and pass a group of buildings with a sign that says, "Argonne West." Sounds like a plush apartment complex for retired joint chiefs of staff. I have also learned that INEL has been designated a "National Environmental Research Park." But where are the rangers? The campgrounds? The pit toilets?

I drive on, and in the approaching dusk, other words come to mind in a flood of contaminated verbiage: *abnormal occurrence* (accident); *energetic disassembly* (explosion); *uncontrollable power surges to the point of criticality* (explosion); *health effects* (death).

We all carry around self-evident truths—things that when our souls have been split, scraped, and skewered, we still hold to be right. And one such common truth today is that even if institutions like tabloids (or television or advertising) *do* use standard propaganda devices such as "big lies," misleading headlines, omniscient narrators, allness orientation, repetition, and association, what they do in their quest for sales is less harmful than what nuclear advocates do in their quest for "defense." Not to worry, the reasoning goes: tabloids and television may contribute to a climate of unconsciousness, but at least they won't fry us in a radioactive skillet.

But are we able to shed the influence of tabloids and other media whenever we grapple with issues like nuclear power? Are we able to recognize, evaluate, and act upon these issues? In the blur of twentieth-century life, do language, thought, and action quietly reside in separate boxes, each neatly wrapped and tied with string?

And will it be easier for us to be poisoned and fried in a nonthinking climate? First, ask Winston Smith.

Works Cited

Abrams, Bill. "National Enquirer Starts Drive to Lure Big-Time Advertisers." *The Wall Street Journal*, 18 Mar. 1982. Western ed.: Sec. 2:27, 29.

Goebbels, Joseph. *The Goebbels Diaries*, 56. Edited and translated by Louis Lochner. Garden City, New York: Doubleday, 1948.

Heidt, Werner. "Dieting Hubby Goes Nuts and Drives Wife Bananas." *Weekly World News,* 20 Oct. 1987: 23.

Moran, Terence P. "Propaganda as Pseudocommunication." *ETC.: A Review of General Semantics* 36, no. 2 (1979): 188–190.

Turner, John. "Hitler Is Alive." *The National Examiner,* 6 July 1982: 2–3.

U.S. Department of Energy. "Idaho National Engineering Laboratory." Pamphlet no. BO 47-0382-R-5M.

18 The Pop Grammarians— Good Intentions, Silly Ideas, and Doublespeak

Charles Suhor
National Council of Teachers of English

The pop grammarians mean well. All they are asking is that people stop talking and writing in nonstandard usage, clichés, jargon, and other unworthy language. Never mind that they disagree wildly among themselves as to which usages are nonstandard, what constitutes a cliché, where legitimate technical language leaves off and jargon begins. Never mind that when they quote scholarly sources at all, their sources disagree on the very points in dispute. The pop grammarians mean well in that they believe that somewhere, out there, there is a best way to say just about everything, if people only would listen to reason.

If you describe the pop grammarians as naïve, expose their erroneous historical arguments, or point to their inconsistencies and flimsy logic, you're liable to be called a linguistic anarchist. But my goodness, they do say some silly things. John Simon described the use of *I* in the objective case as a fickle linguistic innovation, despite the thoroughly respectable history of that usage, easily found in the Oxford English Dictionary, among other places. Thomas Middleton denounced the content of John Mellon's research summary on writing and grammar because he found the style jargonish; indeed, Middleton suggested that Mellon leave the profession. The late Theodore Bernstein, alone a language scholar among the pop grammarians, denied that he called nonstandard usages "good" and "bad," even as he used those very terms in his syndicated "Bernstein on Words" column. Richard Mitchell claimed a direct causal relationship between nonstandard usage and the Three Mile Island accident, reasoning that someone carelessly schooled in grammar probably would be careless enough to muck up a nuclear reactor.

Some of this silliness is laid bare in the pages of journals like *Esquire* and *Saturday Review*. Other examples were included in letters from the

©Copyright 1984 by *VERBATIM,* The Language Quarterly. Used by Permission.

pop grammarians themselves, in response to my queries over the years. Writing letters to pop grammarians isn't just a matter of intellectual jousting; it is a way of lowering the ego stakes in discussion of the volatile issues at hand. Without a wide public audience to dazzle, a flamboyant writer will sometimes approach questions with a bit less swagger. This was certainly the case with Theodore Bernstein and Thomas Middleton. (In fact, Middleton apologized for the arrogance of his comment about Mellon.) At the very least, the pop grammarians who respond to well-reasoned letters are forced to whip up newer and ever more tenuous rationalizations for their positions.

So far, though, I have been dealing only with good intentions and silly ideas—neither of which is doublespeak. By definition, doublespeak involves "deliberate distortion"—or in Bruce Reeves' phrase, "active use of language to hide the truth." If the pop grammarians were *merely* earnestly dogmatic and grossly inaccurate, there would be no call for a chapter about them in a book on doublespeak. So I will move to my assignment here, relegating to the bibliography (especially Baron, 1982; Lutz, 1981; Quinn, 1980; Wolk, 1972) commentaries on the pop grammarian as linguistic/historical dunce.

I will concentrate on six doublespeak techniques used by pop grammarians, citing examples along the way. An element of deceit or conscious retreat from rational investigation is embedded in each of the techniques. They are (1) the overloaded metaphor; (2) bogus ambiguity; (3) the lucky exception; (4) the unfortunate exception; (5) cubing the opposition; and (6) antiscience.

1. In *the overloaded metaphor,* the pop grammarian uses analogy—certainly a legitimate rhetorical device—but tries to invest it with disproportionate argumentative power. Cleverness, not a demonstration of the aptness of the analogues, must carry the argument. For example, there is some wit in John Simon's comparisons of nonstandard English to a life-threatening fever; of a rhododendron, sprouting flowers in accordance with its nature, to a flawless speaker spouting nominatives where nominatives belong. But Simon fails to show, through historical analysis or logical argument, that the terms of his metaphors relate to the circumstances he is trying to characterize.

Richard Mitchell, who calls himself the Underground Grammarian, actually invents a bungling primitive tribe called the Jiukiukwe to warn his readers about the dangers of using the passive voice. I hesitate to call this extended metaphor clever, but Mitchell is clearly having one hell of a good time with it. Because the nincompoops in his allegory use the passive voice, they are a passive people. They lack technology, sophistication, and common sense. So it will be with us, if we continue our wasty, passive ways instead of putting those actor-subjects up front. (Perhaps we and the Jiukiukwe will contract Simon's life-threatening fever, to boot.)

Gentlemen, you can only get so much mileage out of a unicorn; so many real toads out of imaginary gardens. It is shallow, and in the long run unconvincing, to overwork metaphors in argumentative discourse. As Sir Philip Sydney said, "The poet affirmeth nothing."

2. The *bogus ambiguity* technique is the pop grammarians' way of demonstrating that usages they don't like will create semantic ambiguity. In *Strictly Speaking*, Edwin Newman claims to be baffled by a sentence such as "Hopefully, something will happen" (33). Who, he wonders, is doing the hoping in such an utterance? Will something happen in a hopeful manner? Is a puzzlement.

No native speaker can honestly pretend that such a sentence is ambiguous. The sentence is as clear (and structurally as valid) as "Certainly, something will happen," which apparently doesn't bother Newman. He just happens to dislike "hopefully" as a sentence modifier, so he cooks up some ambiguity to justify his position. Irrelevantly, Newman makes negatives of the first two words, driving his point home by noting that people don't say "Hopelessly, nothing will happen" (34). (If you're keeping score on the "hopefully" debate, know that the cons are Newman, Simon, Jacques Barzun, and William Zinsser. The pros include Bernstein, William Safire, Jim Quinn, and most post-1970 dictionaries.) John Simon strains mightily in *Paradigms Lost* to invent a sentence in which a substitution of the nominative *she* for the objective *her* might result in a misunderstanding: "Would you rather that I take you or she?" (21). When I debated Simon at Tulane University in March 1981, he invented an absurd sentence in which failure to observe the standard forms of *lie* and *lay* supposedly led to an obscene interpretation: "Last Sunday I laid in bed for several hours."

I sometimes think Simon receives sentences one at a time from random sources, or finds them tucked individually in envelopes left on his doorstep. In any real communication setting, the context would clearly reveal, even to Simon, whether the *laid* of his sentence meant "rested" or "screwed around." And both the context and the stress would reveal who is the taker and who is taken in his improbable *Paradigms* sentence. (Stress one: would you rather *I* take you, or *she?*" Stress two: "would you rather I take *you*, or *she?*")

The question of clarity in human interaction is an important one, so the pop grammarians are wise to try to link essentially irrelevant questions of usage to problems of ambiguity. But their methods are fraudulent. Garbled syntax is confusing; so is poor development of ideas in a conversation or essay; so are pronunciations from unfamiliar dialects, at least until one's ear grows attuned. But only in the world of textbook examples and pop grammarians' analyses do we find rampant cognitive confusion over the "misuse" of *hopefully*, *lie* and *lay*, *she* and *her*.

3. In *cubing the opposition*, one makes a point; the pop grammarian ridicules it by raising it to the third power. Theodore Bernstein was one of the first to cube the legitimate feminist arguments against sexism in language. In a 1976 "Bernstein on Words" column, he evoked images of a chaotic world in which, among other things, Ann Speakman would technically have to change her name to "Ann Speakperson." I have since heard other examples of the manhole/personhole, woman/woperson variety—but always from people who don't like to pursue problems of sexist language beyond jocular attempts at cubing the opposition.

At the Tulane debate with John Simon, I praised a third-grade student's stunning image—"Flowers feel like rain"—as a creative response to a bland writing assignment, and I criticized her teacher's niggling red-pencil tactics (Suhor, 1975b). Simon cubed the point by saying that the child's metaphor (besides being dumb luck) should not prompt us to "proclaim her the new Marianne Moore" and "fall at her feet in adoration." I have to admit that his comment was amusing, but the idea of declaring the child a genius was his, not mine. By exaggerating my modest claim in an erudite way, Simon avoided addressing the issues I had raised—viz., children's capacity for creating metaphor, and the effects of empty formalistic feedback.

Note that cubing the opposition is not the same as the legitimate rhetorical technique of stating the opposition's argument forcefully, then disassembling it piece by piece. Nor is it the same as bald ridicule, name-calling, or other covert devices usually woven into the pop grammarian's discourse (and mine). Cubing involves adding amusing features to the opposing argument, features that were not there in the first place, to achieve a humorous distortion.

4. *The lucky exception* is the pop grammarian's way of dealing with evidence that speakers designated as "unskilled" can actually express themselves with clarity and invention. If nonstandard dialect speakers come up with interesting figures of speech or unusual turns of phrase, if they advance ideas cogently in their own dialects, the pop grammarians will explain these events as isolated incidents or charming

flukes. For them, nonstandard English is ipso facto unsuited to the expression of complex ideas and sensibilities.

There is no empirical basis for the lucky exception claim, and it is clear that John Simon and Edwin Newman do not spend a great deal of time sampling the nonstandard language of, say, jazz musicians or ghetto youth. But Simon *does* have an overloaded metaphor to explain lucky exceptions. A clumsy dancer, he says, will in the course of inept fumbling sometimes stumble luckily over a new step. This is different from the experienced dancer who, working from a deep understanding of the art, acts consciously to expand its horizons.

The metaphor is interesting, but its terms are not referential to their analogues, i.e., the way people make language in the real world. Teachers and researchers have long known that many students from nonstandard dialect communities are capable of thoughtful, powerful expression in their native dialects, and that a command of standard usage in no way guarantees clear or imaginative use of language.

Nor can it be counted as mere luck, as Simon suggested, that a third grader would come up with an expression like "Flowers feel like rain." Admittedly, children's metaphors are probably rooted in lack of differentiation among elements in their experience rather than in the creative re-fusion represented by adults' poetic imagery. But metaphorical expression can be nurtured among children, as evidenced by poet Kenneth Koch's work, numerous Poets-in-the-Schools programs, and parents' and researchers' observations of children's language. But Simon rarely deals with informed testimony or research data—hence, the convenience of the lucky exception claim.

Edwin Newman treats lucky exceptions with patronizing good humor. In *Strictly Speaking* he is tickled, really, over colorful expressions uttered by a union leader, a cab driver, Harry Truman, a gardener, and other no-class types. Their deviant language—sometimes errors, sometimes highly memorable personal statements—is in the world for Newman's entertainment and smarmy commentary. When a bozo talks to Newman about teachers and says "Them is my chief dread," Newman remarks, "There is no way to improve on that" (6).

5. The *unfortunate exception* is alter ego to the lucky exception. In *Paradigms*, John Simon speaks of "the giants of the English tongue who preceded us, all of those great writers and speakers who were . . . in the ballgame that counts" (147). When someone points out that these giants used virtually every nonstandard form that the pop grammarians consider to be destructive of civilized communication, Simon talks about "slips" and "lapses," atypical events that can be dismissed as if they had never occurred (36).

In a different context, I once tested the unfortunate exception idea (Suhor, 1975a). After noticing that several well-known essayists used clichés now and then, I decided to find out whether or not these apparent slip-ups were truly unusual. So I proceeded to analyze some of my favorite prose stylists disrespectfully, i.e., as if they had punched me in the face the night before.

My cliché hunt revealed that E.B. White's essays were well laced with phrases like *when I first laid eyes on it* and *a tremendous shot in the arm.* I found that William Buckley used clichés like *Passing along the torch, an air of finality,* and *we look forward to the experience.* Tom Wolfe saw things *as clear as day,* was *profoundly moved,* and was willing to *stand up and be counted.* It would seem, then that respected writers from both the past and present use language far more playfully and freely than we normally admit. Excellent writers apparently are confident enough to use nonstandard forms and commonplaces when doing so works well within the overall texture of a work.

Pop grammarians, being committed to the notion of perfect expression, often feel obliged to indulge in public breast-beating when "unfortunate exceptions" show up in their own speech. The result of such a mentality is a tortuous self-consciousness that breaks the narrative flow for parenthetical apologies and amendments of previous statements. A gathering of language purists on *The Dick Cavett Show* was an interesting case in point. By the end of an hour, Simon, Agnes de Mille and Edwin Newman were reduced to continuous self-correction as they became increasingly analytical about each sentence they uttered. Instead of exchanging ideas about language in a fluent way, they ended up backtracking and making self-referring comments on their usage. The pop grammarians were gagging on their own obsession with perfection, unable to admit that the inevitable unfortunate exception is a function of the dynamic qualities of human expression, not an effect of Original Sin.

6. *Antiscience* is a recurring theme in the pop grammarians' writing and speech. Sometimes the theme is expressed subtly, as in Simon's *Paradigms Lost* swipe at the lengthy scholarly bibliography appended to CCCC's *Students' Right to Their Own Language* (163–64). At Tulane he declared that language is an art, not a science. Simon was consistent in this: his talk was artful, but he made scant reference to scholarship. He expressed fond hope that research like sociologist William Labov's studies of dialects would be discontinued. He pooh-poohed the idea that useful bibliographies of language research exist. He allowed that he knew of no data on the harmfulness of television but claimed nonetheless that it is a pernicious force.

It has often been said that you can prove anything by citing research. Simon's counter-principle appears to be that you can prove anything, as long as you ignore research.

Richard Mitchell's contempt for scholarship is revealed in dozens of ways. He shows slim understanding of the purposes, history, and procedures of holistic and primary trait test scoring, even as he condemns them. His program for teaching young children to write, described in *Instructor* magazine, flies in the face of virtually all research. ("First, children must learn all the conventions of writing: punctuation, capitalization, spelling"[35]). To him, intellectual rigor is a matter of enforcing the purist view of language and closing one's eyes to linguistic scholarship and the uses of language in the real world.

It is ironic that the pop grammarians claim to be champions of high standards in language, yet they often operate as saboteurs, subverting the communicative functions of language with trashy argumentation—sly irrelevancies, curmudgeonly posturing, and outright grandstanding. Joseph Epstein (1981) put the situation in perspective when he said that people like John Simon give high standards a bad name. He recommended, moreover, that the language purists stop quibbling over minutiae and turn their guns on the real enemy—namely, "deception in its various forms, deliberate, unconscious, and self-. With . . . the wondrous cant from politics and psychology and education, we have all the means at hand to be lied to or to lie convincingly to ourselves" (45). In other words, they should be joining in the war against doublespeak.

Works Cited

Baron, Dennis. *Grammar and Good Taste.* New Haven: Yale University Press, 1982.

Conference on College Composition and Communication (CCCC). "Students' Right to Their Own Language." Special Edition of *College Composition and Communication* 25 (Fall 1974).

Epstein, Joseph. "Why Madame Bovary Couldn't Make Love in the Concrete." *Commentary* 71, no. 2 (1981): 42–47.

Lutz, William. "Politics and the English Language." *Quarterly Review of Doublespeak* 7, no. 4 (1981): 1–3.

Middleton, Thomas. Personal correspondence.

Mitchell, Richard. "We rob students of power when we fail to teach them English." *Instructor* 90, no. 8 (1981): 34–37.

Newman, Edwin. *Strictly Speaking: Will America Be the Death of English.* New York: Bobbs-Merrill, 1974.

Quinn, Jim. *American Tongue and Cheek*. New York: Pantheon, 1980.

Simon, John. *Paradigms Lost*. New York: Crown, 1980.

Suhor, Charles. "Clichés: A Re-Assessment." *College Composition and Communication* 26, no. 2 (1975a): 159–62.

———. "Linda's Re-Write." *Learning* 4 (August-September, 1975b): 20–25.

Wolk, Anthony. "Linguistic and Social Bias in the American Heritage Dictionary." *College English* 33 (1972): 930–35.

Appendix A

Recipients of the George Orwell Award for Distinguished Contribution to Honesty and Clarity in Public Language

The Orwell Award was established in 1974 to recognize each year a work which has made an outstanding contribution to the critical analysis of public discourse.

1988: Donald Barlett and James Steele. Reporters for *The Philadelphia Inquirer.* In a series of articles (April 10–16, 1988), Barlett and Steele revealed how hundreds of deceptive passages in the Tax Reform Act of 1986 granted billions of dollars in tax exemptions to corporations and influential, wealthy individuals, all done through the use of deceptive language.

1987: Noam Chomsky. *On Power and Ideology: The Managua Lectures.* Boston: South End Press, 1987.

1986: Neil Postman. *Amusing Ourselves to Death: Public Discourse in the Age of Show Business.* New York: Elizabeth Sifton/Viking, 1985.

1985: Torben Vestergaard and Kim Schroder. *The Language of Advertising.* New York: Basil Blackwell, 1985.

1984: Ted Koppel, Moderator of ABC-TV program "Nightline." For his long-sustained role as moderator of an important news program which has contributed to the common good by its extensive analysis of topical news. Koppel has been a model of intelligence, informed interest, social awareness, verbal fluency, and fair and rigorous questioning of controversial figures. The national audience, the citizens in this democracy, have benefited from his attempts to seek honesty and openness, clarity and coherence, to raise the level of public discourse.

1983: Haig A. Bosmajian. *The Language of Oppression.* Lanham, Md.: University Press of America, 1983.

197

1982: Stephen Hilgartner, Richard Bell, and Rory O'Connor. *Nukespeak: Nuclear Language, Visions, and Mindset.* San Francisco: Sierra Club Books, 1982.

1981: Dwight Bolinger. *Language: The Loaded Weapon.* New York: Longman, 1980.

1980: Sheila Harty. *Hucksters in the Classroom.* Washington D.C.: Center for Study of Responsive Law, 1979.

1979: Erving Goffman. *Gender Advertisements.* Cambridge: Harvard University Press, 1979.

1978: Sissela Bok. *Lying: Moral Choice in Public and Private Life.* New York: Pantheon, 1978.

1977: Walter Pincus, Reporter for the *Washington Post.* One of those reporters to whom the term 'gadfly' truly applies. The government's attempt to slip the neutron bomb through, unnoticed, in an ERDA appropriations bill was deceptive—and it was caught because this methodical, patient journalist knew his job, knew the jargon.

1976: Hugh Rank. *Intensify/Downplay Approach.* Park Forest, Ill.: Counter-Propaganda Press, 1976.

1975: David Wise. *The Politics of Lying.* New York: Random House, 1973.

Appendix B
Recipients of the Doublespeak Award

The Doublespeak Award is an ironic "tribute" to American public figures who have perpetrated language that is deceptive, evasive, euphemistic, confusing, or self-contradictory. Following George Orwell's intention of exposing inhumane, propagandistic uses of language, the committee restricts the Award to misuses of language with pernicious social or political consequences that are more worthy of censure than the kind of garden-variety jargon, gobbledygook, or solecisms emphasized by many current critics of language.

1988: Secretary of Defense Frank Carlucci
Admiral William Crowe
and Rear Admiral William Fogarty

The language used in the report, *Formal Investigation into the Circumstances Surrounding the Downing of Iran Air Flight 655 on 3 July 1988,* and the language used during the press conference held on 19 August 1988 to release and discuss that report, was filled with the doublespeak of omission, distortion, contradiction, and misdirection. One reporter called the report an "enormous jigsaw puzzle with key pieces missing."

In addition to censoring essential information, such as the names of almost all the participants—including the former commander of the cruiser USS Vincennes—the report also lacks any original source information such as statements by participants and any of the data recorded by the ship's computers.

While the report pretends to be detailed and complete—by giving such information as the air and sea temperatures, the wind speed and direction, the relative humidity, the evaporation duct height, the surface pressure, the visibility estimate, and the ceiling at the time of the shooting—it does not contain something as basic and as important as a map showing the course, over time, of the Vincennes, its sister ships, the Iranian airliner, and the Iranian gunboats. As one reporter noted, such a map would show important information such as

> whether or not the plane was headed directly toward the Vincennes, or if it made any last-minute turn toward the ship that could have been interpreted as a fighter rolling in to attack.

199

Yet Secretary of Defense Frank Carlucci said that

> I believe the facts to the extent they can be known are clearly
> presented in the report. . . . We chose not to withhold anything.

At the news briefing held to release and discuss the report, Admiral
William Crowe said that "a number of mistakes were made." Despite a
"catalog of errors committed by the crew," according to *Time* magazine,
and despite Crowe's admission that "some of the information given to
Captain [Will] Rogers during the engagement proved not to be accurate," Carlucci said "these errors or mistakes were not crucial" to the
decision to shoot the airliner down. Crowe claimed that "to say there
were errors made . . . is not necessarily to suggest culpability."

When a reporter asked, "Are you saying that these mistakes are in
no way responsible for the downing of this airliner?" Carlucci replied,
"It is the judgment of those who have investigated this, and it is
Admiral Crowe's judgment which I accept, that the errors were not
crucial to the decision."

According to the official report as endorsed by Crowe and Carlucci,
it was not any mistake by the crew of the Vincennes which led them to
shoot down the airliner; indeed, the report never states that anyone on
the Vincennes was responsible. Instead, the report, and Crowe, blame
the Iranians for making the Vincennes destroy the plane. The report
states that:

> Iran must share the responsibility for the tragedy by hazarding one
> of their civilian airliners by allowing it to fly a relatively low altitude
> air route in close proximity to hostilities.

This statement contradicts an earlier section of the report which found
that the airliner was taking off and climbing steadily to its assigned
altitude at the time it was shot down. In his memorandum endorsing
the report, Admiral Crowe states:

> I believe that the actions of Iran were the proximate cause of this
> accident and would argue that Iran must bear the principal re-
> sponsibility for the tragedy.

When a reporter asked Crowe: "You said the Iranians are partially
responsible. Do you have indications that the Bandar Abbas Airport
was aware that there was fighting going on?"

Crowe replied, "When we say Iranians we don't distinguish between
the people at Bandar Abbas Airport and the people controlling the
ships that are engaged in the fire fight."

Another reporter asked Crowe, "You're making the assumption
that they work together on joint operations. Is that really the case?"

Crowe replied that "whether it's the case or not, the point is they were all Iranians."

1987: Lt. Col. Oliver North and Rear Adm. John Poindexter

In addition to using the words *residuals* and *diversions* to refer to the millions of dollars of profits which were intentionally created by overcharging Iran for arms so that the money could be used to finance the contras, Lt. Col. Oliver North also said that he "cleaned things up," he was "cleaning up the historical record," he "fixed" things up, and that he "took steps to ensure" that things never "came out," meaning he lied, destroyed official government documents, and created false documents. According to North, some documents weren't destroyed, they were *non-log* or kept "out of the system so that outside knowledge would not necessarily be derived from having the documents themselves."

North never called any of his actions lying. In speaking of a false chronology of events which he helped construct, North said that he "was provided with additional input that was radically different from the truth. I assisted in furthering that version." He mentioned "a different version from the facts" and called the chronology "inaccurate." North also described how he and William Casey, then head of the CIA, together falsified the testimony that Casey was to give to Congress. "Director Casey and I fixed that testimony and removed the offensive portions. We fixed it by omission. We left out—it wasn't made accurate, it wasn't made fulsome, it was fixed by omission." And official lies were *plausible deniability*.

North said that he had participated in drafting a letter to Congress which stated that "we are complying with the letter and spirit of Boland." However, North admitted that what the letter really meant was that "Boland doesn't apply to us and so we're complying with its letter and spirit." In other words, non-compliance is compliance.

According to the testimony of Rear Admiral John Poindexter, one does not lie but *misleads* or *withholds information*. Likewise, one engages in *secret activities* which are not the same as covert actions. In Poindexter's world, one can *acquiesce* in a shipment of weapons while at the same time not authorize the shipment. One can transfer millions of dollars of government money as a *technical implementation* without making a *substantive decision*. One can also send subordinates to lie to congressional committees if one does not *micromanage* them. For Poindexter, *outside interference* occurs when Congress attempts to fulfill its constitutional function of passing legislation.

Yet Poindexter can protest that it is

> not fair to say that I have misinformed Congress or other Cabinet officers. I haven't testified to that. I've testified that I withheld information from Congress. And with regard to the Cabinet officers, I didn't withhold anything from them that they didn't want withheld from them.

1986: NASA, Morton Thiokol and Rockwell International

Throughout the Challenger tragedy and the subsequent investigation of the accident by a presidential commission, the language used by officials of the National Aeronautics and Space Administration (NASA), Morton Thiokol, and Rockwell International was filled with doublespeak. NASA officials called the temporary coffins of the astronauts *crew transfer containers,* the bodies of the astronauts were referred to as *recovered components,* and the explosion of the Challenger was called an *anomaly.*

When one NASA administrator was asked during the official investigation of the accident if the performance of the shuttle program had improved with each launch or if it had remained the same, he answered:

> I think our performance in terms of the liftoff performance and in terms of orbital performance, we knew more about the envelope we were operating under, and we have been pretty accurately staying in that. And so I would say the performance has not by design drastically improved. I think we have been able to characterize the performance more as a function of our launch experience as opposed to it improving as a function of time.

Another official said that:

> The normal process during the countdown is that the countdown proceeds, assuming we are in go posture, and at various points during the countdown we tag up the operational loops and face to face in the firing room to ascertain the facts that project elements that are monitoring the data and that are understanding the situation as we proceed are still in the go direction.

Other testimony included these sentences:

> I made the comment that lower temperatures are in the direction of badness for both O-rings, because it slows down the timing function.

The criticality in answering your question, sir, it would be a real foot race as to which one would be considered more critical, depending on the particular time that you looked at your experience with that.

I felt that by telling them we did not have a sufficient data base and could not analyze the trajectory of the ice, I felt he understood that Rockwell was not giving a positive indication that we were for the launch.

Officials of Morton Thiokol, when asked why they reversed earlier decisions not to launch the shuttle, said the reversal was "based on the re-evaluation of those discussions." The presidential commission investigating the accident suggested that this statement could be translated to mean that there was pressure from NASA.

1985: The Central Intelligence Agency

The Central Intelligence Agency prepared a "Psychological Warfare Manual" for rebels fighting the government of Nicaragua. The manual gave advice on the "selective use of violence" to "neutralize" Nicaraguan officials, such as judges, police, and state security officials; suggested hiring professional criminals to carry out "selective jobs"; proposed arranging the death of a rebel supporter to create a "martyr" for the cause; and gave directions on "the agitation of the masses in a demonstration" with men equipped with "knives, razors, chains, clubs, bludgeons" joining a peaceful demonstration and marching "slightly behind the innocent and gullible participants." William Casey, director of the CIA, said the manual's purpose was "to make every guerrilla persuasive in face-to-face communication" and to develop "political awareness," adding that its "emphasis is on education."

1984: The U.S. Department of State

In the weeks after the invasion of Grenada, U.S. and Caribbean occupation forces arrested an estimated 1,100 Grenadians and others suspected or accused of opposing the invasion. A U.S. State Department official denied that U.S. troops were making arrests. "We are detaining people," he said. "They should be described as detainees." The State Department also announced that it will no longer use the word *killing* in its official reports on the status of human rights in countries around the world. Instead, the word "killing" will be replaced by the phrase *unlawful or arbitrary deprivation of life.*

1983: President Ronald Reagan

In a speech to deputies of the Costa Rican National Assembly, President Reagan said:

> Any nation destabilizing its neighbors by protecting guerrillas and exporting violence should forfeit close and fruitful relations with any people who truly love peace and freedom.

Subsequent news reports revealed that the United States, through the CIA, was recruiting, arming, equipping, training, and directing "clandestine military operations against Nicaragua." President Reagan also named the new MX intercontinental ballistic missile the *Peacekeeper,* and later said that "a vote against MX production today is a vote against arms control tomorrow."

1982: The Republican National Committee

A television commercial produced by the Republican National Committee pictured a folksy postman delivering Social Security checks

> with the 7.5 percent cost-of-living raise that President Reagan promised. . . . [He] promised that raise and he kept his promise, in spite of those sticks-in-the-mud who tried to keep him from doing what we elected him to do.

In fact, the cost-of-living increases had been provided automatically by law since 1975, and Reagan tried three times to roll them back or delay them but was overruled by congressional opposition. One Republican official was quoted by the *Chicago Tribune* as calling the commercial "inoffensive" and added: "Since when is a commercial supposed to be accurate? Do women really smile when they clean their ovens?"

1981: Secretary of State Alexander Haig

In testimony before the House Foreign Affairs Committee, Secretary Haig, in commenting on the murder of three American nuns and a layworker in El Salvador (they had been shot in the back of the head and three of them raped) said:

> I'd like to suggest to you that some of the investigations would lead one to believe that perhaps the vehicle that the nuns were riding in may have tried to run a roadblock, or may accidentally have been perceived to have been doing so, and there'd been an exchange of fire and then perhaps those who inflicted the casualties sought to

cover it up. And this could have been at a very low level of both competence and motivation in the context of the issue itself. But the facts on this are not clear enough for anyone to draw a definitive conclusion.

1980: President-elect Ronald Reagan

During the 1980 presidential campaign, Reagan's oratory was filled with inaccurate assertions and statistics, and misrepresentations of his past record. He claimed that, as governor of California, he had refunded $5.7 billion in property taxes but failed to mention he had raised taxes by $21 billion. Even after it was disproved, he continued to claim Alaska had more oil than Saudi Arabia. He claimed General Motors had to employ 23,300 full-time employees to comply with government-required paperwork. However, General Motors pointed out it had 4,900 persons to do all its paperwork. Reagan continued his misstatements, omissions, misrepresentations, and exaggerations throughout his campaign, even though his misuse of language was constantly pointed out by others.

1979: The Nuclear Power Industry

The nuclear power industry has invented a whole lexicon of doublespeak used before, during, and after the Three Mile Island accident, which has served to downplay the dangers of nuclear accidents. An explosion is called *energetic disassembly* and a fire *rapid oxidation.* A reactor accident is an *event,* an *incident,* an *abnormal evolution,* a *normal aberration,* or a *plant transient.* Plutonium contamination is *infiltration,* or *plutonium has taken up residence.*

1978: Earl Clinton Bolton, Executive Vice President University of California

A memorandum written by Bolton for the CIA in 1968 titled "Agency-Academic Relations" advises academics to defend themselves by explaining their CIA involvement as a

> contribution to . . . proper academic goals. . . . It should be stressed that when an apology is necessary it can best be made: (1) by some distant academic who is not under attack, (2) in a 'respectable' publication of general circulation (e.g., *Harper's, Saturday Review, Vital Speeches,* etc.) and (3) with full use of the jargon of the

academy. . . . Two doctrines fiercely protected by the academy are "academic freedom" and "privilege and tenure." . . . When attacked for aiding the Agency the academic (or institution) should base a rejoinder on these sacred doctrines.

1977: The Pentagon and the Energy Research and Development Administration

For calling the neutron bomb an *enhanced radiation device* and a *radiation enhancement weapon* which is "an efficient nuclear weapon that eliminates an enemy with a minimum degree of damage to friendly territory."

1976: The U.S. Department of State

The Department announced plans to appoint a consumer affairs coordinator who would "review existing mechanisms of consumer input, thruput, and output, and seek ways of improving these linkages via the 'consumer communication channel.'"

1975: Yasser Arafat, Leader, PLO

In answer to a charge that the PLO wanted to destroy Israel, he was quoted as saying, "They are wrong. We do not want to destroy any people. It is precisely because we have been advocating co-existence that we have shed so much blood."

1974: Colonel David Opfer
U.S. Air Attaché in Cambodia

After a U.S. bombing raid in Cambodia, he told reporters, "You always write it's bombing, bombing, bombing. It's *not* bombing! It's air support!"

Appendix C
Quarterly Review of Doublespeak

Published in January, April, July, and October, the *Quarterly Review of Doublespeak* brings together in one publication examples of current doublespeak as well as articles, book reviews, cartoons, and other material illustrating, criticizing, and analyzing doublespeak. The January issue carries the announcement of the winner of the annual Doublespeak Award for language that is grossly deceptive, evasive, euphemistic, confusing, or self-contradictory. This issue also carries the announcement of the winner of the Orwell Award for the work which has made an outstanding contribution to the critical analysis of public discourse. Each twelve-page issue includes a bibliography of resources such as books, articles, and other materials which aid in the study, analysis, and teaching of public language in general and doublespeak in particular.

Subscription: $8.00 (U.S.) per year.

Address: Quarterly Review of Doublespeak
        National Council of Teachers of English
        1111 Kenyon Road
        Urbana, IL 61801

Selected Bibliography
on Doublespeak

Alexander, Larry. "The Seven Deadly Sins of Corporate Doubletalk." *Business and Society Review* 48 (Winter 1984): 41–44.

Althiede, David L. *Creating Reality: How TV News Distorts Events.* Beverly Hills, Calif.: Sage, 1976.

———. *Media Power.* Beverly Hills, Calif.: Sage, 1985.

Aubrey, Crispin, ed. *Nukespeak.* London: Comedia Publishing, 1982.

Baker, Samm Sinclair. *The Permissible Lie: The Inside Truth About Advertising.* Boston: Beacon Press, 1968.

Bennett, James R. *Control of Information in the United States: An Annotated Bibliography.* Westport, Conn.: Meckler, 1987.

———. "Oceania and the United States in 1984: The Selling of the Soviet Threat." *Social Theory and Practice* 10 (Fall 1984): 301–18.

———. "President Reagan's Panegyric for the Marines Killed in Lebanon." *North Dakota Quarterly* 55 (Spring 1987): 35–47.

Berman, Ronald. *How Television Sees Its Audience: A Look at the Looking Glass.* Newbury Park, Calif.: Sage, 1987.

Black, Edwin. "Ideological Justification." *Quarterly Journal of Speech* 70 (1984): 144–50.

Bloom, Alfred. *The Linguistic Shaping of Thought: A Study in the Impact of Language on Thinking in China and the West.* Hillside, N.J.: Lawrence Erlbaum, 1981.

Bolinger, Dwight. *Language: The Loaded Weapon.* New York: Longman, 1980.

———. "Truth Is a Linguistic Question." *Language* 49 (1973): 539–50.

Bolton, W. F. *The Language of 1984: Orwell's English and Ours.* Knoxville: University of Tennessee Press, 1984.

Bosmajian, Haig. *The Language of Oppression.* Washington, D.C.: University Press of America, 1983.

———. "Reaganspeak as a Case Study in the Use of Godterms, Adwords, Euphemisms, and Faulty Metaphors." *ETC.: A Review of General Semantics* 42, no. 2 (1985): 101–108.

Bryant, Jennings, and Dolf Zillmann, eds. *Perspectives on Media Effects.* Hillsdale, N.J.: Lawrence Erlbaum, 1986.

Carey, Alex. "Word-Power in Politics: 'Terror,' 'Agression,' and 'Refugees' in the Semantics of Violence and Repression." *ETC.: A Review of General Semantics* 37, no. 1 (1980): 53–64.

Carey, James W., ed. *Media Myths and Narratives: Television and the Press.* Newbury Park, Calif.: Sage, 1987.

Carroll, John B., ed. *Language, Thought, and Reality: Selected Writings of Benjamin Lee Whorf*. Cambridge, Mass.: MIT Press, 1956.

Chilton, Paul, and Crispin Aubrey, eds. *Nineteen Eighty-Four in 1984*. London: Comedia, 1984.

Chomsky, Noam. *On Power and Ideology: The Managua Lectures*. Boston: South End Press, 1987.

The Classics of Political Television Advertising. 60 minute videocassette. Washington, D.C.: Campaigns & Elections, 1986.

Cohn, Carol. "Sex and Death in the Rational World of Defense Intellectuals." *Signs: Journal of Women in Culture and Society* 12 (1987): 687–718.

Collins, Richard, James Curran, Nicholas Garnham, Paddy Scannell, Philip Schlesinger, and Colin Sparks, eds. *Media, Culture & Society: A Critical Reader*. Newbury Park, Calif.: Sage, 1987.

Commercial Mania. Videocassette. Santa Monica, Calif.: Rhino Video (1201 Olympic Blvd., Santa Monica, CA 90404), 1986.

Corcoran, Paul E. *Political Language and Rhetoric*. Austin: University of Texas Press, 1979.

Czitrom, Daniel J. *Media and the American Mind: From Morse to McLuhan*. Chapel Hill: University of North Carolina Press, 1982.

Delgado, Richard. "The Language of the Arms Race: Should the People Limit Government Speech?" *Boston University Law Review* 64 (1984): 961–1001.

Diamond, Edwin, and Stephen Bates. *The Spot: The Rise of Political Advertising on Television*. Cambridge, Mass.: MIT Press, 1985.

Ekman, Paul. *Telling Lies: Clues to Deceit in the Marketplace, Politics, and Marriage*. New York: Norton, 1985.

Engel, S. Morris. *The Language Trap, or How to Defend Yourself Against the Tyranny of Words*. Engelwood Cliffs, N.J.: Prentice-Hall, 1984.

Enright, Dennis J., ed. *Fair of Speech: The Uses of Euphemism*. New York: Oxford University Press, 1985.

Geis, Michael. *The Language of Television Advertising*. New York: Academic Press, 1982.

Gerbner, George, Larry Gross, Michael Morgan, and Nancy Signorielli. "Chartering the Mainstream: Television's Contributions to Political Orientations." *Journal of Communication* 32 (Spring 1982): 100–27.

Gervasi, Tom. *Soviet Military Power: The Pentagon's Propaganda Document, Annotated and Corrected*. New York: Vintage, 1988.

Ginsberg, Benjamin. *The Captive Public: How Mass Opinion Promotes State Power*. New York: Basic Books, 1986.

Gold, Philip. *Advertising, Politics, and American Culture*. New York: Paragon House, 1986.

Govier, Trudy, ed. *Selected Issues in Logic and Communication*. Belmont, Calif.: Wadsworth, 1988.

Green, Jonathan. *Newspeak: A Dictionary of Jargon*. Boston: Routledge & Kegan Paul, 1984.

Gyi, M. "Semantics of Nuclear Politics." *ETC: A Review of General Semantics* 41, no. 2 (1984): 135–47.

Hardin, Garrett. *Filers Against Folly: How to Survive Despite Economists, Ecologists, and the Merely Eloquent.* New York: Viking, 1985.

Hawthorn, Jeremy, ed. *Propaganda, Persuasion and Polemic.* Baltimore, Md.: Edward Arnold, 1987.

Hayakawa, S. I. *Language in Thought and Action.* 4th ed. New York: Harcourt Brace Jovanovich, 1978.

Howe, Irving, ed. *Orwell's Nineteen Eighty-Four: Text, Sources, Criticism.* 2nd ed. New York: Harcourt Brace Jovanovich, 1982.

If It Bleeds, It Leads. 14 minute film. New York: The Cinema Guild, 1987.

Information Ltd. 27 minute film. New York: The Cinema Guild, 1980.

Johannsen, Richard L. *Ethics in Human Communication,* 2nd ed. Prospect Heights, Ill.: Waveland Press, 1983.

Jowett, Garth and Victoria O'Donnell. *Propaganda and Persuasion.* Beverly Hills, Calif.: Sage, 1986.

Kahane, Howard. *Logic and Contemporary Rhetoric: The Use of Reason in Everyday Life.* 5th ed. Belmont, Calif.: Wadsworth, 1988.

Keen, Sam. *Faces of the Enemy: Reflections of the Hostile Imagination.* New York: Harper and Row, 1986.

Kenner, Hurnard J. *The Fight for Truth in Advertising.* New York: Garland, 1985.

Kimble, Gregory R. *How To Use (and Misuse) Statistics.* Englewood Cliffs, N.J.: Prentice-Hall, 1978.

Kuppig, Christopher J. *Nineteen Eighty-Four to 1984: A Companion to Orwell's Classic Novel.* New York: Carroll and Graff, 1984.

Lambdin, William. *Doublespeak Dictionary.* Los Angeles: Pinnacle Books, 1979.

Lang, Gladys Engel, and Kurt Lang. *Politics and Television Re-Viewed.* Beverly Hills, Calif.: Sage, 1984.

Lazere, Donald, ed. *American Media and Mass Culture: Left Perspectives* Berkeley: University of California Press, 1987.

Lee, Alfred McClung and Elizabeth McClung Lee. *The Fine Art of Propaganda,* San Francisco: International Society for General Semantics, 1972.

Leiss, William, Stephen Kline, and Sut Jhally. *Social Communication in Advertising: Persons, Products, and Images of Well-Being.* New York: Methuen, 1986.

Lesher, Stephen. *Media Unbound: The Impact of Television Journalism on the Public.* Boston: Houghton Mifflin, 1982.

Lewis, Flossie. *The Involuntary Conversion of a 727 or Crash! Some Ways and Means to Deflate the Inflated Style with a New Look at Orwell's "Politics and the English Language."* Bay Area Writing Project (5635 Tolman Hall, University of California, Berkeley), 1979.

Lutz, William. "The 'American Economic System': The Gospel According to the Advertising Council." *College English* 38 (1977): 860–865.

———. "Corporate Doublespeak: Making Bad News Look Good." *Business and Society Review* 44 (Winter, 1983): 19–22.

———. *Doublespeak: From Revenue Enhancement to Terminal Living.* New York: Harper and Row, 1989.

———. "Doublespeak At Large." *English Today* 3 (October 1987): 21–24.

————. "Involuntary Conversions, Pre-Dawn Vertical Insertions, and Negative Deficits: The World Of Doublespeak," in *The State of the Language 1990*. Edited by Christopher Ricks and Leonard Michaels. Berkeley, Calif.: University of California Press, 1990.

————. "Language, Appearance, and Reality: Doublespeak in 1984." In *The Legacy of Language: A Tribute to Charlton Laird*. Edited by Phillip Boardman. Reno, Nev.: University of Nevada Press, 1987: 103–19.

Making the News Fit. 28 minute film. New York: The Cinema Guild, 1987.

Marchand, Roland. *Advertising the American Dream: Making Way for Modernity, 1920–1940*. Berkeley, Calif.: University of California Press, 1985.

Miller, Don Ethan. *The Book of Jargon*. New York: Collier, 1982.

Nelkin, Dorothy. *Selling Science: How the Press Covers Science and Technology*. New York: W. H. Freeman, 1987.

Nimmo, Dan, and James E. Combs. *Mediated Political Realities*. New York: Longman, 1983.

Ohmann, Richard. *The Politics of Letters*. Middletown, Conn.: Wesleyan University Press, 1987.

Pateman, Trevor. *Language Truth and Politics*. 2d ed. East Sussex, England: Jean Stroud Publishers, 1980.

Postman, Neil. *Amusing Ourselves to Death: Public Discourse in the Age of Show Business*. New York: Elizabeth Sifton/Viking, 1985.

Rank, Hugh. *Analyzing Persuasion: 10 Teaching Aids*. Park Forest, Ill.: Counter-Propaganda Press (Box 365, Park Forest, IL 60466), 1987.

————. ed. *Language and Public Policy*. Urbana, Ill.: National Council of Teachers of English, 1974.

————. *The Pep Talk: How to Analyze Political Language*. Park Forest, Ill.: Counter-Propaganda Press (Box 365, Park Forest, IL 60466), 1984.

————. *Persuasion Analysis: A Companion to Composition*. Park Forest, Ill.: Counter-Propaganda Press (Box 365, Park Forest, IL 60466), 1988.

————. *The Pitch: How to Analyze Ads*. Park Forest, Ill.: Counter-Propaganda Press (Box 365, Park Forest South, IL 60466), 1982.

Rasberry, Robert W. *The "Technique" of Political Lying*. Lanham, Md.: University Press of America, 1981.

Rawson, Hugh. *A Dictionary of Euphemism and Other Doubletalk*. New York: Crown, 1981.

Ricks, David A. "Products That Crashed into the Language Barrier." *Business and Society Review* 45 (Spring 1983): 46–50.

Rohatyn, Dennis. "Propaganda Talk." In *Selected Issues in Logic and Communication*. Edited by Trudy Govier. Belmont, Calif.: Wadsworth, 1987: 73–92.

Rothwell, J. Dan. *Telling It Like It Isn't: Language Misuse and Malpractice—What We Can Do About It*. Englewood Cliffs, N.J.: Prentice-Hall, 1982.

Rowe, Jonathan. "Modern Advertising the Subtle Persuasion: Advertising and Children's TV." *The Christian Science Monitor*, 29 Jan. 1987: 16–17.

————. "Modern Advertising the Subtle Persuasion: Gauging the Impact of Advertising." *The Christian Science Monitor*, 28 Jan. 1987: 1, 14–15.

Schudson, Michael. *Advertising, the Uneasy Persuasion: Its Dubious Impact on American Society.* New York: Basic Books, 1986.

Scott, David Clark. "Modern Advertising the Subtle Persuasion: Finding Out What Makes Us Tick." *The Christian Science Monitor,* 27 Jan. 1987: 1, 16–17.

———. "Modern Advertising the Subtle Persuasion: Networks' Role in Keeping Rein on Ads." *The Christian Science Monitor,* 30 Jan. 1987: 16–17.

Severin, Werner J., with James W. Tankard, Jr. *Communication Theories,* 2d ed. New York: Longman, 1988.

Shapiro, Michael, ed. *Language and Politics.* New York: New York University Press, 1984.

Six O'Clock and All's Well. 60 minute film. New York: The Cinema Guild, 1980.

Smith, David, and Michael Mosher. *Orwell for Beginners.* London: Writers and Readers Publishing, 1984.

Stansky, Peter, ed. *On Nineteen Eighty-Four.* New York: W. H. Freeman, 1983.

The 30-Second Seduction. 27 minute film. Chicago: Films Incorporated, 1986.

Vestergaard, Torben, and Kim Schroder. *The Language of Advertising.* New York: Basil Blackwell, 1985.

Wander, Philip. "The Rhetoric of American Foreign Policy." *Quarterly Journal of Speech* 70 (1984): 339–61.

Weinstein, Brian. *The Civic Tongue: Political Consequences of Language Choices.* New York: Longman, 1983.

Weiss, Philip, and Laurence Zuckerman. "The Shadow of a Medium: How TV Has Transformed the Telling of the News." *Columbia Journalism Review* (March-April 1987): 33–39.

Wheeler, Michael. *Lies, Damn Lies, and Statistics, the Manipulation of Public Opinion in America.* New York: Dell, 1976.

Winnifrith, Tom, and William V. Whitehead. *1984 and All's Well.* London: Macmillan, 1984.

Woodward, Gary C., and Robert E. Denton, Jr. *Persuasion and Influence in American Life.* Prospect Heights, Ill.: Waveland, 1988.

Editor

William Lutz is associate professor of English at Rutgers University, Camden, New Jersey, where he has served as director of the Writing Program (1971–77) and chair of the Department of English (1979–85). He has published over two dozen articles and reviews, and is author of *Doublespeak: From Revenue Enhancement to Terminal Living* (Harper and Row, 1989). He is editor of *Webster's New World Thesaurus* (Simon and Schuster, 1985) and the *Age of Communication* (Goodyear, 1974). With Harry Brent, Lutz has coauthored or coedited a number of books, including *The Critical Reader: Responding through Writing* (Harper and Row, 1989) and four editions of *Rhetorical Considerations: Essays for Analysis* (Winthrop 1974, 1977, 1980; Little, Brown, 1984). After receiving a J.D. degree from Rutgers University in 1983, he was admitted to the Pennsylvania bar, and in that same year he became probably the first American to teach a graduate course in the History of the English Language in the People's Republic of China. He is a member of the Executive Committee (Division on Language and Society) of the Modern Language Association and has served as chair of the Committee on Public Doublespeak since 1978. He has been editor of the *Quarterly Review of Doublespeak* since 1980.

Contributors

George R. Bramer is chair of the Department of Communication at Lansing Community College, Michigan. He is the coauthor with Dorothy Sedley of *Process One: A College Writing Program* (Charles E. Merrill, 1977) and *Writing for Readers* (Charles E. Merrill, 1981). He has contributed articles to *College English, College Composition and Communication, English Journal,* and a chapter to *Rhetoric and Praxis: The Contribution of Classical Rhetoric to Practical Reasoning* (Catholic University of America Press, 1986). He is a member of the NCTE Committee on Public Doublespeak.

Harry Brent is associate professor and former chair of the English Department at Baruch College of the City University of New York. He has authored a number of articles on rhetoric and composition, and has coauthored with William Lutz several books including *The Critical Reader* (Harper and Row, 1989), *The Perennial Reader* (Harper and Row, 1985), *Rhetorical Considerations* (Little, Brown, 1984), and *On Revolution* (Wadsworth, 1970). He is former chair of the College Section of NCTE and has served on numerous NCTE committees. He is currently a member of the Committee on Public Doublespeak.

Scott Buechler received his Ph.D. from the University of Utah and has taught in the English departments of Radford College, Virginia, and Virginia Polytechnic and State University. While teaching, he designed a freshman composition course around the connections between science, technology, and the humanities. He is currently a technical editor with Martin Marietta Energy Systems of Oak Ridge, Tennessee, and a part-time student in the University of Tennessee MBA program.

Frank J. D'Angelo is professor of English at Arizona State University, Tempe, where he directs the graduate emphasis in rhetoric and composition. He is former chair of both the Conference on College Composition and Communication and the Modern Language Association Division on the Teaching of Writing, and a former member of the Executive Committee of NCTE. He is the author of *A Conceptual Theory of Rhetoric* (Winthrop, 1975) and *Process and Thought in Composition* (Little, Brown 1985), and has published more than sixty articles in journals and books.

Roy F. Fox is director of writing at Boise State University. He has published articles in many journals, including *Research in the Teaching of English, Media and Methods, English Journal, English Education,* and *Quarterly Review of Doublespeak.* He is a member of the Committee on Public Doublespeak.

Walker Gibson was one of the original members of the Committee on Public Doublespeak in 1972, and as president of NCTE that year he encouraged and promoted the committee's early development. He is the author of several books and articles on language and style, including *Tough Sweet and Stuffy* (Indiana, 1966), *Persona* (Random House, 1969), and *Euphemism* (Harper and Row, 1974). He has taught at Amherst College (1946–57), at New York University (1957–67), and, since 1967, at the University of Massachusetts at Amherst, where he is now professor emeritus. He has conducted a number of seminars for college teachers of writing under the auspices of the National Endowment for the Humanities. He received the Distinguished Service Award from the National Council of Teachers of English in 1988.

Dan F. Hahn received his Ph.D. in political science from the University of Arizona. He is a professor in the Department of Communication Arts and Sciences, Queens College, Flushing, New York, where he teaches courses in political communication and presidential rhetoric. He is a member of the Board of Editors of the *Presidential Studies Quarterly* and former chair of the Speech Communication Association Task Force on Presidential Communication.

D. G. Kehl is professor of English with specialization in American literature at Arizona State University, Tempe. He is the author of several books, including *Poetry and the Visual Arts* (Wadsworth, 1975) and *The Literary Style of the Old Bible and the New* (Bobbs-Merrill, 1970). He has written over one hundred articles on literature and such interdisciplinary studies as literature and the visual arts, literature and popular culture, literature and gerontology, literature and theology, and rhetoric and composition. He has been a visiting scholar at Harvard and research fellow at Yale, Princeton, and Texas. He is a member of the Committee on Public Doublespeak.

Donald Lazere is professor of English at California Polytechnic State University, San Luis Obispo, and holds graduate degrees from Columbia University and the University of California, Berkeley. He is the author of *The Unique Creation of Albert Camus* (Yale University Press, 1973) and the editor of *American Media and Mass Culture: Left Perspectives* (University of California Press, 1987). He has been a member of the Committee on Public Doublespeak since 1973.

Don L. F. Nilsen is professor of English at Arizona State University, Tempe, and chair of the English department's linguistics program. He is coauthor with Alleen Pace Nilsen of *Language Play: An Introduction to Linguistics* (Newbury House, 1978). With Francine Hardaway he served for three years as coeditor of the *Doublespeak Newsletter,* which later became the *Quarterly Review of Doublespeak.* He is former chair of the General Linguistics Executive Committee of the Modern Language Association, and a member of the International Advisory Committee of the Workshop Library on World Humour. For the past six years he has been coeditor with Alleen Pace Nilsen of the *World Humor and Irony Membership Serial Yearbook* (WHIMSY).

Richard Ohmann is professor of English and American Studies and director of the Center for Humanities at Wesleyan University, Connecticut. He is author of *Politics of Letters* (Wesleyan University Press, 1987) and *English in America: A Radical View of the Profession* (Oxford University Press, 1976). In 1971 he helped draft the resolutions that led to the founding of the Committee on Public Doublespeak and he has been a member of that committee since its inception in 1972.

Julia Penelope is a freelance writer and speaker who has served on the NCTE Committee on Public Doublespeak for fourteen years. Her work has appeared in NCTE journals and publications such as *College English, Quarterly Review of Doublespeak, Teaching about Doublespeak,* and *Sexism and Language,* as well as in *Foundations of Language, Linguistics, Bucknell Review,* and *Papers in Linguistics.* Her book *Speaking Freely: Unlearning the Lies of the Fathers' Tongues* (Athene Series of Pergamon Press) will be published in 1990.

Hugh Rank is professor of English at Governors State University, Park Forest, Illinois. He organized the NCTE Committee on Public Doublespeak in 1972, and served as its first chair. His publications include *Language and Public Policy* (NCTE, 1974), *The Pitch: How to Analyze Ads* (Counter-Propaganda Press, 1982), *The Pep Talk: How to Analyze Political Language* (Counter-Propaganda Press, 1984), and *Analyzing Persuasion: 10 Teaching Aids* (Counter-Propaganda Press, 1987). He is a member of the Committee on Doublespeak, and in 1976 he was awarded the George Orwell Award "for distinguished contributions toward honesty and clarity in public language."

Dennis Rohatyn is professor of philosophy at the University of San Diego, where he has taught since 1977. His publications include *Naturalism and Deontology* (The Hague: Mouton & Co., 1975), *Two Dogmas of Philosophy* (Associated University Presses of N.J., 1976), *In Our Own Image* (Ginn, 1985), *Insight, Prophecy and Moral Vision: Critical Essays on George Orwell* (Special issue, *Cogito* 1, no. 3–4, 1983), and *The Reluctant Naturalist: A Study of G. E. Moore's 'Principia Ethica'* (University Press of America, 1986). He is the founder of the Society for Orwellian Studies, cofounder of the G. E. Moore Society, and a member of the Committee on Public Doublespeak.

Charles Suhor is deputy executive director of the National Council of Teachers of English. He has published over two hundred articles, reviews, and poems in popular and scholarly journals, including *College Composition and Communication, College English, Educational Leadership, English Journal, Humanities Report,* and *Quarterly Review of Doublespeak.* His current interests include K–12 curriculum and applied semiotics.

Charles Weingartner has been professor emeritus at the University of South Florida, Tampa, since 1982. He is the coauthor with Neil Postman of *Linguistics: A Revolution in Teaching* (Dell, 1966), *Teaching as a Subversive Activity* (Delacorte, 1969), *The Soft Revolution,* (Delacorte, 1971), and *The School Book* (Delacorte, 1973). With Neil Postman and Terrence Moran he

coedited *Language in America* (Pegasus, 1969), and with Herb Karl and Larry
Broer he coedited *The First Time* (Bobbs-Merrill, 1975). He is an associate
editor of *ETC.: A Review of General Semantics,* and is a member of the
Editorial Advisory Board of *The High School Journal.* He has been a member
of the Committee on Public Doublespeak since its founding.

Edward M. White is professor of English at California State University, San
Bernardino. He is the author of *Developing Successful College Writing Programs* (Jossey-Bass, 1989) and *Teaching and Assessing Writing* (Jossey-Bass,
1985), and editor of the textbooks *The Writer's Control of Tone* (W. W. Norton,
1970) and *The Pop Culture Tradition* (W. W. Norton, 1972). His articles and
monographs on writing assessment, writing research, and literary figures
(Jane Austen and William Makepeace Thackeray) have appeared in a variety of journals. He is director of the Consultant/Evaluator Program of the
Council of Writing Program Administrators.